A GAME FISHER IN IRELAND

Colin Laurie McKelvie

ASHFORD

Southampton

Published by Ashford, 1 Church Road, Shedfield, Hampshire SO3 2HW

British Library Cataloguing in Publication Data

McKelvie, Colin Laurie, *1950–*
  A game fisher in Ireland.
  1. Ireland: (republic). Angling
  I. Title
  799.1'2'09417

  ISBN 1-85253-147-9

Typeset by Acorn Bookwork, Salisbury, Wiltshire
Printed by Hartnolls Limited, Bodmin, Cornwall, England

Contents

Map	iv
Acknowledgements	vi
Preface	vii
Introduction	1
1 Fish of the Far North-West	7
2 Northern Ireland	44
3 From Leitrim and Sligo Westwards	60
4 West Sligo and Mayo	79
5 The Galway Fishery	96
6 The Wild Fisheries of the West	105
7 'Twixt Galway and Limerick	129
8 The Midland Lakes	135
9 The Great Loughs	156
Select Bibliography	186
Useful Addresses	187
Travel	189
Fishing Licences, Permits and Permission	191

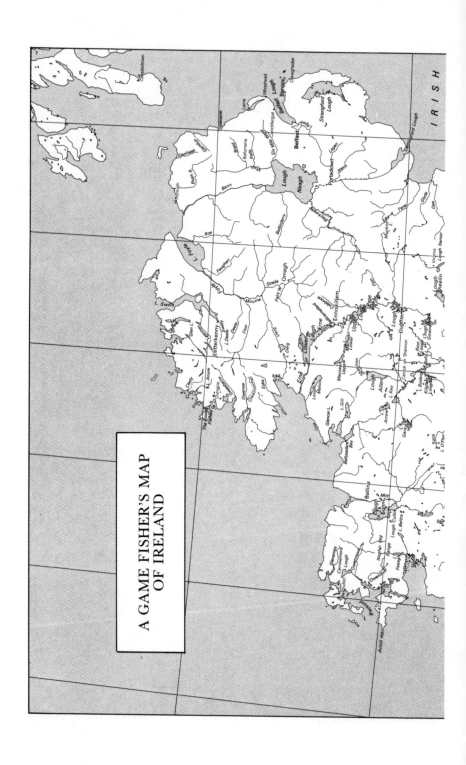

A GAME FISHER'S MAP
OF IRELAND

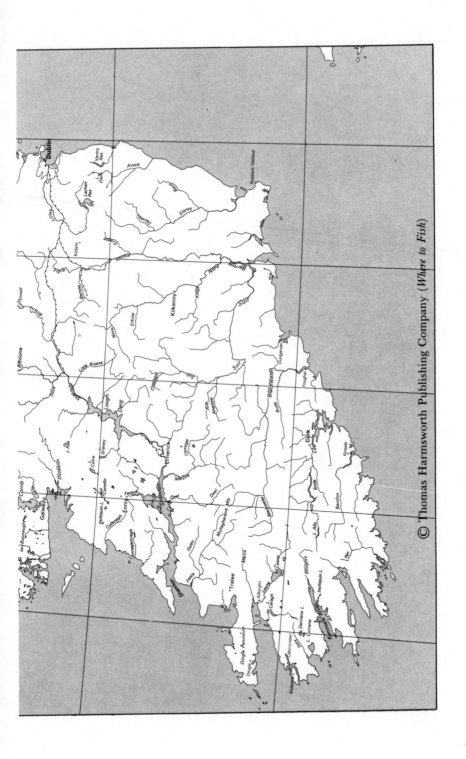

Acknowledgements

In the preparation of this book little could have been achieved without the help, advice and encouragement of a great many people. The Northern Ireland Tourist Board, and especially Eric Thurley, gave invaluable support and guidance on game fishing in Northern Ireland, and gave me access to some of their finest photographic material. For information and photographs relating to waters in the Irish Republic I am indebted to Bord Failte Eireann (the Irish Tourist Board), and especially to Paul Harris and Mark Rowlette. I must also record my thanks to the Central Fisheries Board in Dublin, and to its various regional officers and other staff, with particular thanks to the personnel of the Western and North-Western Regional Boards for their very enthusiastic help.

It is difficult to begin adequately to record my gratitude to the many fisheries owners, local anglers and fellow sportsmen from almost every corner of Ireland who have been such an unfailing source of advice and help to me. To mention them all individually would be impossible, but I must offer particular thanks to the following: Thomas Gallaher, Thomas Kelly, Vinny Battisti, Terence Bradley, Ian Holman, the late Major Alec Perceval, Howard Black, Chris Donegan and Peter Mantle.

I reserve a very special debt of gratitude for the memory of the late Rev. Canon J. I. Lea, of Ardara and latterly of St Ernans, Donegal, for giving me my first fishing rod in the mid-1950s and thereby setting my youthful feet on the piscatorial path.

Preface

Ireland is both entirely surrounded by water and endowed with innumerable inland waters, from tiny streams to massive rivers, from little hill lochans to wide and windswept loughs covering many thousands of acres, as well as the longest river and the largest lake in the British Isles, the Shannon and Lough Neagh. It would be surprising if such a wealth of waters did not afford good fishing, and Ireland has had a reputation for the variety and excellence of its fresh-water fisheries since the earliest records of medieval chroniclers. More recently, Ireland's potential for magnificent coarse fishing has also been discovered and exploited by visiting enthusiasts and by the specialist competitive match fishers.

Since Victorian times the quality of Irish salmon, trout and seatrout fishing has been widely recognised, in game-fishing literature and by successive generations of annual visiting fishers, especially from Britain. When, in the 1970s, what is euphemistically referred to as 'the troubles' erupted in parts of Northern Ireland, many game fishers crossed Ireland off their list and looked elsewhere for their sport. This is understandable, but it is also a very great pity. The news media tends to highlight what is sensational and grim, but most of rural Ireland remains as tranquil, as friendly and sporting as ever. I derive great pleasure each year from taking groups of friends from Britain to fish for the first time in Ireland, north and south, and from hearing their expressions of delight at the quality of the sport and the warmth of the welcome they receive.

It is ironic to see that while many British game fishers have largely avoided Ireland since the early 1970s, there has been a notable influx of enthusiasts from elsewhere in Europe, especially from Germany and Holland. By the early 1990s we will have reached the point where we are in danger of losing all the wonderful continuity which used to exist between Irish game fishing and British game fishers. A whole new generation of eager and sporting game anglers in Britain has grown up, but very few have ever wet a line on Irish waters. This book is an attempt to give some glimpses of the quality of the sport, the landscape and the whole feel of game fishing in some of Ireland's finest game fisheries, large and small, famous and obscure.

In writing this book I have tried, in words and pictures, to draw on my own experiences of a selection of game fisheries, and to use memories, descriptions, anecdotes and pictures to convey the flavour of Irish game fishing – rather like assembling the bits and pieces necessary to tie a fishing fly. And in many ways this book is my attempt to tie a fishing fly and to cast it over the reader, to encourage him to rise, gather up his rods and tackle bags, and come game fishing in Ireland.

Already, there are encouraging signs that British game fishers are gradually trickling back to Ireland and if the following pages can encourage this trend the book's main objective will have been achieved. If, as a result, a few more game fishers have sampled Irish sport and the special ambience and flavour of the Irish fishing experience, and go home with tales of what sport Ireland can afford, there will surely be a steadily increasing return of British visitors to the loughs and rivers of Ireland.

Colin Laurie McKelvie
County Down
1989

Introduction

In thinking about Irish game fishing and looking at the various fisheries I have chosen for this book, I have been guided by certain basic principles. First, I have used the term 'game fisher' as being largely synonymous with 'fly fisher', and there are a number of reasons for doing this. It is generally true to say that the majority of game fishermen get more pleasure from fishing with a fly rod – and from *catching* fish on fly – than by other methods. This is not to decry or devalue other methods like bait fishing, spinning or trolling, all of which can take fish in circumstances when the blinkered purist who stubbornly sticks to his fly tackle is guaranteed to have a blank day. The complete angler's repertoire of tackle and methods should include every sporting technique. And I have good personal reasons to know what excellent sport can be had, especially with salmon, big lough trout, char and seatrout, by adopting a pragmatic approach and using the most appropriate methods for the prevailing conditions. But fly fishing is usually the prime method of fishing for all game species during the months from May to September, which tends to be the time of year when the visiting holiday game fisher will choose to make his trip to Ireland. In a book intended primarily for the holiday game fisher there is all the more reason to concentrate on fly fishing as the method which is likely to be the most preferred and most productive.

Second is the inevitable and invidious task of selection. Nothing written about Irish fishing could ever pretend to be comprehensive or definitive. How do you even begin to discuss the game fishing of a country where the environmental conditions are ever changing; where the still waters, loughs large and small, can be numbered in tens of thousands; and where the rivers and streams which hold trout, seatrout and salmon are almost as numerous?

Instead, I have tried to take the reader on a fairly informal tour around northern and north-western Ireland, through the great chains of loughs which thread the Irish Midlands, across into wildest Connemara and the western province of Connaught, and south-west to Clare and the limestone streams of the Fergus and its neighbouring river-and-lough systems. Trying to select game fisheries is rather like choosing poetry for an anthology – you have to be selective, and you are sure to omit items which other people will regard as vital. In the end I have simply opted for those I know and love best, and can recommend to others who may choose to follow the paths I have trodden.

Third is my firm belief that Irish game fishing, famous though it has always been, still deserves to be very much better known. Here, on the westernmost fringes of Europe, can be found some of the very finest sport with truly wild fish, brown trout, seatrout and salmon, often in breathtakingly lovely surroundings and in an environment uncluttered by too much humanity and the noise and debris it brings with it. Innumerable waters exist, many of them very underfished. Some do not see an angler during an entire season. This book is an attempt, however inadequate, to give some personal impressions of the richness and variety that is available for the wanderer in Ireland with a fishing rod, especially in the northern, western and central parts of Ireland.

A Game Fisher in Ireland is primarily a book for the visiting game fisher, whether he may come from Britain, very much further afield or be a resident Irishman who simply decides to take a brief farewell of his familiar local waters and set off in search of unfamiliar fisheries outside his own county or province. Whatever the distance travelled, it is assumed that the reader will wish to know at least something about the history of the river or lough, its track record as a producer of fish, the patterns of movement of migratory fish and the annual cycles of insect emergence, and thus the flies which can best be used to imitate the hatch and attract feeding fish. This book aims to provide background information on these and other matters of interest for the newcomer: Where can one stay? Is a permit or licence needed; and if so, where can it be bought? Where is the nearest tackle shop? What about hiring boats?

As far as accommodation goes, Ireland abounds in possibilities of every kind, from the five-star delights of some of Europe's most famous hotels, to the snug comforts of a village pub with bedrooms for guests, and the family hospitality of one of Ireland's countless farmhouse guesthouses and bed-and-breakfast places. Both the Irish Tourist Board (Bord Failte Eireann) and the Northern Ireland Tourist Board publish excellent guides to accommodation of all kinds and in every locality, and these can be obtained quickly through your local travel agent or directly from the Boards' offices. With a wealth of information-packed guides, booklets and pamphlets at your elbow, you can make an informed choice of where to go and where to stay, and the same high standard of hospitality can be guaranteed everywhere. Wherever you go in Ireland, do not be in too much of a hurry. Remember the Irish saying, 'A stranger is really only a friend whom you haven't yet met'.

Once accommodation has been sorted out, there is the urgent but equally pleasurable priority of seeking fishing information. It is helpful to know in advance, of course, what conditions generally are likely to be: is such and such a river large or small? Will you need chest waders or will thigh boots suffice? These and many other questions can be answered to a large extent by reference to books and magazines. (See, for instance, 'Useful Information' in this book which provides basic information, names, addresses and telephone numbers.) However, the printed word can never be a substitute for the immediacy of local intelligence and up-to-the-minute information. Even then, the picture can change suddenly. For instance, you are sitting on a sunny afternoon and listening as the ghillie (or the bailiff, or the fishery manager, or the local poacher) is shaking his head and bemoaning low water and lack of fish. Then a fresh face arrives in the bar, orders a drink, and announces that he has just driven over the mountain road and through a torrential cloudburst 10 miles (16 km) upstream. The river is rising, a big summer flood is on its way down at this instant, and all those seatrout and grilse jumping in the bay will shortly be feeling the fresh invitation of the stained water, the irresistible chemical summons of their natal rivers and streams and will come hurtling upstream into these pools and lies which have been rocky, bare and sunbaked for days. Suddenly, the seemingly dour prospects for your fishing holiday have been magically transformed.

Time spent in reconnaissance is never wasted. Maps are not only fascinating documents in themselves: they are also vital aids to the game fisher. Ireland has been well served by the map-makers, with a superb series of 1:50,000 (slightly more than one inch to the mile) scale maps for Northern Ireland (nine sheets in all); and a really excellent series of twenty-five half-inch (1:126,720) sheets produced by the Republic of Ireland Ordnance Survey and covering not only the Republic but the whole island of Ireland and most of the offshore islands. For a complete coverage of the roads and the waters of Ireland your best combination will be a good road atlas or general route-planning map and a series of these larger-scale Ordnance Survey sheets for your specific chosen areas. Every bay of every big lough, every turn of every stream, and almost every cottage is clearly marked, which is a great help when planning your day's fishing and locating your lough or river beat. These maps become really vital if you are to find some of the more remote hill loughs with certainty and to get safely back to your car should the mist descend. Basic map-reading skills and the correct physical and psychological preparation for moderate hill walking are proper insurances against the risks of a good day's fishing ending in disorientation, discomfort, anxiety and (heaven forbid) tragedy. But wild hill land is an unforgiving environment, and sensible planning and preparation are a small price to pay for the pleasures of fishing for wild game fish.

What of tackle and tactics? You could quite easily fill a large estate car with a dozen rods, a score of reels and a couple of hundredweight of other assorted equipment, if you were determined to be perfectly prepared for every game-angling eventuality. The art of successful travelling – and of being a successful travelling angler – is knowing what to leave out.

For successful fly fishing for salmon, seatrout and brown trout in Ireland during the months from May to September – what we can conveniently call summer game fishing – a relatively small range of tackle is sufficient. Like most fly fishers, I passed through the successive stages of cane and fibreglass to carbon and graphite, and my rod rack is now dominated by the products of one maker in particular, Bruce & Walker of Cambridgeshire. I first encountered their rods when this firm was making the changeover from fibreglass to carbon, and I have stuck with them ever since. Tubular carbon, a revelation when it first appeared, has now been joined by Bruce & Walker's newer range of hexagonally sectioned rods, built up from compound tapered triangular strips to give a rod which is superficially similar to the old hexagonally built cane rods with which most of us grew up. There is all the advantage of a hexagonal structure with only a fraction of the weight which cane necessarily entails, and several seasons' experience with rods of the Hexagraph design has convinced me that they are ideal for all my fishing, in Ireland or further afield.

For summer salmon and grilse a 12- to 13-ft (365–395 cm) two-handed rod, capable of casting a moderate length of floating line, probably in the range # 8–# 10, will be more than adequate to cover all but the widest pools and all but the heaviest and most unseasonable floods. For most grilse and salmon a 10-to 10½-ft (305–320 cm) single-handed rod casting a #8 line will be all you will require.

Anyone visiting Ireland to fish, whatever the time of the year, can expect to spend a goodish amount of time in a boat on loughs large and small. You can fish a gentle drift on a small lough quite effectively using conventional wet-fly tactics and a 9-ft (275 cm) medium-action trout rod casting a #5–#6 floating or slow-sinking line. But on larger loughs and in the biggish, rolling wave which is the classic lough fishers' delight, you will benefit from something longer and stronger. Length gives you more command over a fish, and on some of these loughs it may be a biggish fish, especially at mayfly and sedge time, while a bushily-dressed bobfly, so deadly as an attractor of fish, can be tripped and danced over the waves more effectively and enticingly with a rod of 11–11½ ft (335–350 cm) and with a medium action.

The old greenheart lough rods which were so familar to our fathers and grandfathers, and which they used to such good effect, are still occasionally to be seen, although most have collapsed through heavy use and the notorious tendency of greenheart to rot steadily but undetectably. But those which have survived are, to modern tastes, intolerably heavy, although there is no denying the charm of their languid, slow action – perfect for rolling a short line over the front of a drifting boat. The best modern equivalent I have encountered is the carbon-fibre Technocrat loch rods made specially for this style of fishing by Bruce & Walker. The 12-ft (365 cm) Technocrat is unrivalled as a 'Scotch-actioned' boat rod, while the slightly stiffer 11½ ft (350 cm) version also doubles as a very workmanlike grilse and light salmon rod. I first used both rods during the Irish mayfly season of 1983 and have stuck firmly with them ever since.

Dapping has a special place in the tactical repertoire of the Irish lough fisher (and occasionally on rivers, too). On a lough the wind strength has a large part to play in the proceedings, and even a 9-ft (275 cm) river-trout rod can be made to dap quite nicely, provided the fisher does not mind coming in with a rather tired arm at the day's end. Something rather longer, and especially the Technocrats at 11½ ft and 12 ft (350 and 365 cm), is much preferable, and a dapped natural or artificial pattern can be manipulated with considerable accuracy and minimal effort on rods of this length. Some dapping enthusiasts opt for a special dapping rig, comprising a telescopic rod which may extend to 15 ft (455 cm) or even 17 ft (520 cm), with a large-diameter centre-pin reel holding heavy monofilament line to which is attached an appropriate length of blow-line. These are undoubtedly effective and have great power, adequate to subdue even the biggest trout very rapidly. They are also comparatively inexpensive and when fully retracted take up little room in your car or in a boat. But they should be considered as optional extras by all but the most regular and devoted dapping enthusiasts.

On smaller loughs and on most rivers the best all-purpose rod is a medium-to-fast actioned 9-ft (275 cm) rod, of which the best I have used is the Bruce & Walker Hexagraph River Trout model, in the slightly stiffer-actioned 'Walker' form and casting a #5 floating line. This has accounted for a great many trout and seatrout of all weights from dozens of different waters, and has sufficient backbone to handle grilse and small salmon without difficulty.

In the pages which follow we encounter various small streams, often lacking any official name and marked only on the maps by a short and thin blue line. Yet these often hold good numbers of lively brown trout, some of a decent size, and many have many useful runs of small seatrout from late spring onwards. Yet you may find yourself crawling through tunnels of almost impenetrable overhanging vegetation to reach some of the pools, and much of the time your casting will call for little more than a slight sideways flick to land a fly barely a rod's length away. Compactness and ease of handling are at a premium on such Lilliputian waters, and a little brook rod is ideal. Once again, my personal favourite is the wonderfully light and deceptively powerful little 7½ ft (230 cm) Bruce & Walker Hexagraph, married to a light magnesium reel and a #4 floating line. The Ryobi 255MG weighs a mere 2¼ oz (64 g) and is a perfect reel for this rod.

For similar conditions, but with a very different action which is ideally suited to the accurate delivery of a dry fly or a nymph, there is the Bruce & Walker Hexagraph 8¼-ft (250 cm) A.R.T. with a #5 line. This is a little rod with lightning speed and amazing power, ideal for waters where you can cast to individual fish which you have marked down and can see feeding on nymphs or emergent flies.

Finally, in our angling travels across Ireland, we encounter waters for which there is only one approach – on foot, across miles of heather and hill grass. Here it is vital to travel light, and a small, multi-sectioned rod is absolutely perfect for this purpose. You might risk putting one of your smaller carbon two-piece trout rods in a plastic sleeve or an alloy tube and slinging it somehow across your back. But at best you will be uncomfortable, and at worst you may slip or take a tumble on rocks or in a bog-hole, to the accompaniment of the sickening crunch of a carbon-fibre rod snapping as you fall. Far better to have a rod which breaks down to a mere 15 in (38 cm), like the neat little Shake-speare Graphite Travel Fly, whose seven sections make up quickly into a crisp-actioned 8-ft (245 cm) fly rod which is best suited to a #7 line. What its multi-sectioned structure may lack in sweetness of action it more than makes up for in handiness and portability. With a light reel, a spool of spare leader monofil and a box of flies your entire fishing kit may weigh less than one pound – and will almost certainly weigh very much less than your day's basket of hill brownies as you walk back over the heather to your car.

But already we are in danger of over-tackling ourselves, and of setting off on a brief holiday looking like the White Knight. We do not need all eight or nine rods just mentioned, and three will suffice. If I ever manage to discipline myself sufficiently to do this, I shall take a brook rod of 7½–8 ft (230–245 cm), a 9–9½-ft (275–290 cm) river-trout rod and a 10–11 ft (305–325 cm) lough and light salmon rod, with a detachable butt extension. With this small but adaptable battery of rods, and reels, lines and other tackle to suit, anyone should be capable of tackling any Irish game-fishing situation in the months from late spring to early autumn.

Who knows what luck we will have? Only time will tell. But books can give glimpses of what has happened in past seasons. We can find out something about when fish are likely to run, what conditions have proved best in the past, the average catches, the locally favoured techniques and flies, and other fragments of local lore and historical background which should make fishing, and the preparations for fishing, more successful and agreeable. And so there is a suggested selection of books about Irish game fishing, past and more recent, which should provide pleasure in the anticipation of your trip and practical guidance in the detailed planning of it.

There is also a pardonable and pleasurable degree of satisfaction to be derived from 'armchair fishing'. Half the year is ruled out for the trout fisher, and most of us are further limited in our fishing opportunities by pressures of work, family commitments and other duties and responsibilities. If we cannot escape from our office desks to the waterside immediately, we can at least read about what others have done and dream of what we might – some day – do ourselves. We can begin to form some mental picture of this lough or that river, of its setting, its scenery, the sort of fish it can yield. In imagination and in spirit we are already there.

1 Fish of the Far North-West

County Donegal

County Donegal and County Cork are the two largest counties in all Ireland; but while Cork lies in the far south-west, County Donegal is Ireland's northernmost county, and includes Ireland's northernmost mainland point at Malin Head on the Inishowen peninsula, and the most north-westerly promontory of the Irish mainland at Bloody Foreland. But misunderstandings may arise when, as often happens, someone refers in conversation to 'the north of Ireland' or 'the south of Ireland', intending thereby to indicate the separate political units of Northern Ireland and the Republic of Ireland.

Although Donegal is one of the Republic's twenty-six counties, most of which happen to lie in the south of the island, it is most definitely not part of 'the north' in the political sense of that term. In fact, Donegal is one of the nine counties which together comprise the ancient province of Ulster, of which three – Donegal, Cavan and Monaghan – are part of the Republic, with the remaining six together comprising Northern Ireland. This brief digression into political geography may not be unhelpful to the visiting fisherman, especially if you are trying to work out which currency, rod licences and other requirements you need for fishing in a particular part of the country. In County Donegal you are in the Republic, within the territory of the Northern Regional Fisheries Board, and you will need currency and licences accordingly.

Donegal is such a large county, and its loughs, rivers and streams so varied and numerous, that a lifetime's dedicated exploration and fishing would barely suffice to scratch the surface of its game-fishing potential. No book or guide can expect to do more than provide a general introduction, with some more detailed remarks about one or two particular fisheries.

From Inishowen to Millford

Throughout these pages I have made the general assumption, for the sake of convenience, that the reader and the visiting game fisher will be happy to follow a more or less anti-clockwise tour of Ireland's fisheries, in which case

County Donegal makes an excellent starting point. The historic city of Londonderry, just across the county and international boundary, lies at the 'top dead centre' of the island of Ireland, and it takes only a few minutes' easy drive along the A2 trunk road northwards from the city centre to cross the border at Muff and find yourself in County Donegal, close by the western shore of Lough Foyle. This road (now designated the T73) hugs the shoreline north-eastwards towards Moville, and your progress will take you across a succession of a dozen or more little streams and burns which tumble down from the low hills of east Inishowen. Few are marked with an official name on any map, and the passing fisherman's best bet is to pause and look over the bridges to see if water conditions look promising.

All of these streams are short and spatey in character, and all receive modest runs of seatrout during the summer and early autumn when the flow is sufficiently strong to encourage fish to run. Alas, on the average summer's day most of the streams will be down to their bare bones, in which case you should pass on quickly. But if the water is high and begins to look fishy make immediate enquiries locally and prepare for what might be an hour or two of lively sport as a run of fish moves in, always remembering that such sport is always short-lived and conditions can taper off as suddenly as the flood began.

From Moville you may either press on north-eastwards to visit Inishowen Head and enjoy some magnificent views and scenery, or you may prefer to swing north-westwards towards Leckeny and Gleneely, which will take you anti-clockwise around the peninsula past Malin and Carndonagh. As you turn south from Ballyliffin towards Buncrana you pass close to a cluster of attractive hill loughs, of which the largest is Lough Fad. Access to this large hill lough is easy from the by-road which passes southwards through Meendoran, and to the south lies the smaller Lough Naminn. Both are attractive brown trout fisheries, their fish averaging about ½ lb (0.25 kg) and with the sturdy conformation and startling, carmine-spotted livery typical of the little brown trout of acidic upland waters.

These twin loughs can readily yield good baskets of breakfast-sized trout, and both are free fisheries, requiring only the statutory State Trout Licence. The geography of the area should tell you at once a good deal about the characteristics of these two loughs, for the hills drop steeply towards the water's edge, and both loughs are deep, glaciated troughs. Trout therefore always rise best to a traditional three-fly team of wet flies, and occasionally to a dry fly, fished close in by the shore in relatively shallow water. If you take to the water and fish deep and slow with a heavy sinking line and appropriate single fly or lure you might catch something a good deal larger than the 6–8 oz (0.15–0.25 kg) average of these loughs – and you may also encounter one of the many char which inhabit them, as they do so many of the deeper waters of Ireland and Scotland.

Not far away to the south, and still on the road to Buncrana, is Mintiaghs Lough, and the main road follows close by its western shore. This long, narrow lough can also provide excellent sport, but it is exceptionally difficult to fish adequately without a boat owing to the vigorous growth of reeds around most of its shore. Perhaps it is this relatively profuse growth of vegetation, compared to the more arid and rocky environs of the twin loughs to the north, which accounts for the rather larger average size of the trout here, many of which are well above the ½ lb (0.25 kg) mark; and you may be lucky enough to include one or two in your basket weighing rather over 1 lb (0.45 kg). Here, as on most of the hill loughs of Donegal, you will be well served by a traditional three-fly cast of proven wet-fly patterns, of which the Black Pennell, the Mallard and Claret and the Bibio seem to work particularly well on Mintiaghs. The usual sizes 12 and 10 are normally perfectly adequate, but you might find it preferable to drop down to size 14 or even smaller, especially if conditions are warm and calm.

If the weather is kind and you feel like trying your luck on a truly wild and remote lough, why not don your walking boots and equip yourself for a stiff hike up the hill to little Lough Doo. This attractive and rarely fished hill lough lies about a mile (1.6 km) south of the mountain road running westwards from Glasmullan, and your best approach is probably made by striking off to the south-west and up the hill. Travel light, taking a minimum of equipment, and remember to adopt the basic principles and precautions of hill walking. A summer's day can be abruptly transformed by low cloud, heavy rain and chill temperatures.

Do not expect to find Lough Doo yielding large trout, but trout there are in plenty, and the walk and the view are sufficient justification for the effort involved in getting there. Take a picnic, sit down in the heather and enjoy wonderful vistas to the north and west. You might even broil two or three Lough Doo trout, wrapped in damp newspaper and placed in the embers of a fire of heather stalks lit by the water's edge. There could be no finer way to savour in full the pleasures of fishing a Donegal hill lough, but please remember to light fires with care; to keep them strictly under control, especially in dry summer weather when a fire might spread into the heather; and be sure to take home or bury all debris after you have finished. Leave delightful little Lough Doo as you would like to find it, an unspoilt sapphire ornament set in the high hills of north Donegal.

As you pass southwards through Buncrana and Fahan your route takes you south-westwards towards Newtown Cunningham, unless you want to make a detour westwards towards Inch Island and the Inch Level Lough. Inch Island is joined by a causeway and road access is easy. The road marks the northernmost extent of a large and shallow lough of brackish water, which is dammed at the south-western end, where sluices control the water levels. You might be lucky enough to catch a summer salmon here, or to connect with one of the many seatrout which come nosing up the estuary from Lough Swilly and the Atlantic beyond. But this fishery has been greatly altered and has much deteriorated as a result of damming and drainage. It used to be one of the most outstanding seatrout fisheries in the whole of Ireland, but nowadays its glory has sadly departed. You may be lucky, but you are more likely to wish to press on south-eastwards towards Letterkenny, where you cross the river Swilly and turn north again towards Rathmelton and a number of excellent lough and river fisheries.

A drive of about 6 miles (10 km) out of Rathmelton to the west takes you to Lough Fern, which is certainly not to be missed when the fishing conditions are right and a run of fish has taken place. Lough Fern is a large lough by Donegal standards, and receives the substantial flow of the River Lennon which rises in the mountains to the south-west and flows to Lough Fern via Kilmacrennan. The Lennon and Fern fishery used to be regarded as one of the very earliest and best salmon fisheries in Ireland, with fresh spring salmon running into the system from December onwards, a pattern followed by various other rivers of north-west Ireland, including the Drowes on the borders of south Donegal and Leitrim, and also the Garavogue Fishery at Lough Gill.

Sadly, however, the salmon of the Lennon and Lough Fern were decimated by UDN disease in the mid 1960s, and salmon numbers have failed to recover to anything more than a fraction of their pre-disease levels. The ravages of UDN have been compounded by a falling-off of what little spring salmon run remained, just as so many other fine salmon fisheries throughout Ireland and Britain have seen their spring runs reduced to near insignificance since the last war. But if the salmon fishing on Lough Fern has declined, it is consoling that Lough Fern is now a first-class brown trout fishery, and the superb brown trout which were once treated with contempt as virtual vermin when this was primarily a salmon fishery are now highly regarded and give excellent sport throughout the season.

Lough Fern is shallow throughout and its best potential will be realised by taking to the water in a boat in the early part of the season. When trout are on the move and taking insects near the surface almost any drift will produce good fish, which are likely to average ¾ lb (0.35 kg) and may be up to 2 or 3 lb (0.9–1.35 kg) if you are really fortunate, and if some of the larger, bottom-feeding fish have been tempted up to the surface. You may find difficulty in hiring a boat locally, so here is one lough on which the touring angler towing his own boat will find himself at an immediate advantage. However, it is rare to find any lough in Ireland on which a boat cannot be procured by making a few judicious enquiries locally.

The shallowness of Lough Fern makes for excellent boat fishing in the early part of the season, and also promotes the weed and insect life which gives the lough its healthy population of good-sized fish. However, problems can arise with low water levels and uncontrolled growth of vegetation during the summer months, when oars and propellers get repeatedly snagged in weeds, and the boating fisherman will find he probably loses valuable fishing time – and also his temper – in an unequal struggle with difficult conditions. But this is not a time to go ashore and think of going on to fish elsewhere, for Lough Fern can be profitably fished from a good many points along the shore, especially on the western side. This lough rarely fails to provide reasonable sport, and when the trout are properly 'on the take' it can be quite superb. Part of this lough is a free fishery, while other sections are ably managed by the Letterkenny and District Anglers' Association.

This should not be confused with the rather similarly named Letterkenny and Swilly Angling Club, which manages part of Lough Columbkille, another important brown trout fishery in this part of County Donegal. It lies a mile (1.6 km) east of Millford and close to a small country road where you can park your car and stroll down to the water with ease. Your most direct route takes you to the north-western corner of this little lough, and the north and west shores are easy to fish. There is no need to cast a long line, for this is a rather deep little lough, especially towards the eastern side, and the best fly fishing is to be had in the northern and western shallows. As always, traditional wet-fly patterns in sizes 10 and 12 will rarely let you down, and while the average size of the Columbkille trout is rather below the 1 lb (0.45 kg) mark it is unwise to fish with too fine a leader. Trout of up to 5 lb (2.25 kg) were taken from this lough in the 1980s, and you might fare especially well when there is a hatch of sedges and the larger fish are tempted to feed close to the surface.

Columbkille can be an excellent place on which to practise the interesting and often deadly method of skimming the sedge, using either a large, bushily dressed and buoyant traditional pattern such as the Murrough, or one of the many sedge patterns which incorporate deer hair. The ever-dependable Muddler Minnow has accounted for a high proportion of sizeable trout on Columbkille when its larger occupants are coming up for sedges.

If you have time while fishing Columbkille, or if by chance your creel remains empty or lighter than you would have wished, take a gentle stroll to another neighbouring lough just a short distance away to the south. It appears to have no particular name, either on the map or among the local fishermen, but it has a considerable reputation for consistently producing good baskets of excellent trout averaging around ½ lb (0.25 kg). This lough appears to provide excellent feeding for trout, and its fish are unusually plump and their flesh is vividly pinkish-red. The relatively small size of the fish is probably accounted for by the fact that spawning and recruitment in the feeder streams and the shallows is rather too good, and beyond what the nourishment of the lough can sustain. Consequently, this is one of many little loughs which would probably benefit from being fished very much harder and having its trout population significantly reduced. Fewer trout would each enjoy a bigger share of the available food, whose quality is seemingly excellent, and some very fine specimens might develop as a result.

Apart from the change of scene from Columbkille to 'the wee lough', you might also take a moment or two to compare the appearance of the fish from the two loughs. Those from Columbkille are fairly typical of the wild brown trout of north and north-west Ireland, predominantly dark in colour and somewhat white-fleshed, while the fish from its smaller neighbour are outwardly very much paler, with less prominent spotting and speckling and showing hints of silvery hues reminiscent of salmon smolts, and with startlingly bright pink flesh. It is surprising how two such adjacent waters can sustain two such very different styles of brown trout; and little wonder that the fisheries experts of the last century tried to categorise so many different species of non-migratory brown trout.

Although the twentieth-century game fisher has been brought up to believe that all our native trout, both non-migratory and the migratory seatrout, are merely variations on a single large but highly variable species which we know as *Salmo trutta*, some of the most recent freshwater fisheries research has shown that within the brown trout family there can be some very marked genetic differences, not only between distinct and isolated waters but between trout occupying the same lough or river. It seems the game-fish enthusiasts of a century and more ago were wiser than we used to think.

Onwards to Glenveagh

West and north from Millford the hills are scattered with loughs large and small, all of which hold abundant wild brown trout, but none of them is likely to provide anything larger than the typical breakfast-sized trout of 6 oz (0.15 kg) or so. Nevertheless, this is a wonderfully attractive area, very sparsely inhabited and with superb scenery in good weather. The ridge of hills which runs north-east from Loughsalt mountain includes half a dozen excellent little loughs which are well worth a visit in the course of a summer day's hill walking. Take a small, light rod, perhaps one of the purpose-built telescopic or multi-sectioned fly rods designed for the hill-walking fly fisher, and you can cast a line on waters which may never see another fisherman for the rest of the season.

An excellent walk is to follow the ridge from Lough Reelan, to the north of Loughsalt Mountain, and strike off north-eastwards over Crocklaght and past Lough Nacreaght, dropping down to meet the hill road which runs from Glen to Streamstown; and this can best be done if you can arrange to be dropped off at the start of your walk and collected at the other end. But remember to check the weather forecast, go well equipped with map, compass and other hill-walking necessities, and pick your way carefully. This is wonderfully spacious and exhilarating country for hill walking, but bog-holes and sphagnum pools can be traps for the unwary, especially if you are tired or disorientated in mist or low cloud. The risk of bad weather is present in every hilly part of Ireland and Britain, but do not let the need for simple precautions deter you from tackling some of the finest walking and the most peaceful fishing you may ever encounter.

The village of Glen lies at the north-eastern end of Lough Glen, which is fed by the Owencarrow River from the south-west, and which flows out into Sheep Haven Bay via the short Lackagh River, with its estuary at Cashel. As a salmon fishery Lough Glen is in many respects a carbon copy of what has happened on Lough Fern. It was once famous for its large runs of exceptionally early spring fish, and there was great local rivalry between the devotees of the Lennon and Fern system and those who fished the Owencarrow–Glen Lough–Lackagh river system just over the hills to the north-west. The devastating outbreak of UDN disease in the 1960s caused massive losses on the Owencarrow and the Lackagh, and the fishery has only slowly begun to recover. There is also little doubt that such recovery as has taken place on both the Lackagh and Lough Fern has occurred despite intolerably high levels of off-shore fishing, both legal and often illegal, by high-seas netting and off-shore drift-netting. Few salmon are likely to be encountered in the Lackagh or Glen Lough before late spring, although May and June have produced some notable fish during the 1980s, including one celebrated salmon of just over 28 lb (13 kg) caught in 1985. There is also local talk of another fish, allegedly of almost 30 lb (14 kg), caught there in 1987.

As so often happens, the loss of one type of sport in a fishery can be compensated for by improvements in other ways. When Glen Lough and the Lackagh was regarded primarily as a very early spring salmon river, few fishers, local or visitors, gave much thought to the seatrout which also run up the river and into the lough from spring onwards. Disease affected their numbers too, but recovery has been much better, and seatrout are not quite so vulnerable to the depredations of drift-netting, although many illegal operators use monofilament nets of a quite disgracefully small mesh size, and far too many seatrout perish in this way. Glen Lough is now a really excellent seatrout fishery, and in a wet season good numbers of fish may run from June onwards. Unless conditions are unusually dry the system should have an excellent head of seatrout by early August and there should be fine sport from then until the end of the season on 30 September.

The seatrout here are of a good average size, and a typical basket will contain fish of 1½–2 lb (0.7–0.9 kg). This is rather higher than the general average for the famous and highly specialised seatrout fisheries of Galway and Connemara, and recent fisheries research seems to show that better feeding is available for migratory trout along the north coast of Ireland and within the Irish Sea itself, compared with the rather poorer fare available to seatrout feeding offshore on Ireland's Atlantic seaboard. Although much of this impor-tant information is tucked away in obscure scientific papers and in learned journals, a good deal of it has been made available to the layman and the seatrout fishing enthusiast in Edward Fahy's superb book, *Child of the Tides: A Seatrout Handbook* (Dublin 1985), which is a vital addition to every Irish game fisher's library, and deserves a place alongside other Irish classics like Kings-mill Moore's *A Man May Fish*.

The fishing on Glen Lough is in the control of four proprietors, including the Letterkenny and District Anglers' Association, and the visitor should contact John Doherty at Derryscleagh (Tel: 074-38057), who can also advise on the hire of boats and the availability of outboard motors. A well-equipped boat is essential if you are to be able to cover Glen Lough adequately during seatrout time, and there are few parts of the lough which do not provide productive drifting in the classic 'over the front' lough style, fishing a fairly short line and a trio of classic flies. While your choice of point and dropper flies will probably be made from among the traditional ranks of Peter Rosses, Butchers, Black Pennells and others, do not neglect to have a good bushy pattern on your top dropper, to be used as a bob fly.

The choice of a precise pattern seems largely unimportant, and the fly may be anything from a Muddler Minnow to any of the more traditional, bushily

13

dressed patterns. The important thing is that it should be large, buoyant and capable of creating a good deal of wake and general surface disturbance, and that you should fish it by dancing and tripping it across the top of the water, using a shortish line and a longish rod. Use the smaller sizes in calm conditions and your biggest and bushiest flies on the bob when there is a stiff breeze and a good rolling wave. Such tactics seem to have an irresistibly magnetic attraction for seatrout (and many brown trout, too) and the pattern and style are not particularly critical, since the dancing, tripping bob fly acts chiefly as an attractor, catching the eye of the fish and bringing it close enough to see and, with luck, take either the dropper or the point fly.

The movement of a large insect, or insect imitation, on the surface of the water is also the essence of the dapping technique, and this too can be a deadly method of taking seatrout on Glen Lough. Few local fly fishers or visitors seem to have experimented with any of the natural insects, but some large baskets of seatrout, and some very large individual fish, have fallen to the bushily dressed Loch Maree-style dapping flies, tied on hooks size 10 or 8, and sometimes even larger, and possibly with the addition of a small flying treble hook.

A good relief map of northern Donegal, such as the excellent Sheet 1 of the Irish half-inch series, will show that a deep and prominent glen runs south-westwards through the Derryveagh Mountains. This glen has the Owencarrow river at its north-east end, and further south is the long, deep trough of Lough Beagh (sometimes called Lough Veagh).

This is a spectacular lough, both for its magnificent setting, with high rocky crags and soaring heathery slopes all around, and also for the strikingly positioned Glenveagh Castle, a nineteenth-century mock-Norman castle with crenellated battlements, towers and all the other features characteristic of so many shooting lodges and grand houses built on sporting estates in Ireland and the Scottish Highlands in Victorian times.

Glenveagh Castle and its surroundings have a great deal in common with the classic Scottish sporting estate, most notably the presence of large numbers of magnificent red deer on the hills. Like many a Scottish landed property, Glenveagh also had to endure the human miseries of land clearances and evictions when its proprietor, John Adair, implemented his plans for the development of the estate's sporting potential. He was fired with enthusiasm to create a Scottish-style Highland sporting estate, and he and his wife largely succeeded in turning their property into a very fair replica of a west Highland deer forest, with some good grouse shooting, and fishing in the lough over which the castle presides with such self-conscious grandeur. But this was achieved at the cost of large-scale clearances of his tenantry from their little cabins and cottages, and the evictions were unpleasant affairs, carried out with ruthless efficiency by bailiffs supported by police and militia. Tenant families were removed bodily from dwellings which were then pulled down or burnt behind them. John Adair and his neighbour Lord Leitrim were two of the most notorious and unpopular landlords in Victorian Ireland, and this part of Donegal was shaken by repeated outbreaks of agrarian unrest for much of the last century.

Curiously, John Adair's widow, who continued to live at Glenveagh after her husband's death in 1885, appears to have been as popular and widely respected as her husband had been detested. After his death she pressed ahead with the development of a Scottish-style deer forest, which involved the monumental task of erecting a high deer fence of iron stanchions running for some 25 miles (40 km) around these rugged hills, and enclosing over 22,000 acres (8900 hectares) of hill land around Lough Veagh. Deer were imported from Scotland and England, and they thrived in excellent habitat, with good pasture, a mild climate and the careful management of a succession of professional Scottish stalkers who were charged with looking after Ireland's only 'Highland' deer forest. There were visits from notable sporting guests, too, and among the many visiting 'rifles' who stalked on Glenveagh was H.R.H. the Duke of Connaught.

In 1937 the Glenveagh estate was bought by Henry McIlhenny, who also was briefly owner of the neighbouring Dunlewey estate. There is a certain poetic justice in the fact that Henry McIlhenny was a direct descendant of one of the peasant tenants who had been evicted from Glenveagh by John Adair almost a century earlier. He had returned to Ireland from the USA a very rich man, his fortune made from sales of millions of those familiar little bottles of fiery chilli sauce whose labels still bear the name McIlhenny. Shortly before his death in the late 1970s he made a gift of Glenveagh to the Irish people, and handed over the entire estate to the Government of the Irish Republic, whose Office of Public Works is now responsible for its management and maintenance.

The twin influences of glaciation and volcanic action mean that Lough Beagh (or Veagh – call it what you will) lies in a long, deep trench, and the best fishing for brown trout is around the margins where the water begins to become shallow. Bank fishing is not allowed here, and in any case a boat is by far the most effective way of covering the productive marginal waters and also the shallows around the various small islands which are clustered towards the north-eastern end of the lough. The average run of brown trout here is not particularly large, and may reasonably be expected to weigh around ¾ lb (0.35 kg), although fish of 3 and even 4 lb (1.35 and 1.8 kg) occur regularly each season. However, this lough is also a really excellent seatrout fishery, particularly in the latter part of the season. The seatrout here run late, which is typical of most of Ireland's northern and and western waters, but fish should be moving in during July if the summer is at all wet. However, in a dry season it may be August before big numbers have moved up and into the lough.

In late August and September the sport can be really fast and furious, and the Lough Beagh seatrout have a reputation as free risers, not only on the trout drifts and around the islands but over almost all the surface of the lough. Traditional wet-fly fishing from a boat drifting broadside-on to the breeze is highly effective, as also is Loch Maree-style dapping with large, bushy flies, and no other fishing method would be any more productive, even if this were not a strictly fly-only fishery. The necessary arrangements for permits and the use of boats must be made with the staff of the Glenveagh National Park at

Church Hill (Tel: 074-37088), and visitors should book well in advance, especially at the prime seatrout times in late August and September, when demand for fishing on this increasingly popular lough can be quite high.

Lough Beagh is a uniquely attractive fishery, set in magnificent surroundings which are, as their Victorian owners intended, rather like a little corner of the West Highlands of Scotland transplanted into north Donegal. On a good day it can provide seatrout fishing of a consistent quality to equal any British seatrout fishery, although you must be prepared to brave roughish weather and squally conditions when a strong south-westerly wind is blowing. The glen, with its high hills and craggy slopes, is a natural wind tunnel, funnelling the breeze and sometimes producing alarmingly rough conditions, for which the fly fisher needs to be well prepared.

Also within the confines of Glenveagh National Park are two good-sized hill loughs, Nambraddan and Inshagh, both of which used to provide excellent sport with pan-sized brown trout. However, the policy of the park is now to forbid fishing on either of these loughs, as part of the general management strategy for conservation of the deer and other upland wildlife.

After your visit to Glenveagh you should back-track slightly and head northwards via Creeslough towards Ballymore and Dunfanaghy. Here, at one of the most attractive spots along the dramatic north Donegal coast, you can find a number of excellent hotels, guest-houses and bed-and-breakfast places where you can stop and take a few days to explore the excellent fishing of the area, most of which is controlled and managed by the Dunfanaghy Anglers' Association. Your first call should be at Arnold's Hotel in Dunfanaghy (Tel: 074-36208), where you will find a warm welcome and all the information you require about a number of excellent local brown trout loughs. Sessiagh Lough, Port Lough and Kill Camble Lough are all well worth a visit, but perhaps the most interesting of these waters is the so-called New Lake.

This is a good-sized water, almost 250 acres (100 hectares) in total and exceptionally shallow, averaging only 5–7 ft (1.5–2 m) deep. It was unknown to earlier generations of anglers, simply because the lough is a recent natural creation, formed by a prolonged and violent storm in the 1920s which caused sand and silt to seal off an arm of the sea and create a new fresh-water fishery within sight and sound of the Atlantic in Sheep Haven Bay. Limited natural spawning and recruitment have been given a helping hand by some enlightened stocking and management, and now the brown trout fishing here is excellent. It is reasonable to expect your basket to comprise a number of good trout averaging well over 1 lb (0.45 kg), with perhaps one or two a good deal larger.

Although the season starts slowly, this lough is normally in consistently good fishing condition from late April onwards, and the emergence of natural flies appears to follow a fairly typical pattern of buzzers followed by lake olives, sedges and even some mayflies, with good potential for dry-fly fishing, especially towards dusk on warm evenings in late summer. The shallowness of the water and its general clarity, except after a stormy spell when it may be muddy and turbid for a while, mean that you generally have a clear view of the bottom, and of fish coming up to your flies – an exciting sight but one which should not be allowed to tempt you into over-excitement and tightening too soon.

Afloat on the shallow waters of the New Lake you may occasionally glimpse the submerged remains of old field boundaries on what used to be farmland, before the storm and the silting up caused permanent flooding of land which was once part of the Horn Head House estate of the Stewart family. The ruinous remains of Horn Head House can be seen to the north of the lake and beyond the road causeway, and it is well worth while taking a drive out onto Horn Head peninsula and wandering over the heather to see the spectacular cliffs and view the prolific bird life to be found there, especially in the breeding season and the early summer. Peregrine falcons still nest on these wild, precipitous cliffs, and the young peregrines bred in the age-old traditional eyries of Horn Head were highly regarded by the falconers of Victorian and Edwardian times, who took the well fledged eyasses from the eyries in June and trained the young birds for grouse hawking in August and September. The ancient art of falconry still flourishes as a sport, but those who have the skill, time and opportunity to fly trained peregrines at grouse are few in number. The wild peregrines of Ireland and Britain enjoy special legal protection, and most falconers' birds are now bred in captivity.

Dunfanaghy and Gweedore

From Dunfanaghy the road westwards towards Falcarragh passes close to little Drumlesk Lough, and this free fishery holds some excellent and obligingly free-rising brown trout averaging just over ½ lb (0.25 kg). A quick glance will show you that bank fishing is virtually impossible because of the prolific weed growth, so you will need a boat to make the most of what Drumlesk has to offer. Another 3 miles (5 km) drive westwards brings you to a road bridge across the Lough Agher River, formed by the confluence of the stream out of Lough Agher with the Ray River, both of which rise to the south in the foothills of Muckish Mountain, whose distinctive profile dominates the landscape for miles around. Though spatey in its upper reaches, this river settles down to a more steady flow in the last 3 or 4 gentle miles (5–6.5 km) of its course to the sea, during which it winds through low, fertile grazing lands. It receives a good run of late-summer seatrout, and also some smallish salmon, and if conditions look promising you should make enquiries in Falcarragh or from the farmers whose lands border the river to secure the necessary access and permission to fish.

From Falcarragh and the neighbouring village of Gortahork you have a choice of two routes, taking you clockwise or anti-clockwise around the hills of Gweedore. The northern road takes you westwards towards Bloody Foreland and past a scattering of small loughs close to the road, all of which hold small, lively brown trout. Once you have rounded Bloody Foreland and swung south towards Bunbeg you will pass another scattering of loughs before you come to the Gweedore River. This is fed by the waters of three large and connected loughs, Dunlewy, Nacung Upper and Nacung Lower. This used to be an excellent spring and summer salmon fishery, but the runs have been much reduced by the twin effects of UDN disease and the presence of an enormous hydro-electric scheme which harnesses the considerable power of this river, and on whose flows the runs of salmon depend so heavily.

There is enormous scope for brown trout fishing in the spacious waters of the three loughs which together make up a virtually unbroken stretch of almost 6 miles (10 km), and you may fish either from the bank or from your own boat, which you can launch on payment of the small licence fee to the Fisheries Manager at the Power Station. It has to be said, however, that the chances of a salmon are rather slight, and the seatrout fishing can be slow and dour, and certainly cannot be compared to the wonderful sport available on Lough Beagh, which lies only a few miles away, as the crow flies, over the Derryveagh Mountains. It is sad to reflect that this once-excellent fishery appears to have been in steady decline for over a century. In the 1860s the lucky few who had discovered this corner of Ireland were already beginning to lament the effects of over-fishing, which they attributed to the development of the railway system and, later, to the building of a hotel to accommodate the increasing number of anglers who came to the Gweedore fishery. Even so the fishing, particularly for salmon, remained excellent until the coming of the hydro-electric scheme and, most recently, the effects of UDN disease and netting at sea.

The Rosses

Another look at that invaluable map of north-west Donegal will show you that the coastline from Bunbeg follows a contorted and ragged course out into the Atlantic, its shoreline deeply indented by innumerable bays, each dotted with a sprinkling of islands, and with Aran Island out to the west. (Incidentally, this Aran Island should not be confused with the Aran Islands off Galway, which lie much further to the south.) The coastline turns back in towards Dungloe and this whole area is known as The Rosses. It is every game fisher's idea of paradise, and The Rosses loughs and rivers thoroughly deserve a full-length book all to themselves. Perhaps one day someone will write one, if he can find time to explore the endless variety of waters which exist here, and if he can then tear himself away from the sport they provide to sit down and start scribbling.

This wonderful area is extremely fortunate in being under the management of a most enthusiastic and active local angling club, The Rosses Anglers' Association. They now oversee well over 120 loughs on five different river catchment areas, almost all of which are within an easy twenty minutes' drive of Dungloe Village. Anyone heading for The Rosses should make a point of contacting the Association, either by enquiring in Dungloe or by writing or telephoning to Charles Boner, Bridgend, Dungloe (Tel: 075-21004). Advice will be freely given, day tickets or plans for a longer visit can be procured, and you can make all the arrangements you need for bank fishing or boat fishing in

The author fishing under low cloud and a leaden light on a Rosses lough in June.
Tripping a bushy bob-fly over the waves can be deadly for trout and seatrout.

pursuit of brown trout, seatrout and salmon, depending upon your inclinations, the time of the year and the state of the waters at the time of your visit.

It would be a hopeless task – and unfair to the local Association, to the visiting game fisher and to these wonderful waters themselves – to attempt to single out particular fisheries for special discussion in this general book. Such an invidious choice would inevitably mean neglecting countless superb fishing spots. Suffice it to say that it is simply impossible to get bad sport in The Rosses, and at their best these waters can provide some of the very finest seatrout and brown trout fishing anywhere in Ireland.

But let us risk making some of these invidious choices, and pick out at least a couple of The Rosses waters in passing. Lough Anure should certainly not be missed, a large and attractive lough pleasantly situated among the low hills of the eastern Rosses, with the heights of Crocknafarragh and the Derryveagh Mountains beyond. A road runs along the western shore and passes through the little village of Loughanure, and you can park your car and launch your boat just a short distance away. Boats are available, with or without outboard engines, and you will have a great deal of pleasure in exploring the 350 acres (140 hectares) of this big, straggling lough, with its many bays, inlets and islands large and small.

The trout are of a good size for these western parts, averaging around ¾ lb (0.35 kg), which is probably attributable to the surprisingly good insect life of this otherwise rather acidic lough. Perhaps this is due to the general shallowness of the waters, which allows good light penetration and the development of some sub-surface vegetation, so that insects and other invertebrates are thereby encouraged. Lough Anure gives good trout fishing right from the start of the season, but its real peak comes in the summer, usually from late July onwards when the summer salmon and seatrout have begun to run. Salmon are not especially numerous, it must be admitted, and to bring one to the net would be a bonus, especially if you hooked it on relatively light wet-fly trout tackle. But the seatrout of Lough Anure are numerous, free-rising and an almost certain guarantee of good sport in late summer and through to the end of the season on 30 September. This is a fly-only water, and you will find that the most productive tactics, adopted by visitors and locals alike, involve the classic traditional drift beam-on to the wind, with dapping as an alternative.

A word of caution will not go amiss here, and indeed it applies also to many other loughs in The Rosses region. Lough Anure is shallow and very rocky, and it is fatally easy to get into trouble, bumping on submerged rocks or suddenly finding yourself on a lee shore. Then the boat may take a bad battering and possibly suffer damage, especially if you are using one of the traditional clinker-built wooden boats, when you may spring a plank and effectively put the boat out of action until skilled and probably costly repairs have taken place. The propellers and shear-pins of outboard engines are also at risk, so when fishing Lough Anure it is no bad thing to have someone permanently on the oars, keeping the boat in safe waters and allowing the other occupants of the boat to give their full attention to fishing.

Apart from the danger and the risk of damage, there is nothing more maddening than to have your sport spoilt, and perhaps miss good numbers of fish, because you are frustrated by repeated runnings aground. Two friends sharing a boat might do best to take turn about on the oars, changing every hour or so, and very best of all will be to secure the services of a local boatman. This will not only allow you to concentate fully on your fishing, but will probably mean you have a real expert on board, with a lifetime's knowledge of the ways of the lough, its fish, and the best drifts for you to try on your chosen day.

Another Rosses lough, but of a rather different character, lies a few miles away to the north-west beyond Annagary village. Mullaghderg Lough is another sizeable, shallow piece of water, but it is in an altogether lower, gentler setting, and not far from the coast at Inishfree Bay and Cruit Island. There is an abundance of good brown trout here, averaging rather more than ½ lb (0.25 kg) and a boat is really vital if you are to make the most of its potential. Launch your own, or inquire locally, and once afloat use the classic lough-drifting tactics which are so productive on all these western fisheries.

But for something really different, move on from Mullaghderg Lough to little Kincaslough, which lies only a short distance to the west. This is, at first glance, a rather unpromising-looking little lough, but its special attraction and challenge is the fact that it holds some really enormous wild brown trout. Fish of up to 9 and 10 lb (4 and 4.5 kg) have been taken here in recent years, and no one locally is likely to be at all surprised if you manage to extract something weighing 5 or 6 lb (2.25 or 2.7 kg). Known locally as 'slob trout' or 'bull trout', these big fish of Kincaslough are, as you might expect, heavy and fat because of the rich bottom feeding to be found here, although the extent to which they actually feed in semi-salt or brackish water has not been fully studied. Nevertheless, 'slob trout' is their local name.

Wet-fly tactics of the traditional style which are a fairly sure bet on other loughs are most unlikely to impress these unusually large specimens with their deep-water feeding habits. This situation, which might at first appear to pose something of a problem, may actually be to the advantage of the visiting British fly fisher, who may have cut his piscatorial teeth on fly fishing for trout in deep, man-made stillwaters such as the great Midlands reservoirs, where sinking lines, shooting heads and slow fishing at considerable depths are the normal equipment and procedures. Such tactics and tackle are not generally required on the average run of Irish loughs, but Kincaslough is an exception. A careful fishing of this water, working a single large lure-type fly (but not too bright in colour) slowly and cautiously close to the bottom might produce a wild brown trout of a lifetime. These massive fish do not give themselves up readily, but perseverance may be rewarded by something really memorable.

Finally, before we leave The Rosses, we must really not forget Lough Meela, another sizeable lough which lies midway between Burtonport and Dungloe, the road running close by its south-western shore, and with good access from another road along the north-eastern side. Like Lough Anure, Meela is shallow and rocky, and requires careful boat handling and constant vigilance to avoid damage to boats and engines. This lough also has the significant additional hazard of being more exposed to the prevailing westerly winds which sweep in directly from the Atlantic. A balmy westerly breeze may suddenly blow up into a gusty, squally storm. At such times you definitely must set down your rod and give the oars your full energies and concentration, unless of course you have a friend or a local boatman to look after that department.

This said, however, Meela is an excellent fishery, regularly stocked with good brown trout of keepable size. This is a management policy designed to compensate for the paucity of natural food in the lough, which means that the myriads of little trout which hatch and grow so successfully in the nursery areas rarely get a chance to attain a worthwhile size. However unlikely it is to produce sizeable wild brown trout, it is this acidic, nutritionally impoverished environment which makes Meela a particularly good seatrout fishery, for the best potential for growth is for the young trout to migrate downstream to find the richer feeding available in the estuary and offshore. The seatrout return to this and the other Rosses loughs from late June onwards, and can give excellent baskets to the wet-fly fisherman or dapping enthusiast who happens to be there at the right time.

Finn, Owenea and West Donegal

We tear ourselves away from The Rosses with the greatest reluctance and the L75 road takes us southeast towards Fintown and, as the name suggests, the valley of the river Finn. It rises in the Aghla Mountains to the south, and the waters of Lough Finn flow eastwards from Fintown through some of the most attractive and underestimated scenery of central Donegal. The progress of what begins as an upland spate stream is swelled by the addition of waters from numerous tributary rivers and streams flowing in from the hills to the north and south. The river at Cloghans has always enjoyed a good reputation for salmon from late spring onwards, since the days when it was a private sporting estate. Today Cloghan Lodge Hotel is run as a hospitable and progressive sporting hotel, which offers excellent fishing for residents and casual visitors alike. There are some outstandingly fine fly stretches when water levels are right, and this is one river on which a shrimp or prawn pattern is sure to be your best choice. The Curry Red Shrimp is a perennial favourite among Finn enthusiasts, as also is the General Practitioner in its smaller sizes, and the purple variants of all the shrimp and prawn patterns will take fish on this delightful, lively river.

Westwards and across the watershed towards Glenties flow the waters of the Owenea river, shorter than the Finn but with a notable reputation as a summer salmon and seatrout river since the mid-nineteenth century. Along with its smaller sister river the Owentocker, the Owenea has a reliable series of sizeable runs of seatrout and salmon from late May onwards, with an exciting grilse run from June onwards. Water levels are all-important to fishing success on these short, rocky rivers, and when conditions provide a good, steady flow of water at a height which is conducive to running fish the sport can be excellent. On both rivers the variant forms of purple shrimp and prawn patterns are very successful, as also is the Dunkeld dressed on a size 10 low-water double hook.

The town of Ardara marks the mouth of these lively and productive west Donegal rivers, and from Ardara onwards the game-fishing visitor should drive westwards around the Glencolumbkille peninsula, a rounded promontory which forms the northern extremity of Donegal Bay, and which sweeps in a wide and scenically attractive curve out into Ireland's Atlantic seaboard and then turns back into the deep and generous sweep of Donegal Bay itself.

North-west of Ardara lie a trio of attractive little loughs, all of which can give fine sport, and which are managed by the Ardara Anglers' Association. Loughs Doon and Fad are both within easy striking distance of the towns of Ardara and Portnoo, and both can provide good baskets of wild, hard-fighting brown trout averaging a typical ½–¾ lb (0.25–0.35 kg), but with the ever-present possibility of something a little bigger. Both can be fished from boats, which can be hired locally. Third and perhaps the finest of the trio is Kiltooris Lough, an elongated lough set amid gentle green hills and with an island nestling in its south-eastern corner. Kiltooris is less acid than its neighbours, with clear waters and a bottom composed of rock and fine, silvery sand. Light penetration is good, the invertebrate life of the waters is prolific, and trout of around ¾ lb (0.35 kg) are fairly typical when you have a few hours afloat in a boat and fish in typical lough style with a short, floating line cast over the front of the boat.

But Kiltooris can yield bigger fish when the time and the tactics are right. Despite its western location and seeming isolation, Kiltooris has a small but important mayfly hatch which occurs sporadically from early June onwards. When this is in progress, and if you are there at the right time to look out over the water from a good vantage point on one of the many grassy knolls which occur around the lough, you will see plenty of really good trout rising, whose average weight is well in excess of the 10–12 oz (0.35 kg) average which you can realistically expect to take on a traditional team of wet flies almost any time from April to September. Big, stockily-built fish of up to 2 and 3 lb (0.95–1.42 kg) can then be seen on the move, cruising steadily to take advantage of the annual but short-lived bounty of the mayfly hatches, and the best opportunities for getting on terms with these biggish trout is on a calm evening when there is a good fall of spent gnat and the bigger fish are intent upon eager feeding. Then all the classically stealthy methods come into their own, including the cautious and careful stalking and casting of a biggish spent gnat imitation to an individual feeding fish which you have marked down and whose cruising course you have tried to estimate and calculate to a nicety. Drop your fly accurately and gently and you may have a strong, assertive take from a big, confident fish. Miss him an inch or two behind, or drop your fly with splashy carelessness, and the most you may see might be a humping, V-shaped surge as your frightened fish comes off station and heads for the safety of an undercut bank or down into deeper water.

Kiltooris trout are handsome fish, bright and golden with prominent speckling and a spangling of brilliant ruby-red spots. And if I seem to be unduly enthusiastic about this lovely, lonely, trout-rich lough it can probably be explained by the fact that it was here that I first fished for trout, with the first trout rod I ever owned, which I wielded with more enthusiasm than skill under the careful supervision of the man who gave me that rod, and who first introduced me to trout fishing. Canon J. I. Lea was a former rector of Ardara and Glenties, a canon of the diocese of Derry and Raphoe, and a retired missionary who had spent most of his life in India. He and his wife had returned from India to Ireland, first to Ardara and then to retirement near Donegal town. It was there, in the late 1950s, in Canon Lea's study with its innumerable treasures like pig-spears, leopard- and tiger-skin rugs, racks of rods and reels and guns and rifles, and row upon row of books about sport and wildlife, that I first fell under the spell of his tales of fishing and shooting – the introduction to a sporting addiction which took hold instantly and which has not diminished with the passing of more than thirty years.

From Ardara the main road takes you westwards towards Glencolumbkille and the eventual prospect of sea and cliffs from the breathtaking heights of Slieve League, which drops over 600 ft (200 metres) sheer to the wild Atlantic surge below. From there the road doubles back on itself via Carrick, Kilcar and the attractive little fishing village of Killybegs. At Glencolumbkille and again at Carrick you find the road crossing two lively little spate rivers, and the procedure is always the same. Unless you have telephoned ahead and got the latest local intelligence on the condition of the water and the state of the fishing, you stop your car and look over the bridges. A quick glance should tell you whether you should take the rod out of its car-top clips and linger, or press on eastwards towards Donegal town and the hill loughs which lie inland to the north, to the left of the road.

Lough Eske and South Donegal

At Donegal town you are back within a few miles of the border with Northern Ireland, and the town lies at the innermost recess of Donegal Bay, where the River Eske slips down to the sea from its sources in the upland slopes of the Blue Stack Mountains. The Eske has a good run of seatrout and little summer salmon and grilse from late May onwards, especially if the iniquitously heavy pressure of illegal off-shore drift netting has chanced to miss a run of fish and let them slip past and upstream to their natal sources. In the long, lingering western gloaming of a July evening it can be very pleasant to work your way upstream along the few miles of the Eske, fishing from just above Donegal towards the remains of Lough Eske Castle, near where the river flows out of the long, delta-shaped lough.

From late June onwards Lough Eske can give some excellent sport with both seatrout and salmon, fishing in traditional fashion from a drifting boat with a three-fly cast and something especially bushy and buoyant on the bob as an attractor. But the lough is deep and lies in a glaciated cleft in the high hills, which can funnel the westerly and south-westerly winds coming in off Donegal Bay. When there is a stiff breeze on the bay conditions on the lough may be choppy or rough to the point where effective boat handling for fly fishing ceases to be a pleasure. Trolling can be a most productive way of taking salmon and seatrout on Lough Eske, especially if you take your trolling seriously and not as a mere mindless exercise in moronic motoring to and fro with two or three lines trailing behind. Look at the contours of the lough shore and imagine in your mind's eye how they continue under the water, and regulate your trolling lines so that your baits are working at the appropriate levels. Better still, use downriggers and a modern compact electronic depth-finder and fish-finder, and you may finish the day with a basket of fish which will demonstrate to the cynics that trolling is, and should be, a skilled and thoughtfully executed form of sporting game fishing. An added incentive is the fact that Lough Eske has produced some very large salmon indeed, with records of 20-pounders-plus (9.5 kg+) not uncommon.

Lough Eske is temperamental and often dour, but there are compensations. One is the scenery, which is unsurpassed in this corner of south Donegal. The lough is set in the southern slopes of the Bluestack mountains and is flanked to west, north and east by sweeping slopes of heathery hills, although the

June on the Delphi fishery in Connemara. Setting out in ideal conditions.

A tide-bright Irish spring salmon caught on fly.

Firmly into a grilse at dusk on Lough Beltra.

creeping menace of dark green blanket commercial afforestation has begun to encroach here, as in so many once-beautiful places in upland Britain and Ireland. Lough Eske Castle, at the southern end of the lough, is a handsomely situated property, and another delightful house, though on a very much smaller scale, is Ardnamona Lodge, set on the western shore of the lough. During the 1980s Ardnamona declined from being a welcoming and handsomely furnished little sporting hotel to a deserted and decaying shell, but its abiding glory is its gardens, which surround the lodge and sweep down to the lough shore. In late spring it is a riot of azalea and rhododendron blossom, with countless varieties of these acid-loving shrubs to delight the eye and to fascinate the gardening enthusiast. The gardens are seen to best advantage from a boat out on the lough or from the road which runs along the eastern shore.

Sheet 3 of the Irish Ordnance Survey's half-inch series will show you a scattering of enticing looking hill loughs to the north of Lough Eske, of which the most prominent is Lough Belshade. This is a wonderful hill lough, in remote and tranquil surroundings which will remind you of some of the wildest parts of the Scottish highlands. I have fished Lough Belshade on a good many occasions since I first made its acquaintance in the mid-1960s, but repeated inquiries have failed to reveal who owns the fishing rights, or from whom the visitor should seek permission. If I have been transgressing on someone's private fishing I apologise, but in mitigation I must plead that it has not been for lack of trying to establish the sporting ownership. But I suspect that Belshade is one of the countless Irish hill loughs on which the sporting rights are indeterminate and could probably never now be fully established. The gradual decline of so many old landed estates, throughout the nineteenth century and in the aftermath of the Land Acts of Victorian and Edwardian times and after 1921, have made sporting rights on many properties obscure and uncertain, and Belshade seems to be one such. It is so rarely fished, so remote and sequestered, that even the local people seem almost to have forgotten about it.

But for all Belshade's beauty, this is not a lough to tackle in bad weather, or if you are unwilling to tackle a stiff and energetic hill walk of an hour or more up a steep gradient and over rough ground as you strike off from the road at the northern end of Lough Eske. This is a perfect lough to fish with light, easily portable tackle, and a telescopic or sectional fly rod such as the excellent little Shakespeare graphite model is ideal. Good footwear, physical fitness and the ability to use a map and compass should low cloud or mist descend are all vital here, but the rewards are those of fishing in wild and beautiful surroundings. Best of all is to take a tent or make a bivouac by Lough Belshade, and spend a day and a night by its shores in summer. There are few more lovely places in Ireland. Golden eagles, some of Ireland's very last, used to nest here, and you may still see merlins, peregrine falcons and hen harriers. The trout are small but obliging (and taste delicious), and you may be the only fisherman to wet a line on the lough for months on end.

From Donegal to the Dunragh Loughs

From Donegal town two principal roads lead to the south and to the east. The new and much improved N15 whisks you fast southwards past Ballintra to Ballyshannon, while the T35 winds uphill and rises eastwards over the switchback road towards Pettigo and the border crossing on the main road leading back into Northern Ireland and on through Kesh to Fermanagh's historic county town of Enniskillen. These two roads form two sides of a large triangle, the base of which is supplied by the road from Ballyshannon eastwards through Belleek (famous for its fine porcelain) and across into Fermanagh over the long and sinuous Boa Island and its connecting bridges and causeways at the western extremity of Lower Lough Erne. And within this triangle lies a wonderful and largely undiscovered selection of excellent game-fishing waters.

If you begin your exploration of this little corner of Ireland from Donegal town itself, the road leads you past the village of Laghey and then turns up towards the long ridge of hills which is not designated on the maps by any particular name, but which is known locally and by all who know it as 'the Pettigo mountain'. The course of the road runs through a wealth of fine trout waters, but the lie of the land is such that you may not be immediately aware of all of them from the windows of your car. Off to the south, and down over the heather and rough moorland grasses and young conifer plantations to your right, you will catch one fleeting glimpse after another of loughs large and small. All are worth visiting, all hold good brown trout, and all give the best sport to those who devote a little preliminary time to reconnaissance and local inquiry.

A good relief map, like Sheet 3 of the Irish Republic's Ordnance Survey half-inch series, will show the full picture of this wonderful scattering of waters. Many are looked after by the Pettigo Anglers' Association, for which your best contact is Desmond Egan in Pettigo village. Others are virtually free fisheries, for which no formal permission is normally required, although it is always best to inquire locally as a matter of courtesy, and to ensure that your car is parked in a place where it will cause no inconvenience to landowners or farm workers. It may pay dividends in other ways, too, for a straight line is not always the shortest or easiest way between two points, especially if your way lies across thick heather and quaking bog, and through broken peat hags and turf cuttings. The local small-holder, who walks the mountain every day of his life, can quickly put you on the right track, thereby avoiding irritating or danger-ous flounderings over unsure and unfamiliar terrain.

To the north of the road, and up the hill to your left as you drive out from Donegal town, lie a number of important loughs. Three small but interesting waters are strung out over the hill in an almost straight line from north to south, and these are Loughs Keeran, Sand and Sallagh. All are small, and seem like typical hill loughs, although they produce fine brown trout of a surprisingly good average weight. Lough Keeran is a pleasant, intimate little mountain lough which is fishable around much of the shore, and if you have a small portable boat you may fare even better. The lough has good spawning and feeding facilities, which enables the trout to achieve an average mature size of almost 1 lb (0.45 kg), and they are well muscled, pink fleshed specimens which are free-rising and make excellent eating.

Immediately to the south and a short stroll over the hill is the Sand Lough, which is small and can be rather dour. The spawning here is out of all proportion to the feeding available to the growing fish, and you will do well to catch anything over ½ lb (0.25 kg), although there is no denying the tooth-some sweetness of these little breakfast trout. The same comments apply to Lough Sallagh, the last and most southerly of this little trio of loughs. When these little lough trout are on the take a three-fly cast of small, dark-hued flies will quickly give you all the fun you could wish for.

Further east along this long, low hill ridge the quality of the fishing becomes decidedly more interesting. 'The Dunragh loughs' is an umbrella term which covers a collection of four or five hill loughs which lie to the west of Lough Derg. Despite their proximity to this great lough and its catchment which flows north-east down the River Derg and into the Foyle system, the loughs of Dunragh are actually part of a quite distinct catchment, which eventually drains westwards and into Donegal Bay. Access to the Dunragh area has been made much easier over the years, first by the improvement of the age-old turf-cutters' tracks to allow tractors and cars to pass where previously only donkeys and men on foot could go, and latterly by the construction of forestry roads in association with the massive hill ploughing and afforestation scheme which is rapidly transforming the landscape of southern Donegal.

The most enjoyable and most effective way to fish these loughs has not changed, and for the best of the fishing and the scenery you should hike out over these gentle hills and pitch a little tent among the heather and the rough hill grasses. You can fish these loughs early in a summer's dawn or far into the gloaming of a warm evening – and that is probably the best time to have sport with these totally wild fish, which may encounter few other fishers during the course of a season. The smallest of the Dunragh loughs is a bit of a scramble to reach, and is unlikely to be worth the effort, since it is widely believed that no one has ever caught anything in it! The best of all the loughs lies between Lough Derg and the biggest of the Dunragh series, although the fishing is not always easy. This lough is not large, but it appears to produce surprisingly good trout, and fish of up to 1¾ pounds (0.7 kg) will figure in a typical day's basket. They are pinker fleshed than most of the trout from the neighbouring hill waters, which may indicate better feeding in the form of fresh-water shrimps and other crustacea, and the fish are often reluctant to rise to surface-fished flies with the same verve as those on neighbouring loughs.

Perhaps this is one lough on which a sinking line and some deep-and-slow tactics might be more productive than the traditional methods we use on most hill loughs. But however you catch them, the trout of this lough are worth the effort, deep in the body, with a silvery hue and a fineness of head and a delicate pinkness of flesh which makes them rather special.

But for most fishers of the Pettigo mountain, 'Dunragh' denotes the largest lough of this group, which lies slightly to the south-west and just north of the rounded outline of Loughfad Mountain. This is an enchanting spot from every point of view. It holds plenty of free-rising trout, which average 8–10 oz (0.25–0.30 kg), and it will be a most unlucky visitor who does not have a few good little trout in his basket by the end of a few hours' fishing. The setting is delightful, among low, rolling hills of heather, and the lough has a scattering of small islands and bays of startlingly white sand – an ideal place in which to fish and camp, to broil your trout in damp newspapers in the embers of a fire of heather stalks, and to have draughts of strong tea freshly brewed in a volcano kettle with water from the lough and fuelled by dry heather stalks. (But remember the Country Code, and keep all fires and litter under control!)

Up here on the low, rolling hills to the north-west of Pettigo the watershed is complex, an intricate network of hill rivulets and streams, of seepage from the perennially wet blanket peat, of swift run-off from the recently ploughed commercial forestry drains and channels, and from a great many natural springs. It is never safe to assume that two or three adjacent loughs are part of the same catchment or within the same watershed, and this has implications for the fishing. One lough may abound with small, dark trout, while another just a few minutes' walk away is devoid of fish, or has a quite different style of trout, perhaps much bigger and more classically golden. All of this makes the game fishing of the Pettigo mountain area especially interesting and intriguing to study.

Lough Derg

For example, the Dunragh loughs are within a short walking distance to the west of the much larger Lough Derg, a broad expanse of just over 2000 acres (810 hectares) of water which is the source of the River Derg, one of the most important rivers in the great Foyle system. But for all their proximity there is no flow from the Dunragh loughs into Lough Derg, which is largely fed by a number of hill streams along its northern and eastern sides, and also a large number of natural springs.

It is easy but unwise to confuse this Lough Derg with its namesake on the Shannon system above Limerick, which has such an international reputation as a mayfly water, and which is discussed in Chapter 8. But Ulster's Lough Derg has some important claims to fame, too, not all of which have to do with its qualities as a fishery.

Lough Derg is internationally known as an important centre for pilgrimage, and many thousands of pilgrims visit the island basilica and perform the arduous penitential and devotional exercises there during the months from June to August. On first glimpsing Lough Derg, either from the main approach road from Pettigo or along one of the forestry tracks, it can be a somewhat surrealistic sight for the newcomer to see what appears to be a Venetian church apparently floating on the grey waters of a lough in a remote corner of west Ulster. The history of Lough Derg and the island pilgrimage site popularly known as St Patrick's Purgatory is a long and fascinating one, and dates from pre-Christian times.

Despite its position among hills of heather and blanket peat, and its surrounding blanket of many thousands of acres of coniferous forestry, the waters of Lough Derg are surprisingly not acidic. The lough's pH is, in fact, almost neutral, and the water is usually very clear. At no point is the lough especially deep, and there is good light penetration which is conducive to a profusion of crustaceans such as freshwater shrimps and snails. These are a very major component in the diet of the Lough Derg trout, making them pink-fleshed and toothsome.

But Lough Derg is not rich in insect life, or in the aquatic plants upon which so many trout insect foods depend. They are therefore not accustomed to feeding regularly on insects, and the fly fisherman may consequently find them dour and unresponsive to traditional tactics. This seems strange, in view of the excellent reputation Lough Derg enjoyed in the last century and up to the 1920s, as a fly fishery in the very top flight. 'My father told me it was the equal of Loch Leven in Scotland,' one elderly Pettigo fly fisher once remarked to me. In his scarce and important book about fishing in this corner of Ireland, entitled *The Erne; its Legends and its Fly Fishing* (1851), Henry Newland describes how a fly fisher in a drifting boat and casting the traditionally short line of the lough-style method could see 'trout rising pretty thick about him'. These daytime one-pounders caught by Newland's anglers were followed by a stupendous but brief rise of much larger trout at very last light, with fish of 4 and 5 lb (1.8–2.25 kg) coming to the fly.

Since the habits of the Lough Derg trout appear to have changed a good deal in the space of a couple of generations, one wonders what environmental factors have been at work. The recent afforestation of vast tracts of the surrounding country is really too recent to be the sole cause. Perhaps there is scope here for a fisheries biologist to study the lough and the history of its trout fishing.

All this may sound gloomy and unpromising for the angling visitor who prefers to fish with a fly rod. In fact, although Lough Derg trout are often reluctant takers of a fly, there can still be some notable exceptions. There are some goodish hatches of duckfly (*chironomid*) species in spring, and the sedge hatches from midsummer onwards can be excellent. Perhaps inevitably, it is the smaller trout which come up to these hatches, but in Lough Derg terms that may still mean you have a nice basket of trout averaging just over the 1 lb mark (0.45 kg).

The other approach – and we must always be pragmatic in these matters – is to remember that if the trout will not come up to the fly, the fly can be made to go down to the trout. Lough Derg is not a deep lough. In fact it is a large and generally very shallow basin, and a weighted lure or nymph on a sinking line can be most effective. When there is a calm breeze and the boat drifts slowly, it is best to cast a long line which has high density and will sink quickly, and then retrieve at the appropriate pace to keep the fly fishing deep and ahead of the boat. With the fresh-water shrimp known to be the staple food of the trout in

Lough Derg, that is the creature your pattern should try to imitate. Alien though this style of fishing may be in Ireland, it has been proved most effective in taking good trout from Derg, with superb wild fish of up to 6 lb (2.7 kg) caught during the late 1980s.

What of salmon in Lough Derg? This is the source of the River Derg, a highly productive part of the prolific Foyle system, and there are no physical barriers downstream of the outflow of the river from the lough's north-east corner. Yet this is where we have to confront a very curious fact – there are no salmon in Lough Derg, and no one can ever recall one being caught in the lough. And yet every summer and autumn good numbers of sizeable salmon can be seen lying in the pools of the river within a few minutes' walk downstream of the lough, and several spawning redds can usually be found there.

There is an interesting piece of folklore relating to the salmonless state of Lough Derg. Legend has it that St Patrick, on one of his visits to the lough which has always been so closely associated with his name, arrived weary and hungry, and sent out one of his followers to catch a salmon from Lough Derg for their supper. Despite his best endeavours the fisherman returned empty-handed, for although Lough Derg was full of good salmon he had been unable to catch one. The saint, according to the story, flew into a passion and pronounced a malediction on the lough, angrily placing a curse on the disobliging salmon and saying that there would never thereafter be a single salmon in its waters.

Good folklore is not always good biology, but the fact remains that Lough Derg has no salmon, and there is absolutely no apparent reason why the fish should not move up the river and into the spacious lough which has so many good lies and resting bays to offer. In the early 1900s an attempt was made to test the truth of the legend that the waters of the lough were somehow repellent to salmon, even though every drop of water in the river flows from the lough. Lough Derg was the joint property of two Ulster landed families – the Alexanders, Earls of Caledon, and the Leslies of Glaslough – whose estates bordered one another here. A joint team of family fishing enthusiasts and estates workers was assembled to conduct and observe the experiment.

Several salmon were netted and taken alive from the river, and marked to make them readily identifiable. A stout net was then strung across the outflow of the river, to ensure that no fish could move down into the river without being caught. The marked salmon were then transported safely across to the most distant point on the far shore of the lough, not far from where the pilgrimage ferry boats now set out. Here the live salmon were duly released into the waters of Lough Derg, to see what would happen, and a deputation made back with all speed to the net at the outflow to see what, if anything, would occur. But by the time the team of men had returned on foot, by horse and across the lough by boat to the outflow of the river, every one of the marked salmon was fast in the nets, having apparently made a direct dash to get out of the lough and back into the river.

The legend may be very ancient, but that experiment was made less than a century ago, and was well attested by a number of reliable witnesses. And so far as I am aware, no one has ever been able to come up with any plausible explanation to account either for the behaviour of these particular fish, or for the general tendency of salmon to stop short of the lough. Now there is a really challenging puzzle for modern fisheries experts to investigate!

From Pettigo back to Donegal

Whatever your success with Lough Derg's trout, your onward route will take you back through Pettigo and over the high hill road towards Donegal town and the west. En route you will pass close to several interesting loughs, all of which are well worth at least an hour or two of your time. Lough Sallagh is a useful little hill lough which lies just a few hundred yards to the north of the road, from a point about half a mile (0.8 km) on the Pettigo side of a spot known locally as 'the Black Gap' and clearly marked as such on the various Ordnance Survey sheets of this area. A conveniently routed turf-cutters' track enables you to take your car part of the way, after which it is a short and easy stroll. The brown trout in Lough Sallagh do not run large, and a realistic expectation is for fish up to ½ lb (0.25 kg). The rise, especially to wind-blown terrestrials, can be very lively, but at other times an intermediate or slow-sinking line and a slow retrieve may serve you better.

Just about 3 miles (5 km) west along the T35 from the Black Gap lies Lough Nadarragh, which you cannot miss as it can be seen immediately to the right of the road, on its northern side. This is an attractive small lough, set in a cupped fold of land and almost totally surrounded by a riotously profuse growth of wild rhododendrons. This, the *ponticum* variety, was one of a number of rhododendron species which came to Ireland as exotic introductions made by a number of large landowners in Victorian times. In Ireland, and also in parts of the West Country, Wales and western Scotland, it has achieved the status of a thriving weed in many places, for it loves acidic, peaty soils and mild, damp climates. Delightful though rhododendron can be, especially in its various unusual types, *ponticum* has little to recommend it, apart from the cover it affords for pheasants and, more particularly, for woodcock. A well-tunnelled and well-patterned mosaic of rhododendron can provide superb winter cover for these mild-weather migrants, but few Irish sporting estates now have the enthusiasm or the resources to keep rhododendron under the strict manage-ment it requires for optimum sporting potential, and to prevent unsightly and solid masses of the shrub from consolidating.

Over much of the Pettigo mountain road *ponticum* rhododendron grows in large and impenetrably thick clumps, the consequences of one of many unwise introductions of exotic plants and animals by earlier generations whose enthusiasm exceeded their consideration for the possible environmental con-sequences of their 'acclimitisation' projects. But one of the very few good points about *ponticum* is the splashes of bright pink blossom it briefly provides in late spring over places like the hills between Pettigo and Donegal.

Nadarragh is often simply referred to as 'the rhododendron lake', and it has been under the management of the Northern Regional Fisheries Board since the mid-1980s. Day tickets can be bought from Gerard McMenamin, whose cottage is snugly sheltered by a trim fringe of high rhododendron hedges just half a mile (0.8 km) along the road towards Pettigo. Lough Nadarragh's natural stock of wild brown trout has been augmented by annual introductions of ready-to-catch brown trout and also rainbow trout, in an obvious attempt to cater for the casual angler who wants the more or less instant results which only put-and-take management tactics can provide. There is a convenient car park and good access to much of the shore, and the bank fishing is quite good where the encircling rhododendrons do not encroach too closely upon the water's edge, and where the weedy and reedy growth of summer is not too dense.

But it still seems unnecessary to have transformed this lovely little lough into something other than a wild brown trout fishery. The artifice of put-and-take stillwater rainbow trout fisheries may be justifiable in the heavily populated south of England, or even close to major Irish population centres like Belfast and Dublin. But why release non-native trout, which are unlikely to spawn, into a jewel of a hill lough in this wonderfully remote corner of Ireland?

Although he will not say it to your face, when Gerard McMenamin sells you your ticket for Nadarragh he will still instinctively feel that stocked rainbows are 'not the thing' in these parts. With a long lifetime's experience of fishing and shooting over these loughs and hills, he has a masterly knowledge of the waters and their wild fish. If you happen to have had a run of bad days and poor catches, he will be glad to point you towards tiny little Lough Aguse More West, only a few hundred yards down the road in a westerly direction and just below the road on the southern side. This is a minute lough, little more than a large bog-hole, but a better morale-booster for jaded fly fishers could not be found. Its dark and reed-fringed depths are full of wonderfully free-rising little wild brownies, dark and blunt-headed but with a vivid spangling of carmine spots, and their pale flesh is sweet and appetising on your breakfast plate. There is sometimes a small boat available on this little lough, which is otherwise almost unfishable owing to the fringe of reeds, which become a particular problem in late summer.

Another lough not far away presents a quite different type of challenge. From the hill road you will not be able to see Lough Nasmuttan, but Gerard will be able to point you in the right direction. Its few acres lie in a gentle fold of the heathery hills behind his cottage, and twenty minutes' walk should take you there. Here is one of those special loughs, dark and mysterious and often downright dour. You might fish it all day and see nothing, for its spawning grounds are very restricted and there are no masses of little brownies to fling themselves at your fly. But the depths of Nasmuttan hold some surprisingly big trout, well-made and buttery-gold fish of up to 3 lb (1.35 kg), which are not often lured to a surface-fished fly or are even to be seen taking flies or nymphs near the surface. 'Deep and slow' might be your best bet here on a normal day, but the magic of Nasmuttan is to be there in the near-dark of a warm summer night, when the plop and slap of big trout on the move can be heard all around this little lough. Try a White Moth or a Coachman, and these are the conditions in which you may take *the* hill lough trout of the season, powerful, wild and a doughty fighter.

The Drowes – A River for All Seasons

Lough Melvin is such a special fishery that it really deserves a book to itself. It has already been the subject of intense and fascinating scientific study by Irish fisheries biologists, and I have tried to convey something of the special qualities and challenges of this wonderful lough and its salmon and trout in the later section dealing with the great lough fisheries of Ireland.

But Melvin is drained by a river which must not be overlooked, the Drowes (or Bundrowes), which flows out at Lareen at the lough's western end and slips quietly down to Donegal Bay and the waters of the Atlantic just 5 miles (8 km) or so to the west.

Lareen is an important spot in Irish fishing, past and present. It is the site of the 'Big House' which played such a prominent part in Kingsmill Moore's introduction to Melvin and the Drowes, and to the waters on which he eventually devised his version of the unassuming little 'Penguin' fly, which we now know as the Kingsmill, and which is such an indispensable pattern in every flybox on western Irish waters.

Of the Big House there is now little to be seen, following a disastrous fire many years ago, but the out-buildings and the old stables remain. The present proprietor of Lareen and the Bundrowes fishery, Thomas Gallaher of Eden-ville, Kinlough (tel: 072-41208), has developed them into an informal and comfortable colony of self-catering cottages and houses, ideal for the angling visitor, especially if you are one of a party or four or six friends who are willing to share. From the front of the cottages at Lareen you look eastwards up the long length of Lough Melvin towards the distant hills of Fermanagh and west Leitrim, across miles of water rich in trout and salmon. Directly in front of the site of the old house is a splendid new pier and slipway, able to accommodate a dozen or more good-sized lough boats in safety and shelter.

Directly below this little harbour lies the top pool on the Drowes, the first of a wonderful succession of 53 named pools which run from Lareen down to the sea just south of Bundoran and close to the Drowes Bar, an aptly named hostelry and much frequented by enthusiasts of this remarkable little 6-mile (10 km) river. It was from this top pool that a German visitor took the largest salmon caught on the Drowes-Melvin system in the 1980s, a splendid 25½ lb (11.5 kg) fish caught in mid-April 1985 on a ledgered worm, and the heaviest Drowes salmon for at least eight seasons.

But more typical of the Drowes and of the lough are the very early spring fish, which often begin to run in late November and average 8–9 lb (3.5–4 kg), and then the sprightly and numerous summer grilse, which are at their peak in late May and June, and average 4–5½ lb (1.8–2.5 kg). (This exceptionally early run has some parallels with the Garavogue/Lough Gill spring run, discussed elsewhere.)

There is a fish counter at the eel weir at Lareen, and this has provided some fascinating data since the early 1980s about the numbers of fish passing through the upper river and entering the lough. The very high water conditions which can prevail from December to late February in some winters can make accurate counting impossible, but the general trend has been to record the passage of spring salmon in many hundreds, and sometimes well over the magic 1000 mark, safely into the lough before April is out. Catches of 200–400 salmon on the river are commonplace in the period from 1 January to 30 April, and in 1989 there was a quite magnificent total of 400 salmon and early grilse caught on the Drowes during the month of May alone.

In the early part of the season spinning, prawning and worming are common, especially when the water is high, but there is a steady trend towards fly fishing, and an excellent middle beat on the river is reserved for fly-only anglers. Early season conditions will usually call for sinking lines and tube or Waddington-type flies in the larger sizes, but by April a floating line and low-water patterns like the ever-dependable Stoat's Tail are best. The Silver Rat, a North American pattern which has become a favourite and highly successful summer salmon and grilse fly in many parts of western Ireland, is also much in evidence once the weather has warmed up, the clocks have changed and the water level has settled at a steady spring and summer height.

The salmon season on the Drowes could scarcely begin earlier in the year, for Thomas Gallaher signals the 'Off!' at about 8 am on New Year's Day. The Drowes is a sight to behold on opening day, with throngs of eager fishers lining the banks and vying with one another to take the first Drowes salmon of the new season – which is often the first salmon from any Irish river, and a prize indeed. There is a handsome cash prize for the lucky captor, and a pleasant tradition has evolved whereby this first fish is offered for sale by auction to raise funds for charity. It is usual for the first salmon of the season to be on the bank by 9 am, and on 1st January 1989 an unusual 'double' was achieved, when two brothers-in-law each caught a first-day salmon.

The green-and-yellow Devon minnow – the 'yellow-belly' – is as successful and popular on the river as it is among the trolling fraternity at the eastern end of Lough Melvin near Garrison, where the salmon season begins a month later, on 1st February. On the river prawn, shrimp and worm all produce these early fish, and there is no reason why sunk-line fly tactics should not do well too, if only more fishers would try them.

Salmon passing upstream from the river into the lough tend to follow the south shore and eventually congregate in Rossinver Bay, at the south-east corner of Lough Melvin, from where they run up the principal spawning stream in autumn. Rossinver Bay afford top-class lough fly fishing for salmon and grilse, but the conditions are rarely right before April, by which time the Drowes may already have yielded the bulk of its salmon for another season.

From May onwards the Drowes is essentially a grilse river, and unless the spring is unusually cold and dry there will be plenty of lively activity in most of the good holding pools in the upper and middle stretches of the river. This is not a good river for wading, and it is positively discouraged. Instead there are

Two tide-bright salmon for two lucky brothers-in-law on Leitrim's Bundrowes river on New Year's Day 1989. This six-mile river seldom fails to yield Ireland's first salmon of each new season.

excellent walk-ways and bankside paths, and the river is nowhere so wide that it cannot be covered by casting a medium length of line from a single-handed rod of 10–11 ft (305–335 cm), although some fishers' preferences may be for a rather longer two-handed rod, which allows greater command of the water and the ability to work your fly methodically over almost every bit of likely fish-holding water. But a light 13-ft (395 cm) rod is the longest you are likely to need, and most successful Drowes regulars are content with their 10-footers (305 cm) for spring salmon and grilse.

Although the Drowes is famous, and justly so, or its wonderful spring salmon and summer grilse, its potential as a top-class trout river is often overlooked. In fact the river holds an excellent head of beautiful brown trout, and these are often best pursued towards last light. The evening hatch of large olives on parts of the Drowes, especially in the upper reaches just below Lareen, can be sensational, and the trout respond accordingly with some frenziedly active feeding. In the last hour before a June dusk finally slides into darkness you might fill a creel with beautiful ¾–1 lb (0.35–0.45 kg) trout, but how much more satisfying to try and mark down the really big fish, casting a dry fly or a nymph to a selected individual. Two and three-pounders (0.9 and 1.35 kg) are not unusual from this river, but they seem rarely to show themselves until the last of the grilse fishers have packed up and gone home.

Only the dedicated few who are prepared to wait long into the gloaming are likely to see them move and have an opportunity of trying for one.

July and August can be dour months on the Drowes, as on so many waters everywhere. But lack of water is rarely a problem, except in the most exceptionally dry summers, for Lough Melvin's waters provide a massive and reliable head of water to maintain a steady flow. Only a prolonged dry spell, especially if it is combined with sustained strong westerly winds which tend to 'back up' the lough's water, can produce such low water that the Drowes becomes difficult to fish productively.

For a final fling, September is a month to bear in mind. The autumn run of salmon on the Drowes/Melvin system is negligible, but the back-end trout fishing can be superb. The *gillaroo* which haunt the rocky shores and sandy bays of the lough drop down-river to spawn, and in September some sizeable fish can be found in the upper pools of the river below Lareen. Large olives and sedge patterns seem to be the most successful, and trout of 3 lb (1.35 kg) and more are not uncommon at this time. (Later, when the game fishing is over and winter eel netting takes place, some really superb *gillaroo* are to be seen in the eel nets and traps, indicating just how fine the really prime specimens can be, running up to 5 and 6 lb (2.25–2.7 kg) and with a magnificent, golden bellied, slab-sided depth and powerful muscular conformation.)

The Bunduff

It would be difficult to find two rivers which are so close geographically but so completely dissimilar in character as the Bundrowes (or Drowes) and the Bunduff (or Duff). Both enter the sea just south of Bundoran, and you can stroll from the sea-pool of the one to the estuary of the other in a few minutes' gentle walk along the course of the old Sligo to Donegal road. Now quiet and almost devoid of traffic, thanks to the new, fast N15 trunk road whose course lies just inland to the south-east, the old, winding road allows you to stop and take time to peer over the bridges.

The Bundrowes is a river with clear water and a steady flow, which are both products of the great header-tank of Lough Melvin. Its wide and deep waters mitigate the effects of cloudbursts and prolonged rainy periods, ironing out the ups and downs to which spate rivers are liable. Instead the Drowes flows with a fairly predictable steadiness on its gentle and direct 7-mile (11 km) course, in which it falls just under 100 ft (31 m) from the outflow from Lough Melvin at Lareen to the sea-pool south of Bundoran, just beyond the old road bridge.

The waters of the Drowes, like those of its parent lough, are of a fairly neutral acidity, inclining slightly towards alkalinity with an average pH of about 7.2. The river water may also be slightly enriched by the effects of fertiliser run-off from the permanent pastures through which it flows, although the grass is naturally lush and local agricultural practice does not involve the heavy use of fertilisers. The water seems dark, partly because it is slightly stained by peat and also because the pools tend to be deep and the river bed is composed of dark-coloured rocks and marls.

The level, speed and strength of flow of the water in the Drowes vary, but fluctuations are gradual and seasonal, rather than sudden and dramatic. A cloudburst or a day of heavy rain over the Aroo hills to the south of Lough Melvin may swell the feeder streams and send floods tumbling down the Glenaniff River and the countless smaller hill streams which spill into it from the south, but the lough's 6000 acres (2430 hectares) of deep waters iron out the vigour of the fresh floods and absorb the peat-stained torrents of water, mud and debris. When salmon fishing on the Drowes begins, on New Year's Day, the water will probably be 2–3 ft (0.6–1 m) higher than when you go to cast a fly for grilse in June or a dry fly for trout in late September. But the rise and fall is gradual, over many days and weeks, and always the water is clear and bright.

Not so on the Bunduff. This bright, lively river is mercurial in its moods, acidic in quality, and it can rise and fall with alarming speed. You might easily miss it as you drive along the main road, so narrow and well sheltered is its course, with thorn bushes and ash trees fringing its lower reaches and arching over the pools near the road and the sea. After breakfast on a morning in May or June you may set off for Ballyshannon or Bundoran for a few hour's shopping in Sligo and, as you stop the car to take a quick look over the Bunduff bridge, you may see its flow reduced to the merest trickle, scarcely any apparent movement of water between one isolated pool and the next. But a morning's heavy rain over Ben Bulben and Glenade may have transformed the scene by the time you return after lunch.

The Bunduff is a typical west-coast spate river, similar to many others in Ireland and western Scotland. It is short, barely 10 miles (16 km) along its winding course from source to sea, and it is directly responsive to recent rainfall within its well-defined catchment. The rains which fall on the heights of Truskmore and Aroo flow quickly into the hill drains and thence into streams which tumble down from the sheer limestone scarp slopes to the main river. But for most of its length the river flows over heavy clays and peaty soils, and it is much more acid than the Drowes. There is little weed growth in the river and natural food is scarce, so that brown trout are not numerous or large, and anything over ½ lb (0.25 kg) would be remarkable. But the fry and parr of salmon and seatrout abound, and this is a river pre-eminently suited to migratory salmonids.

It may have been a dry and pleasant morning in Sligo or Bundoran, but if there has been a rainstorm in the hills you can look over the bottom bridge and see the Bunduff change by the minute. A summer cloudburst over the mountains can send a flood rolling down, turf-brown, foam-frothed and bank-high, to flush the algae and the stale, honey-slick water out of the near-stagnant pools and down to the sea in a burst of vigorous life. The flood carries its energetic surge of fresh water out into the sea beyond the bridge pool, and from April onwards there should be seatrout and salmon waiting to run up. June, July and early August are the best period, however, and a flood at this season should mean fresh fish in the river and an excellent chance of several on the bank, too. Fish waiting close inshore will sense the new conditions as a summer flood comes down, and respond as Nature has intended, 'taking the yellow tilt of the river with a magnet's purpose' as they move in and begin the run upstream.

In fishing the Bunduff timing is all-important. To spend time fishing it in low-water conditions and in bright spring or summer weather is as futile as to do so when the water is colouring and rising with a spate as you watch it, or while the flood is at its height. But when the peak of the spate has passed and the water begins to fine down, you may have two or three hours of superb sport. So critical are the conditions, so brief the duration of the best fishing times, that you must be there at precisely the right time. And then you may have a morning or an afternoon to remember, with your rod bent into a succession of grilse and small summer salmon. There may also be plenty of the lively little seatrout which run up most of these Sligo, Leitrim and Donegal rivers, and which average about 1½ lb (0.7 kg), with plenty of 'harvesters' at around ¾ lb (0.35 kg).

So fast and furious is the sport when the conditions are right, that the syndicate which purchased the Bunduff fishery some years ago and which now administers it, has a policy of limiting individual rod catches. This seems wise, to prevent the over-zealous from indulging in a fishmongering exercise and to conserve stocks of salmon and seatrout for the future, while still allowing every Rod plenty of opportunity to enjoy fine sport. Your limit achieved, and it may be achieved quickly, you may continue to fish, but you must return your fish to the water unharmed, which is best done by changing to barbless hooks or using your pocket pliers to flatten the barbs.

In the interests of flexibility in their management of this fishery, the owners may change the catch limit regulations from season to season. However, you can check these and other details when you buy your daily or weekly ticket for the Bunduff at the little grocery shop by the lowest bridge on the old road. There, too, you will hear the latest intelligence about recent catches and conditions.

There is an all-or-nothing quality about the Bunduff which will be apparent as soon as you get out of your car and peer over the parapet into the bottom pools. A pound to a penny it will be low and clear, its pools reduced to a succession of boulder-strewn puddles. You might be lucky and get a grilse, or more probably a seatrout, if you fish with care and stealth in the deep pots and tight under the undercut banks further upstream. These will probably hold fish which ran up on the last flood and which must have an enforced rest before another rise in the water level enables them to move further upstream.

But low-water conditions on the Bunduff are rarely productive, and then only with stealth, skill and a large measure of luck. The best bet is probably to fish likely-looking spots with an upstream nymph or, better still, a dry fly. In late spring and summer it is not uncommon to see seatrout and even small grilse rising to take surface insects, usually terrestrials blown onto the water from the bankside bushes and the rushes and rough grasses. Try to match the river-borne terrestrials, and you may require anything from a tiny midge-type pattern to something much larger. I have seen August seatrout taking daddy-longlegs, and even managed to catch them on a large and rather extravagantly dressed Murrough, the nearest imitation my inadequate boxful of dry flies could produce that day.

Most exciting, and also the greatest disappointment, was to see and stalk a good grilse, 5 lb (2.25 kg) or thereabouts, which was tucked in a deep pool against the undercut outside bend of the river above Liscally bridge. It was gulping regularly and with evident relish at a steady stream of daddies which were borne down on the current, and I stalked into an excellent casting position just below his lie. The big Murrough was carefully annointed with floatant and flicked into its best shape, and everything was ready. A gentle, steady westerly wind blew from my back, the fish was still taking the daddies with steady dedication, and all I had to do was drop the fly just above his nose.

Suddenly there was a thumping and a crashing. Great dark shadows were cast over the sunlit pool, and there was a surging boil in the water and an urgent, water-humping V-shape as my fish took fright and made off. A small group of bullocks, snorting and pop-eyed with curiosity, stood on the bank opposite. Unseen by me as I stalked up and made ready, the frisky youngsters had presumably spotted the presence of an alien creature behaving in an unusual way and had charged over to take a closer look, as bullocks will. The cattle stood there, stamping, munching and looking gormless; and the fish was gone. I carried on upstream for several hours, enjoying the sun and the scenery, and returning to the scene of my disappointment after almost four hours had passed. The sun was as bright, the wind as warm and gentle, the daddies were still trickling down on the stream. But of that fish, of any fish, there was not a sign. The bullocks were there, but this time they did not even lift their heads to see me pass.

So much for the Bunduff in low water. But if the water is right, you will be in no doubt. First, it will simply *look* right. Then you will see the dedicated locals, already in action or converging purposefully on the river. You should lose no time in getting your ticket, tackling up, and moving quickly off upstream to find a vacant pool where you will not be cutting in too closely just below another angler, nor coming down too hot on the heels of another. The Bunduff is never crowded, but during those prime and precious hours when conditions are good, it will be much less lonely than at other times, when you might have the whole river to yourself.

The Bunduff offers all the typical perils and pleasures of the classic spate river. Since its waters and the quality of its sport go up and down so quickly, there is little point in planning a fishing trip with this river as your main objective. You might spend a week or even a fortnight looking with increasing dismay at the bare bones of a river, with the boulders shimmering in the heat and no sign of a spate in prospect. Or you might encounter a succession of days when the rain falls steadily, the river remains stubbornly and unproductively dirty and bank-high, and the longed-for fining-down of the river and the start of good fishing come on the morning when you must pack your car and head back for the ferry or the airport. If the latter happens, it takes a stout heart to bear the thoughts of the bonanza you may be missing, of the tales of fish caught or lost that will fly about over the glasses of whiskey and stout in the Drowes Bar or Duncarberry Lodge.

Furthermore (and this may be your dubious consolation) there is never any guarantee that a spate will necessarily bring a run of fish and sport to match. The timing may be wrong and the fish may not be there to run yet. Worse, much of the run may have been lost at sea, scooped up by a drift-net, legal or illegal, should the run have had the misfortune to be intercepted. Even if the salmon have returned to Donegal Bay, they and the in-shore feeding seatrout may fall foul of illegal drift-netting just off the coast. The general drift-netting problem around Ireland is a distressing affair, but a full discussion of this very serious ecological and social evil is outside the scope of this book. Suffice it to say that so extensive is the scale of illegal drift-netting off the north-west coast, so long are the nets, and so small is the mesh, that the majority of fish in a run destined for the Bunduff and the Drowes might well be lost. But as these words are written, in April 1989, there are some slightly encouraging signs that the fisheries protection authorities are getting to grips with the illegal netting gangs. The future of all migratory fish in the waters of Ireland and Britain, and indeed throughout the entire Atlantic Basin, depends upon the eradication of the menace of off-shore and high-seas netting.

But back to the Bunduff. The worthwhile fishing season here is fairly short, and the Bunduff is unlikely to be productive before mid June. Better by far to hedge your bets, taking the Lough Melvin area or the Bundrowes as your main base. Both offer excellent prospects for trout and salmon throughout the season, and a totally blank visit is unlikely. And if that cloudburst comes and the Bunduff springs into life, you have only to put your rod in the roof clips and drive a few miles to be by the river and ready for action.

The Bunduff is now owned and conserved by a consortium of local enthusiasts, but it has passed through the hands of various owners and long-term tenants over the years. In former years it was part of the large sporting holdings of the Palmerston estates, the property of the Ashley family. Lord Palmerston, a celebrated British Prime Minister, turned Broadlands in Hampshire into the family's principal house, and the Sligo estates remained a favourite place for summer fishing and grouse shooting and for woodcock and snipe shooting in winter. Eventually, after the upheavals of Irish partition and the tenant buy-outs of many estate farms under the provisions of the Irish Land Acts of the 1920s and 1930s, the estate was much reduced in acreage and it passed by marriage into the ownership of the Mountbattens, for whom it was a favourite summer home.

Unless you are especially unobservant you cannot spend very long in the vicinity of the lower reaches of the Bunduff before you glimpse the distant, dark bulk of Classiebawn Castle. As you drive along the main coast road towards Cliffoney village you cannot miss it, perched high on a sandy hill to the north-west, a dramatic – indeed, rather melodramatic – building. A late Victorian construction, its neo-gothic towers and ramparts give it a Transylvanian appearance, hinting at vampires and mystery. Like a film-set for a Ruritanian epic, the castle looks awkward and out of place there on this part of the Irish coast, above the sand dunes and the twin rushy lakes, while its elegant Palladian counterpart, Broadlands House, is a pleasing and harmonious sight in its rich parkland setting in the Test valley in Hampshire.

Classiebawn Castle looks theatrical and fantastical, an expression of the same widespread Victorian exuberance in baronial-style sporting-lodge design as you may see in countless lodges and castles throughout Scotland. But Classiebawn Castle has had melancholy associations since the bright August day in 1979 when its owner, the Earl Mountbatten of Burma, was assassinated when his boat blew up in nearby Mullaghmore harbour, with the loss of several other lives. That tragedy shook the whole of Ireland and Britain, but perhaps an even greater and deeper tragedy can be seen from the perspective of subsequent events. With the passing of the years, the Mullaghmore explosion has receded into the historical middle distance, and has become just one of many ghastly milestones in the long and woeful annals of Irish–British relations.

As you drive along this coast, perhaps in bright summer sunshine or when the veils of soft mist and rain sweep in from the Atlantic and shroud the tops of Ben Bulben's cliffs, it can be difficult to appreciate how such violence and grief can intrude upon the peace and subtle beauty of this landscape and its people. Perhaps the best expression of this painful, perennial enigma can be found in the poems of W. B. Yeats, who lies in the churchyard under Ben Bulben. He knew how 'peace comes dropping slow' under these western skies, but he also tells how the land, and the people, and the houses, great and small, could be wrought by the twin powers of hate and love.

> *. . . whatever flourish and decline*
> *These stones remain their monument and mine.*

History of another sort, making a lighter subject for consideration, can be found in the old game records of estates like this. The Classiebawn records tell a good deal about the sporting successes of the Ashleys and their guests, who included eminent public figures, obscure and forgotten names, local sportsmen like the lawyers, the clergy and the doctors, and also some decidedly exotic dignitaries. In particular 1912 seems to have been a busy sporting year, and late June and July produced plenty of salmon and grilse from the Bunduff when the three Counts Metternich were the principal guest Rods. Count Albert Metternich is solemnly recorded as having shot 'one seal at Roskeeragh', just below the castle, on 22 July – presumably to pass the time when the Bunduff was not fishing well, and on the assumption that the seal was probably eating salmon and therefore deserved to be shot. (Seals still find few friends among salmon fishers, either Rods or netsmen.)

At Classiebawn, the Ashley family were fortunate in having the services of several generations of the remarkable Bracken family as their gamekeepers. Some also went to work on the English estates at Broadlands, and few keepers can have been exposed to the challenges of working on two such different estates.

Broadlands remains an outstanding sporting estate, with a reputation for its pheasant shooting and the fine quality of its salmon and trout fishing on the Test, the queen of south-country chalk streams. Classiebawn lies in a remote and westerly region, between the high hills and the Atlantic surge, far removed from the bustling over-population of southern England. Sport in north-west Sligo is still characterised by the wildness and unpredictability of the quarry and their habitats. The rocky, tumbling waters of the Bunduff rise and fall in wild, westerly Glenade with a sudden vigour which is a world away from the unruffled and predictable calm of the lower Test. There the river slips with stately, silent power through the rich meadows and finely timbered parkland of south Hampshire, the waters alkaline and food-rich from the chalkland springs.

Massive, multi-sea winter salmon nose upstream from the sea near Southampton, while big trout, native brown and introduced rainbow, both heavily stocked along much of the river, mingle with the grayling (a fish unknown in Ireland) and move with aldermanic poise among the fronds of gently waving weed. In the crystal clarity of the chalk-filtered water they feed with a discriminating delicacy compared to the wild, dashing, slashing rise of a Bunduff fish, and the Test at Broadlands calls for care in the fly fisher's selection of an imitative style and size of dry fly or nymph, and demands precision and accuracy in its upstream presentation. On the Bunduff you cast your team of soft-hackled wet flies or your small salmon fly down-and-across into water the colour of beer, which slides and tumbles in rills and races and eddies. You work methodically as you fish down the pools and through the rocky lies, and your progress is no less careful or skilful than the arts of the chalk-stream fly fisher on the Test – but they are very different.

On the Palmerston estates, as in most of western Ireland in Victorian and later times, the field sports were truly 'wild sports', as contemporary writers called them. Grouse on the hill and snipe in the bogs and along the reedy fringes of the twin Bunduff loughs below the castle were dependent, then as now, on suitable natural habitat, while the woodcock which nested in the woods of ash and hazel were joined in winter by countless more migrants from Europe, fleeing in annual search of the mild, moist winter climate which is typical of Ireland's west coast. The migrant woodcock and snipe were just as fundamental to the shooting at Classiebawn as the migrant salmon and seatrout were for the estate's fishing.

The dedication and natural talents of the Bracken family extended beyond mere keepering and ghillying. Jules, Arthur and Walter Bracken were outstanding field naturalists, and from 1910 to 1937 part of their duties was to search the coverts in spring for woodcock nests. Colonel Wilfred Ashley had a particular interest in woodcock habits and behaviour, which extended far beyond his enthusiasm for shooting them in winter. When nests and eggs at Classiebawn were located by the keepers or other outdoor staff they were watched carefully, and the chicks were later leg-banded with two rings, one on each leg, one engraved 'W. Ashley' and the other 'Sligo 1913', or whatever year was appropriate. The wonderful total of 760 chicks were ringed during those twenty-eight consecutive breeding seasons – a tribute to the enthusiasm of Ashley and the skill of the Brackens.

It is all meticulously recorded in Jules Bracken's neat handwriting in the Classiebawn game book, and was later analysed by Dr S. R. Douglas and published as two scientific papers in the Proceedings of the Zoological Society of London, in 1917 and 1929. One of the most important individual studies of woodcock ever undertaken, this work demonstrated that most Irish-bred woodcock are sedentary, unlike the migratory birds of Scandinavia and northern Europe.

2 Northern Ireland

When you drive in your car or stroll on foot across the border which separates the Irish Republic from Northern Ireland, it can be very difficult to persuade yourself that you are in fact crossing an international frontier between two separate sovereign states. The grass is just as green; the countryside has the same appearance of being parcelled into little, intimate fields between high hedges and stone walls; and the sun shines as brightly and the rain falls with the same relentless softness.

Northern Ireland is a political and administrative unit within the United Kingdom, and is thus quite separate from the Irish Republic. This division of Ireland into two distinct jurisdictions has had the inevitable effect of creating two separate sets of fisheries regulations. This is something which the game fisher must take into account in checking that he knows the close seasons; that he has the requisite licences, permits and tickets for the waters he intends to fish; and that he has the right kind of banknotes in his wallet to pay for them.

In practice, all this is much less complicated and awkward than it might appear. You will normally plan your fishing trip so that your route, the waters to be fished and the places you will stay will be known in advance, and you can then work out what licences will be needed and whether your expenditure will be in pounds sterling or Irish punts. The ubiquitous credit card is accepted everywhere, and as for banknotes, in areas close to the border between Northern Ireland and the Republic you will find either currency will be equally acceptable.

When Ireland was partitioned in 1921 and what was then called the Irish Free State was established, the border was drawn to separate six of the north-eastern counties of Ulster from the twenty-six remaining Irish counties. The division was drawn along the old county boundaries, and this had some significant and curious implications for Irish sporting fisheries.

County boundaries in Ireland, as in many parts of Britain, have tended to take certain obvious geographical and physical features as natural dividers. A ridge of hills might logically be perceived as a natural divide, and the dotted line on the map which marks the county boundary might well run along the top of such a hill ridge like the vertebrae on the spine of an animal. But much more obvious in most parts of the country, and much more important as defining the boundaries of parishes, baronies, counties and whole provinces are *rivers*. Just two examples of this are where the course of the River Foyle separates County Londonderry in Northern Ireland from County Donegal in the Republic; and where the Blackwater (one of Ireland's innumerable rivers of that name) marks the county and also the international boundary between County Armagh and County Tyrone in Northern Ireland and County Monaghan in the Irish Republic.

Happily for the game fisher and for every field sportsman and country lover, wild creatures and natural phenomena do not readily lend themselves to strict regulations devised by politicians and bureaucrats. Lines on a map mean little to wildlife, for their activities are governed by age-old natural ways which long precede man's appearance on the scene. Sport and sportsmen also acknowledge few barriers, and with a little advance planning (which is part of the fun of a fishing trip) you can travel and fish anywhere in Ireland with an absolute minimum of fuss. This is not always appreciated by the visitor who intends to pack a couple of fishing rods with the rest of his luggage, and whose view of Ireland, north and south, may have been coloured largely by the sensational obsessions of the newspapers and the broadcasting media. Ireland has grievous political and terrorist troubles, but that is really nothing new, and the vast majority of people live peaceful and uneventful lives. Fishermen can go fishing with untroubled pleasure in every part of Ireland.

Northern Ireland's 'Public' Game Fisheries

In Northern Ireland, as in the Republic, game fishing tends to fall into one of two general categories – that which is privately owned and managed; and those waters which are under the jurisdiction of a government department or some other centralised authority. In Northern Ireland the Department of Agriculture has had statutory powers and responsibilities since 1966 to acquire and develop lough and river fisheries as public amenities, and over sixty of Northern Ireland's fisheries are now under D.A.N.I. control and management. The majority of these are primarily game fisheries, including thirty-five loughs and reservoirs and a dozen stretches of river, comprising a total length of around 50 miles (80 km).

But figures and statistics are inadequate to convey the enormous diversity and variety of angling environments and types of fishing which are available among the Department's waters. Nor must we overlook the Department's largest single asset, the huge Upper and Lower Lough Erne Fishery and some of the tributary rivers. This comprises a massive 37,000 acres (15,300 hectares) of water within one huge catchment, and while Upper Lough Erne and the Erne River near Enniskillen have established a firm reputation as unquestionably the finest coarse fishery in Europe, it is to the waters of Lower Lough Erne that the game fisher will find himself drawn. But more of Lough Erne anon.

An excellent 100-plus page *Angling Guide* to the D.A.N.I.-controlled fisheries is published by the Department and updated from time to time, as regulations change and as new fisheries become available. This can be obtained either

Dusk and a flat calm on a Tyrone lough. Check locally to ensure you have the necessary permission to fish. In Ireland the visitor will rarely be refused.

directly from the Department, from the Northern Ireland Tourist Board or in most fishing-tackle shops throughout the province, especially those which sell Department licences and permits. Thus while you are topping up your fly box with important local patterns and buying other bits and pieces of tackle, you can also buy all the necessary licences and permits which will give you the freedom of your chosen waters, either throughout the province or on a more local basis according to your choice. Whatever that choice may be, the costs are unlikely to break the bank. A full range of licences and permits for all-season access to all of Northern Ireland's 'public' waters will still leave you with a good deal of change out of £50 (1989 prices).

It is a legal requirement for every rod fisherman over the age of 18 to have a rod licence. This requirement also extends to those aged under 18 if they intend to fish for salmon or seatrout anywhere in the province, or for any game fish, including brown trout in the Foyle system. In 1989 the cost of a game-fishing rod licence for the full season was £13.30, with a fifteen-day game-fishing rod licence, intended primarily for the short-term visitor to the province, and costing £9.20. An additional licence is required for those intending to fish within the Foyle system in the north and west of the province, and this can either take the form of a licence for the full season or for a 14-day period. Inevitably, charges are likely to increase slightly from year to year, and up-to-date information can be obtained from the Department of Agriculture, the

Northern Ireland Tourist Board, the Fisheries Conservancy Board or the Foyle Fisheries Commission, the addresses of which are listed in the reference section at the end of this book.

One of the principal achievements of the Department of Agriculture in providing top quality game fishing at moderate cost in Northern Ireland has been the development of a number of reservoirs in various parts of the province. Although the term 'reservoir' may tend to conjure up unappealing mental images of stark, concrete-lined bowls and craters with unattractive pumping stations and other functional machinery, the reality in almost every instance in Northern Ireland is very different. Although reservoirs are designed and constructed primarily to provide public water supplies, thoughtful layout and landscaping means they are often almost indistinguishable from natural loughs. Where a pleasing and natural setting does not already exist, measures have been taken to landscape the surroundings of the reservoirs, to contour the ground and to plant trees and shrubs in a way which will provide a mature and acceptable environment for these artificially created reserves of water.

The settings in which Northern Ireland's game-fishing reservoirs are to be found varies enormously, from the open and windswept moorland environs of the Antrim plateau where you will find reservoir fisheries like Dungonnell and Killylane, to the near-suburban setting of Portavoe in north Down, and the City Park Lakes in the decidedly urban setting of the new County Armagh city of Craigavon. All have excellent fishing, even in the more exposed waters such as Killylane. This was expected to be a little more than the equivalent of a hill lough, producing an abundance of lively little trout, undiscriminating as to their choice of flies and flinging themselves with reckless abandon onto almost any pattern of fly you might care to cast to them. Killylane does indeed have splendid natural spawning grounds and a productivity rate far in excess of the apparent capacity of its rather acidic waters to nourish the fish and produce sizeable specimens. And yet wild brown trout of up to 5 and 6 lb (2.25–2.7 kg) have been taken there since the late 1980s, especially on flies fished deep and slow on sinking lines – a clear indication that much bigger trout exist in upland reservoirs like Killylane than you might think at a casual glance.

If your particular preference is to fish reservoirs and other stillwaters from a boat, then the D.A.N.I.-controlled reservoirs will probably not appeal to you. Since they are primarily public water supplies various strict measures are enforced to maintain water purity and minimise the risk of pollution. Unfortunately for the boat fisherman this means that fishing from boats, powered or otherwise, is invariably not permitted. But in Northern Ireland, as in every other part of Ireland, there are plenty of other natural loughs, large and small, where the boat fisher will find all the scope he could possibly desire. On the reservoirs, however, the bank fisher will find many compensating advantages, not the least of which is the fact that almost every reservoir can be fished safely and successfully from any point around the shoreline. This is more than can be said for most natural loughs, where soft and treacherous banks, reedbeds and other natural hazards may make life difficult and sometimes dangerous for anyone attempting to fish other than from a boat.

Lough Neagh – Ireland's Largest Lough

One of Northern Ireland's most interesting and mysterious waters is a very familiar sight to anyone who has ever looked at a general map of the British Isles, or even glanced at a television weather forecast picture. This is Lough Neagh, a vast sheet of water which lies almost in the centre of Northern Ireland. Its waters wash the shores of five of Northern Ireland's six counties, and the lough is almost rectangular in shape, averaging about 15 miles (24 km) from north to south and 12 miles (19 km) from east to west. If you look at an outline map of Ireland you might be fanciful enough to see something whose shape resembles that of a rather ragged parrot, facing to the east and turning its back on the Atlantic. The curved peninsula of the Ards forms its stubby beak, while the coastline of north Antrim and Donegal gives it a high, crested head. Mayo and Galway extend westwards like short, stubby and wind-torn wings and its ragged tail is the indented coastline of Cork and Kerry with its prominent peninsulas and inlets. Lough Neagh is the bird's large and prominent eye.

The lough's vast extent, well over 150,000 acres (60,700 hectares), makes it by far the largest lake in the whole of Britain and Ireland. Set in a shallow basin in central Ulster, Lough Neagh averages only 30 or 40 ft (9–12 m) in depth, dropping to a maximum of around 100 ft (30 m) in a few places, and it collects the waters of innumerable rivers and streams which flow in from all points of the compass. Its chief tributary is the Upper Bann, which drains a large area of south County Down and east Armagh and flows into the lough near its south-west corner, not far from the inflow of another of the lough's major tributaries, the Blackwater. The Bann estuary at Castlerock sees the discharge of waters draining an estimated 2100 square miles (c. 544,000 hectares) of Ulster land.

Although there are countless rivers which flow into Lough Neagh, there is only this one outlet, the Lower Bann. All the waters of this huge lough flow out at the north-western corner, where the Lower Bann slips out at the town of Toome. It widens out briefly to form Lough Beg (literally, 'the little lough', although it is by no means small except by comparison with the vastness of Lough Neagh itself), and then follows a steady north-north-west course of some 40 miles (64 km) to the town of Coleraine and the sea just west of the coastal town and holiday resort of Portstewart.

It is fair to assume that such a massive river-and-lough catchment will afford some notable fishing, and some of Ireland's very finest river fishing for salmon and trout is to be found on the Lower Bann and in the larger tributary rivers like the Blackwater, the Moyola, the Maine in County Antrim, and the Ballinderry River in County Tyrone. Salmon and grilse in their tens of thousands nose into the Lower Bann at Castlerock, running miles upstream and through Lough Neagh to spawn in the upper reaches of the feeder rivers and streams. And from the waters of Lough Neagh countless numbers of big brown trout move up the rivers from late summer onwards as spawning time approaches.

The great dollaghan *or lough trout move upstream from Lough Neagh into its principal rivers when water levels are high from July onwards.*

The big brown trout of Lough Neagh are known as *dollaghan*, and they are regarded as unique to this lough system. The precise meaning of the Irish word *dollaghan* is obscure, but it probably means 'a run of fish'. This is an undeniable characteristic of these lough trout, for their appearance in the rivers comes suddenly and impressively, just like a biggish run of salmon or seatrout into a river from the open sea.

Within the general *dollaghan* category are three distinct types of large lough trout – the 'pollan trout', the 'boddagh' and the 'black boddagh'. All are variants on a common theme, and all confirm what recent fresh-water fisheries research has indicated – that one fishery or body of water can accommodate several genetically distinct races or subspecies of fresh-water salmonid, exhibiting distinctive physical characteristics and with little or no interbreeding between the various strains.

The term 'pollan trout' relates to the smallest of the three observed varieties of *dollaghan*, a neat and trimly-shaped little trout with an overall silvery sheen and averaging around 2–2½ lb (0.9–1.2 kg). These are brown trout from the lough, and the name 'pollan' can cause unnecessary confusion, because Lough Neagh is also renowned as the home of the true pollan, *Coregonus autumnalis pollan*, sometimes known around Lough Neagh as the 'fresh-water herring'.

This is a member of the whitefish family, and may possibly be an intermediate phase or hybrid between the vendace and the other whitefish varieties, which may have colonised Ireland via the great Shannon system, which was one of the first waterways to be opened up when the ice retreated after the last glacial period. This assumption would be consistent with the presence of pollan in Lough Derg, lowest of the great loughs on the Shannon system, and also in Lough Ree, which lies some distance further upstream. Just north of the source of the Shannon, in the hills of north Cavan, pollan can be found in the Erne system too, especially the Upper and Lower loughs.

There is little commercial pollan fishing on Lough Neagh nowadays, although this fish once gave a livelihood to a good many families of fishermen around the lough up to the 1960s, when pollan were netted in large numbers and smoked for sale in Belfast or exported in bulk to northern Germany and Poland. These bright, neatly shaped and toothsome little fish average around 10 oz (0.28 kg) and rarely occur above 1 lb (0.45 kg) in weight, although some of the nineteenth-century records from Lough Neagh describe exceptional examples of pollan which must have weighed up to 2½ lb (1.2 kg). They belong to an ancient and isolated breed, and their home is the wide expanse of the lough, in which they feed on crustaceans, plankton and insect life such as *daphnia*. They do not migrate into the rivers to spawn, but deposit their eggs in mid-winter on the bottom of this big, shallow lough.

The neatly formed, silvery lake trout which begin to move up the tributary rivers of Lough Neagh to spawn from late summer onwards look rather similar in appearance to the familiar pollan of the commercial net fishers, and thus the term 'pollan trout' was adopted. But these are true brown trout, heading back to their natal rivers and headwater streams to spawn and renew the perennial cycle of their lives. They look quite unlike any other lake trout, and can perhaps best be compared with the *sonaghan* of Lough Melvin (see page 161). They are racy and trim, neat and small in the head and powerfully muscled. The Lough Melvin *sonaghan* were once thought to be a 'land-locked seatrout' (although Lough Melvin has a perfectly negotiable link with the sea via the Bundrowes river), so similar were the *sonaghan* in appearance and size to the trim, tough and lively little 1–1½ lb (0.45–0.7 kg) seatrout of Ireland's Atlantic coast river-and-lough systems. The reality, which can only be proved by careful electrophoretic analysis of tissues and blood proteins, seems to indicate that Lough Neagh, like other waters, has evolved several races or subspecies of brown trout, which live and move, and feed and breed, in ways which keep the various races quite genetically distinct and pure.

In ascending order of size after the 'pollan trout' of Lough Neagh comes the *boddagh*, Irish gaelic for 'the old man'. These are altogether bigger, stouter fish, and a decent representative specimen would average 3–4 lb (1.35–1.8 kg). These are much darker in colour than the smaller 'pollan trout', and have the dark background colour and the familiar speckling of the biggish brown trout of a sizeable lough. But most significant of all is the build of these fish, which are stout and solid in conformation. They are typically heavy, chunky fish, short in the body and very deep in the flank, with a hump-backed, slab-sided appearance. They can run very big, and one splendid specimen caught in the early 1960s weighed 12 lb (5.5 kg), measured only 32 in long (81 cm), but had a staggering depth in the flank of almost 18 inches (46 cm).

Biggest of the three traditionally recognised forms of *dollaghan* from Lough Neagh are the so-called 'black *boddagh*', the huge, dark-hued trout which ascend the rivers in early autumn. These are awesome fish, massive and doughty fighters, often running to 15 lb (7 kg) and more, and with many well-attested instances of fish weighing as much as 20 lb (9 kg) and even more. Unfortunately the stringent verification requirements of today's various specimen fish committees have made it impossible for them to accept many undeniable records of really massive lough trout, from Lough Neagh and elsewhere – which is a lesson to anyone who catches a really big fish in the future. Make absolutely sure you have your camera, your witnesses and access to properly calibrated and thoroughly reliable scales.

Any rod fisher, whether his tackle is a fly rod or a stouter spinning or worming rig, will have a major battle on his hands if he hooks a typical black *boddagh*. These biggest of all the Lough Neagh trout are less compact and stout than the *boddagh*, and are rather similar to a thick-set salmon in conformation, with massive fins and abundantly evident strength. But their fighting power far exceeds that of any salmon of comparable weight, and a big black *boddagh* is probably unrivalled among British and Irish fresh-water fish for the power and stamina of the fight which it puts up. The proven patterns of fly for these and all the *dollaghan* types are traditionally dark wet flies dressed in sizes 8 and larger, and fished down-and-across in classic fashion. *Dollaghan* fishing is at its best on a higher-than-average river, and the runs depend heavily on good falls of late summer rain. Sink-tip and slow-sinking lines fished on rods with sufficient power to subdue biggish fish in high water are preferred, and a rod which handles grilse and summer salmon is probably best, combining power with a manageable length for the rivers up which the *dollaghan* come.

It is understandable that these big lake trout should move inshore and begin the upstream migration as summer lengthens into early autumn. This is the same migratory spawning urge which is most evident among salmon returning over thousands of ocean miles to the rivers and streams of their birth, and we see it on a less spectacular scale with lough trout, even in little bog-holes of only a few acres, as breeding fish head for the rivulets and feeder streams to spawn. But the great and still unresolved mystery is where and how to find the great trout of Lough Neagh at other times of the year.

Lough Neagh is a big and still largely unknown piece of inland water. It is a rich lough, with a high pH and plenty of insect and invertebrate life, and an abundance of small fish. It is generally believed that immature pollan form the staple diet of the big lake trout of Lough Neagh, especially the smaller fry which shoal in very large numbers. Why rise to feed on emerging insects when the slightly deeper water provides such an abundantly rich source of food? And that richness is reflected in the growth rate of these Lough Neagh trout. One fairly typical example is that of an 8 lb (3.5 kg) trout which was caught in September and taken for careful examination of its scales to determine its age and development. The scales told a clear tale of a four-year-old fish, the first three years having been spent in its natal river. A typical weight for a three-year-old river trout in, say, the Maine or the Blackwater would be 1½–2 lb (0.7–0.9 kg), which seems to indicate that a fish which descends to the richer feeding grounds in the main lough, rather as a salmon smolt goes to sea at the age of about three years, may achieve a wonderful growth rate of up to 7 lb (3 kg) in a single year.

Lough Neagh is a focal point for many trout fishers in Northern Ireland, but their attentions are focused on the tributary rivers from the late summer onwards. The Maine, the Blackwater, the Moyola, the Cusher and the Sixemilewater all give superb autumn sport with these doughty lough trout – but little or no serious trout fishing takes place in the waters of Lough Neagh itself.

This is partly accounted for by the sheer scale of the lough, which is nothing less than an inland sea in its wide immensity, and partly by the frankly rather dull and uninspiring setting of the lough. Lough Neagh can be downright dreary, a wide and seemingly limitless expanse of water with none of the scenic splendour of Lough Erne, Lough Melvin or most of the great loughs of the south and west of Ireland. It lies, flat and vast, like a huge puddle surrounded by rich but low-lying farmland, some of the most productive and best-farmed grazing land in the country. But there is little to uplift your spirits on an unproductive day, and it takes a dogged, determined soul to persevere when this great sheet of water resolutely refuses to yield a fish or two.

But herein lies the challenge for the game fisher, and especially for the growing band of specimen trout hunters. We know there are big – sometimes massive – trout to be caught. Modern technology and the experience of the lake trout anglers of North America and the *ferox* enthusiasts of Scotland has shown what can be done with the aid of depth-finders and fish-locaters; with down-riggers trolling baits and lures at carefully calculated depths and speeds; and with careful monitoring of the temperature gradient of the water as your thermometer is lowered into the depths. Lough Neagh remains the last – and by far the largest – unexploited stillwater game fishery in Europe, and from its moderate depths there may be caught trout of a size which will astound the game-fishing world. But who will be the first to tackle this challenge and to reap the rewards?

Even if your inclinations do not lead you in the direction of down-riggers, deep trolling and specimen hunting, Lough Neagh can still offer you some good sport with smaller but lively brown trout on more conventional fly-fishing tackle. Its rich waters yield good hatches of insects throughout the season, and the lush bankside growth promotes abundant terrestrial insect life which an off-shore wind carries onto the water. Sedges in particular are taken avidly by trout of up to 2 and 3 lb (0.9–1.35 kg) in late summer, and a couple of hours drifting along the lough shore in the balmy warmth of an August evening, skimming a sedge imitation or some similar wake-creating pattern, might bring you some agreeably surprising results.

In the mid-nineteenth century Walter Peard looked at the trout potential of

Lough Neagh in the course of his piscatorial tour of Ireland, which culminated in his classic *A Year of Liberty* (1867). There he lamented what he regarded as the gross over-exploitation of the lough's brown trout by commercial netting, but his worst fears seem to have been unfounded. Some massive hauls of trout have been taken by commercial netsmen in recent years, with tales of up to eight or ten hundredweight (407–509 kg) of trout at a single haul, which would seem to indicate that Lough Neagh still sustains a thriving head of trout. E. J. Malone, in his important *Irish Trout and Salmon Flies* (1984) also regards Lough Neagh as a rod fishery of immense but largely unexplored potential, and the late Dan McCrea, doyen of Ulster game fishers, wrote an important chapter on the 'heavyweight trout' of Lough Neagh in his *Fisherman's Forum* (1961). But the curious fact remains that very, very few Ulster game fishers ever bother to try their luck on Lough Neagh, preferring to flee westwards to the more dramatic environs of Erne, Melvin, Conn or Mask. And so the field is wide open for the enterprising pioneer who, with modern methods and tackle and an open-minded, pragmatic approach, might achieve great things on this mighty lough.

Only one cloud darkens the horizon for Lough Neagh and the future of its trout – the spectre of pollution and progressive enrichment by slurry, silage effluent and nitrogenous run-off from the rich Ulster farmlands which surround it on all sides. Each summer there are signs of algal bloom in the lough, a sure indication that all is not well. There are important lessons to be learned from the near-disastrous events on the lakes of the Irish Midlands in the 1960s and 1970s; and if eutrophication and progressive degradation of Lough Neagh and its fishing potential can be averted it will reflect great credit on the local farming community and the various conservation organisations. It will also be the salvation of one of the great unexploited trout lakes of the world.

But if you visit Lough Neagh or its environs as a holiday fisher you may prefer to play safe, spending your precious and hard-earned hours on rivers and loughs with a proven reputation for producing fish by conventional methods. From mid-summer onwards, provided it has not been too dry, the lough trout should have begun their upstream migratory runs in Lough Neagh's principal feeder rivers, to join the excellent brown trout which already exist there, and which give good sport to traditional wet- and dry-fly practitioners, and to the growing band of nymphing enthusiasts on Irish waters. A call at one of the many tackle shops in any of the towns within striking distance of Lough Neagh will bring you up to date on the latest state of the waters, the killing flies and tactics, and provide you with all the licences, permits, directions and introductions you will need.

The Lower Bann

As we have mentioned, Lough Neagh's vast acreage empties to the sea down the north-flowing course of the Lower Bann. At its outflow from the lough at Toome there is a famous eel weir and some superb pike fishing, and there is first-class trout fishing along almost every inch of its length from Toome to the sea at Castlerock.

But the pride and joy of the Lower Bann is the exceptional quality of its salmon fishing, especially in summer and early autumn. In the last century and up to the 1940s it was a local rule of thumb that the salmon fishing was best from mid-May to mid-August. After that point in the year it was regarded as virtually unfishable, chiefly owing to the influx of foul and poisonous water from the flax-growing farms along its banks. Having referred to Lough Neagh's vulnerability to eutrophication from modern hazards like slurry, fertilisers and silage effluent, it is salutary to reflect on the appalling annual pollution which earlier generations of countrymen and game fishers took for granted, and which we tend to forget when we look back through a roseate grow at the halcyon days of sport in our forefathers' times.

The Irish linen industry grew famous and successful from the widespread growth of flax in Ulster, and an essential part of the process of growing and marketing flax was to immerse the cut stalks in small pools or flax-dams, to allow the outer fibres to rot away and leave the valuable linen fibres exposed. This rotting, technically known as 'retting', produced large quantities of foul and highly toxic water, which was disposed of by the simple expedient of opening the little sluices in the dams and letting the stagnant water simply run away. Inevitably it found its way straight into the water-courses, and who knows the extent of the resulting fish-kills? My own grandfather, born and brought up in the heart of a flax-growing area of south Tyrone in the 1880s, once told me with a mixture of vivid recollection and considerable shame of how, as a boy of seven or eight, he and some friends sneaked away and mischievously opened the sluices of a flax dam, letting the toxic water flow into a trout stream. Scores of lovely trout simply turned belly upwards and expired, to be scooped out by eager little hands before the gang fled guiltily homewards, filled with the fear of being caught and also with a childish pride at the monstrous draught of fishes they had so quickly achieved. Environmental vandalism by youthful pranksters is nothing new, it seems.

From Toome to the sea the Lower Bann is a large, generally slow river, and parts were made into the Lower Bann Navigation Canal in the last century. Immediately downstream of Toome one such stretch has been developed by D.A.N.I. into an excellent coarse fishery, and there are further such facilities at Portna and Movanagher, not far from the town of Kilrea.

Good fishing for brown trout, with fly, spinner and worm, can be found at a great many points along the course of the Lower Bann, by arrangement with riparian owners, local farmers and the various local angling clubs and associations. All have a well-deserved reputation for hospitality to visiting fishers, and by far the best procedure for making contact and acquiring the necessary permission is to call at the nearest tackle shops, especially in Portglenone and Kilrea. And as always in Ireland, a very great deal may be achieved by simply stopping your car and having a chat with a farmer or anyone else you encounter along the road. Above all, never fail to stop and talk to anyone you may see with a fishing rod in his hand. Fishers the world over are only too pleased to meet other enthusiasts, to stop and give you a full situation report on the local conditions and the successes or failures of their sport. The local angler is always the very best source of sound advice about specific waters, and you may find you have acquired an invaluable guide for a few hours' sport.

But back to salmon, the principal game fishing attraction of the Lower Bann. For such a large and relatively long river the good salmon fishing stretches on the Bann are effectively confined to a fairly short stretch of the river upstream of the town of Coleraine. At the Cutts and Carnroe the consistently high quality of the summer salmon fishing is proverbial, and has been since more than a century ago. Like the Erne, in earlier times, between Ballyshannon and Belleek, the Bann is essentially a late spring and summer fishery, and when the conditions are right the sight of a biggish run of fish at Carnroe is simply mouthwatering. Grilse from 5 lb (2.25 kg) upwards abound, and there are thousands of good summer salmon, averaging perhaps 12–14 lb (5.5–6.5 kg), which come up from the sea on the first part of their long run through the huge catchment of the Bann system and its associated rivers on their way to their spawning grounds.

There is some exceptionally fine fly-fishing water at Carnroe, with fast, streamy water and slower, deeper slacks in which the fish lie in large numbers, and where they have a reputation as free takers. Some of the single-day tallies of fresh-run fish caught at Carnroe are simply staggering, and far outstrip anything which most of the world-renowned Scottish salmon rivers have ever achieved, even in their heyday. The Carnroe fishery is not only a strong contender for the title of the most consistently productive summer salmon fishery in the British Isles; it is also one of the best-kept secrets of British salmon angling.

For many years this superb fishery was held and carefully preserved by a syndicate of enthusiasts. The sport they enjoyed was magnificent, and they understandably guarded it jealously and were reluctant to give too much publicity to the supreme excellence of the fishing. And so Carnroe continued to yield its annual rod-caught harvest of many hundreds of magnificent Bann salmon. More recently, however, important changes have taken place on the Bann, which has resulted in a compromise between the former exclusivity of the private syndicate's sport and the opening up of this fishery to more general enjoyment by a wider range of fishers, paying a moderate fee for a single day's fishing. This new arrangement, whereby the best of the Bann salmon fishing is now giving pleasure to a wider range of enthusiasts than ever before, is still in its infancy as these words are written in 1989. But the new dispensation seems to be working fairly harmoniously and the prospects for the future are good, both in terms of the consistent quality of the sport and the conservation of fish stocks for future generations.

The Agivey

An important tributary of the Lower Bann, and a significant trout and salmon fishery in its own right, is the Agivey River, which rises in the north-eastern fringes of the Sperrin Mountains and joins the Bann at a point approximately midway between the towns of Kilrea and Coleraine. Garvagh is the principal town along the banks of the Agivey, and the local angling association controls most of the finest trout and salmon waters within easy reach of the town. In normal years the Agivey will have received good runs of salmon by late May, and provided the water levels do not fall too low and the water does not become too warm and de-oxygenated, sport can be excellent on this delightful little river set in a quiet and unspoilt corner of Northern Ireland.

Sport at both Carnroe and on the Agivey can be savoured in anticipation, thanks to two excellent video films which have been produced by local angling enthusiast John Thompson. 'Tight lines on the Agivey' was filmed in 1987 and its successor 'Angler's Paradise – The River Bann' was made in the summer of 1988. Both capture the full flavour of sport on these waters, and details of these and other game fishing videos are available from John Thompson Video Productions, 159 Main Street, Garvagh, County Londonderry, Northern Ireland.

The Foyle Fisheries System

There can be no mention of game fishing in Ireland without including some details of the Foyle system in Ulster. This is a massive and complex catchment, comprising five major rivers and a host of smaller tributary rivers and streams, many of which give excellent sport with trout, seatrout and salmon, especially in the latter part of the season. Indeed, it has been claimed that the Foyle system receives what is probably the largest run of migratory salmonids of any river system in Europe.

The Foyle system comprises all the waters which enter the sea at Lough Foyle, a wide and spacious bay which opens out to the north-east of the city of Londonderry, and which can be seen on any outline map of Ireland to have a distinctly oval or almond shape. Out from Londonderry its broad waters widen out to more than 7 miles (11 km) at the widest point, and then the bay narrows to barely a mile (1.6 km) between Magilligan Point on the eastern shore and Greencastle to the west.

This most interesting and important river network is also a very good example of the ways in which Nature and natural features cannot readily be confined within the administratively convenient frameworks which bureaucrats and politicians love to construct. At Magilligan Point you are standing at the most north-westerly point in Northern Ireland, and those green and purple hills just across the bay behind Greencastle are in Donegal, and thus within the sovereign territory of the Irish Republic. The rivers which together comprise the Foyle system drain large areas of both parts of Ireland, the eastern rivers rising within Northern Ireland and the western ones in the Republic. The line of the border follows the old county boundary between Donegal and Londonderry, but the river system straddles it. Thus age-old landscapes and natural features successfully combine to defeat mankind's latter-day attempts to establish arbitrary and unnatural divisions.

Adrift on a Rosses lough, County Donegal. Even a small boat can give the fisherman greater freedom.

Lively summer sea-trouting on Lough Furnace.

Lough Conn yields a fine basket of plump trout, caught using traditional western wet-fly and dapping tactics.

And so it is that the Foyle fishery is the joint responsibility of the two jurisdictions of Northern Ireland and the Republic, which is the only logical way of managing this precious and important natural asset. The Foyle Fisheries Commission has its headquarters and administrative offices at 8 Victoria Road, Londonderry (Tel: 42100) and among its various duties and functions is the issuing of licences to fish within the Foyle system. It is the unique cross-border situation which prevails on the Foyle rivers which necessitates a separate system of licensing and regulating game fishing.

It is a fascinating exercise to spread out a good series of relief maps, like the splendid half-inch and one-inch series produced by the Ordnance Survey offices in Dublin and Belfast respectively, and to trace the rivers of this great system back along their courses to their sources. Largest of all the Foyle rivers is the Mourne, which enters the main Foyle river at Strabane. A short distance downstream towards Londonderry the Foyle becomes tidal, and thus the fishing is free; and each year a surprising number of salmon are caught in this brackish water, in addition to the splendid sport which seatrout can always give in estuaries.

South of Strabane and upstream of the town, the Mourne is really the aggregate of a number of important rivers which drain a very extensive area of central and west Ulster. There is the Strule, fed by the important tributary streams of the Camowen and the Drumreagh, and others too; and the Glenelly and Owenkillew rivers flow in from the east and gather their waters from innumerable hill streams in the Sperrin mountains, while the headwaters of the Mourne itself lie more directly to the south, in central Tyrone south of Omagh. From the south-west flows the river Derg, which rises in the lough of the same name, an impressive, mile-wide (1.6 km) sheet of excellent fishing water which lies just within the Republic, in south Donegal. Cupped in a low basin among the gentle hills of southern Donegal, Lough Derg is fed by extensive seepage from the blanket peat of the hills, by a number of small feeder streams, and by a good number of natural springs. Its only outflow is the Derg river, which flows out at the northern point of the lough and follows a north-easterly course past the town of Castlederg before it joins the main Mourne–Foyle system near Ardstraw.

From the west and the high and lonely hills of central Donegal flows the river Finn, which rises at Fintown and Lough Finn and gives excellent salmon fishing and good sport with wild brown trout throughout its long course. The river around Cloghan has always enjoyed a fine reputation, and the Cloghan Lodge Hotel can provide excellent trout and salmon fishing at moderate cost to residents and visitors.

Although the Mourne and its various large and small tributaries comprise the largest section of the Foyle fishery, two other important rivers join the system lower down, their waters discharging into Lough Foyle between Londonderry and the narrows of the lough between Magilligan and Greencastle. These are the Faughan, which rises in the hills above the little town of Claudy in the north of the Sperrin area, and the Roe, which rises in the Glenshane and Banagher areas of the north-east Sperrin hills and flows almost directly northwards past the towns of Dungiven and Limavady to enter Lough Foyle at Bellarena, where the soaring cliffs of Benevenagh rise sharply above the gentle and fertile sandy littoral of Lough Foyle's eastern shore.

The Roe and the Faughan are both essentially seatrout and summer salmon rivers, on which little excitement can be expected before late May at the earliest. In a normal season with average rainfall, good runs of seatrout and small salmon can be expected from early June onwards, with exciting runs of lively little grilse and summer salmon averaging 7–9 lb (3–4 kg). Both rivers have some excellent seatrout fishing, especially in the lower reaches, although salmon will penetrate to the very highest headwaters of both rivers in a rainy autumn when their spawning instincts are firmly intent upon the uppermost reaches of the rivers and their tributaries.

Neither the Roe nor the Faughan is a large river, and although they rise in hill country their courses are for the most part through gentle and low-lying pastures. Nevertheless, the successful fly fisher will take account of the water conditions, which may vary from a well-coloured murkiness to a pellucid clarity, and choose his fly accordingly. Both rivers can be worth trying with a dropper fly on the cast, which is one of those traditional and proven techniques for summer and low-water fish. It is always risky to generalise, but in Ireland the shrimp and prawn imitations and variants have proved their worth, and on all the rivers of the Foyle system it is important to have a selection of prawn and shrimp patterns in your fly-box, in both natural and purple shades, and in sizes from 6 down to 10 or even as small as 14. Some deadly execution has also been done on all these rivers with traditional seatrout patterns such as the Peter Ross, the Zulu and Butcher variants and the Dunkeld, but preferably all on low-water double hooks.

There are 'public' (i.e. Department of Agriculture-controlled) stretches of river on the Roe below O'Cahan's Rock near Limavady; and on the River Mourne from the weir at the village of Sion Mills downstream for about 1¾ miles (3 km) on the left (i.e. western) bank. There is D.A.N.I. fishing on the Strule, too, but this is principally a coarse fishery managed by arrangement with the Omagh Anglers' Association, and the game fishing is reserved by the Association for its members and guests.

The Foyle and its many associated rivers comprise a large and complex variety of waters, most of which are in the hands of private proprietors and also a good many local clubs and angling associations. Local inquiries are always the best means of ascertaining the current state of the fishery and the best ways of gaining access to the water, and most of the private riparian owners and clubs have a well-deserved reputation for their helpfulness and hospitality to the game fishing visitor. As always, the key to these piscatorial doors is via the local tackle shops or an encounter with a local fisherman, either along the roadside or in one of the many cosy hostelries which (most conveniently) tend to be situated not far from the water's edge.

So far we have looked mainly at the rivers and loughs of northern and north-west Ulster, but two of the finest and most important game fisheries in Northern Ireland are tucked away in the south-western corner of the province, in County Fermanagh. Lower Lough Erne is a massive lough with an unsurpassed record for producing fine brown trout, while Lough Melvin lies just to the south, straddling the border and offering the visitor a choice of three distinctive varieties of brown trout, in addition to the early spring salmon and the summer grilse which enter the lough throughout the early months of the season.

But Lower Lough Erne is discussed elsewhere, in the section on Ireland's great loughs; and since much of Lough Melvin and all of its associated river, the Bundrowes, lie within the Irish Republic, they too are looked at in more detail in another section of this book.

3   From Leitrim and Sligo Westwards

. . . in boyhood when with rod and fly,
Or the humbler worm, I climbed Ben Bulben's back
And had the livelong summer day to spend . . .

W. B. Yeats, *The Tower* (1928)

Drumcliff, Sligo and Lough Gill

Ben Bulben juts out like a massive stone bulwark on the Sligo coast, its vertical limestone cliffs the highest and most dramatic scarp slopes in Ireland, where the high plateau with its blanket bogs, rough hill grazings and a scattering of hill streams and loughs drops to the heavy clay soils along the fringe of Ireland's north-western Atlantic coast.

And at Ben Bulben's foot, in the tiny churchyard of the Church of Ireland parish church at Drumcliff, you will find the grave of William Butler Yeats. Arguably the finest poet in English of the twentieth century, Yeats was a Sligo man. He was never more at ease than when he could raise his massive, craggy head and see Ben Bulben's gaunt, familiar profile. North-west Sligo is Yeats Country, by long association with the poet and his family, a link promoted by tourist literature and guided tours. For the international scholars, and for those who find a simple delight in his writings, there is the continuing traditions of the Yeats Summer School which convenes here annually to consider the poet, his work and the landscape which gave birth to both.

But what has Yeats to do with fishing? What has poetry to do with Irish game fishing? Sadly, if you need to ask those questions, you will probably not be satisfied by any answer. *Piscator non solum piscatur* – there is more to fishing than merely catching fish. The art and the craft of skilful, successful fishing demand an understanding of natural things, of wind and weather, birds and animals. No sport calls for such an intimate and personal absorption with the natural scene. And no sport can give such rich rewards from that involvement. That is why a fisherman may be a poet, and that is why fishing, far more than any other sport, has given birth to a wonderfully rich tradition of fine writing, in prose and verse. Thinkers, writers, poets and those of a reflective and poetical cast of mind have often been drawn to fishing. Our heritage of sport and of literature are both the richer for it.

From his early boyhood W. B. Yeats knew the rivers, the hill streams and the loughs of this corner of Ireland. And when he grew older – 'decrepit age', he called it, 'that has been tied to me as to a dog's tail' – he remembered the excitement and the eager anticipation of his youthful days fishing in the Sligo hills. Bowed down with years, with the responsibilities of age, public duties and his political commitment to Ireland in the early and agonised decades of this century, he remembered with delight the freedom and the honest, simple joys of fishing. He recalled it in the simple words with which this chapter begins, and he went on later in the same poem to draw a brief but striking portrait of his ideals of the honest, upright men upon whom the future of mankind and civilisation would depend.

> . . . *upstanding men*
> *That climb the streams until*
> *The fountain leap, and at dawn*
> *Drop their cast at the side*
> *Of dripping stone; I declare*
> *They shall inherit my pride . . .*
> *I leave both faith and pride*
> *To young upstanding men*
> *Climbing the mountain side,*
> *That under bursting dawn*
> *They may drop a fly . . .*

For Yeats, the solitary dignity of the fisherman on the western hills represented goodness and honesty in a world which he believed was suffering from cruelty and cowardice, from wit without humour, from self-seeking cleverness.

No one who enjoys fishing should miss a chance to explore the rivers and loughs and hills which lie within sight of Ben Bulben, and within easy reach of the many hotels and guest-houses within the Yeats Country. And in preparation for your journey, or for your reading on your trip, you can refresh your memory of Yeats's poems, or perhaps discover them for the first time.

Sligo is one of five counties which together comprise Connaught, Ireland's sprawling and sparsely populated western province. Mountainous and grand in many ways, from the soaring escarpments of the north-west coast to the gentler outlines of the Bricklieve and Curlew mountains in the south of the county, Sligo is also rich in other types of landscape. There are long strands of white sand, wide vistas of lush pasture parcelled in small, stone-walled fields, and mild, damp woodlands of native ash, oak and hazel. The blanket peat which covers the high plateaux is spangled with scores of little hill loughs, many of which are unvisited by any fishermen. Elsewhere, glaciation and the folding of the land into hills and deep valleys has created large loughs, where the underlying limestone makes the waters alkaline and rich in fish and fly life.

Spate rivers and hill streams tumble into the bays, and most have good runs of salmon and seatrout, especially in late spring and summer. Lough Arrow lies in the south-east of the county, and is such a celebrated trout fishery, especially in mayfly time, that its very name conjures up visions of the finest brown trout fishing, and we will look at it in more detail shortly. And for the specimen pike angler there are some of the finest and most productive waters anywhere in Ireland. All in all, Sligo is a county no fisherman should overlook.

Sligo town, large, prosperous and friendly, lies towards the northern end of the county, and no river or lough in Sligo is very far away by car. There are tackle shops and, equally important for the family fishing party, gift shops aplenty, and the town and its environs abound with hotels, guest-houses and bed-and-breakfast places offering every level of price and luxury.

But towns, however agreeable, are not always to the liking of the holidaymaker or the visiting angler, who may relish an escape from urban surroundings. Most of us, after all, are obliged to spend much of our working lives surrounded by people, traffic and bustling activity. But out in the Sligo countryside there are countless farmhouse guest-houses and country homes, in peaceful, rural surroundings where the outlook from your bedroom will probably be over a lough or onto rich limestone grasslands which are world-renowned as pastures for fine cattle and bloodstock. There are few houses in Sligo where you can mention fishing, hunting or racing without finding a fellow enthusiast among your hosts.

Sligo's waters can offer you every sort of game fishing, from the pursuit of big lough trout and salmon to dark, free-rising little wild trout in hill loughs, and seatrout in streams so narrow and overhung with bushes that you may find a little 7-ft (215 cm) brook rod seems over-long. But perhaps the best way to begin sampling Sligo fishing and Sligo scenery is to head for the hills. We can begin with a mountain lough which W. B. Yeats knew and wrote about.

From Sligo town you take the main N59 trunk road which runs south to Ballysodare, and then turns westwards towards Easky and the borders of County Mayo. The road follows the narrow coastal strip between the waters of Ballysodare Bay and the lower slopes of the Ox Mountains.

The word 'mountain' is a relative term, whose use in Ireland deserves some explanation. Ireland is not a land of alpine peaks or high ranges. Its highest point is the summit of Carrauntoohil, in the MacGillycuddy's Reeks which soar with majestic green grandeur to the west of the lakes of Killarney, in the far south-west of Ireland. There you stand on the topmost point on Irish soil, at rather less than 3500 ft (1070 m). At the diametrically opposite end of Ireland, in County Down, the slope of Slieve Donard, highest of the mountains of Mourne, sweeps down to the sea, just like the song says, from a height of 2796 ft (852 m). That is the highest point in Northern Ireland.

In cosmic terms both peaks are pimples. In Scotland the Cairngorms sweep across the Grampian region with mile after mile of land at well over 3000 ft (910 m). To an Austrian or a Swiss these are as insignificant as the Alps to a Sherpa, and so on.

Thus an Irish mountain is a modest affair, and so far we have mentioned only two of the highest peaks. There are thousands of lesser hills, eminences and outcrops which are also dignified by the name of mountain, and some may be as low as 300–400 ft (90–120 m). As a rough guide, anything whose name begins with 'Slieve', 'Ben', 'Croagh' or 'Knock' tends to be on the high side; 'Carrick', 'Carn' and 'Craig' are likely to be much lower; and what is locally known as, for example, 'Donnelly's Mountain' is probably nothing more than a piece of gently undulating hill grazing which rises behind a farm owned by a family named Donnelly.

If an Irishman invites you to 'walk over the mountain with me' to fish a little lough or a stream, do not panic at your unfitness and envisage sheer slopes. It is unlikely to involve anything more strenuous than an agreeable stroll over an area of heathery, boggy hummocks and hollows. Heather, in fact, is one of the essential prerequisites of an Irish mountain. In some parts of Ireland a mountain means much the same as a 'moss' in lowland Scotland, an area of raised blanket bog on which ling heather, cotton grass and sphagnum moss are the principal vegetation, and snipe, grouse, golden plover and hares the principal wildlife. Many a Scottish moss and Irish mountain (in this sense) actually lies at or even below sea level.

In Ireland, therefore, we tend to use the word mountain in our own way. It is not hyperbole, and we are not inclined to make great claims for the heights of our hills. It is simply that the Irish language, and thus Irish placenames, include such a wealth of different terms for a high or hilly place that the English vocabulary cannot easily supply adequately subtle equivalents. And so everything is a mountain. This digression seems justified, if only to put Irish mountains (of all types) in perspective. Visitors to Scotland require a comparable explication of the term 'hill'. This can mean anything from the sheep-walks behind the crofter's bothy, the equivalent of 'Donnelly's Mountain', to Ben Nevis and sundry other 4000-ft-plus (1220 m) peaks. When a stalker in a Highland deer forest takes you out 'on the hill' you may have to contend with precipitously steep slopes, soaring peaks wreathed in high clouds, and the possibility that a stag shot at the wrong spot in the forest may tumble, bounce and free-fall hundreds of feet, leaving you with an irate stalker, and a long scramble down to find the pulped remains of your beast and the shattered pieces of the antlers you had envisaged hanging on your wall. The English language is a curious tongue, and Irish mountains are less to be feared than 'the hill' in Scotland.

But *revenons à nos moutons* – or mountains. From the low eastern spur of the Ox Mountains near Collooney the slopes rise steadily, peaking at almost 1800 ft (550 m) on the top of Knockalongy, 7 miles (11 km) to the west. As you drive westwards, and a mile (1.6 km) beyond the village of Dromard, you should turn left. The by-road rises, gradually at first and then with increasing steepness, into the northern slopes of the Ox Mountains, eventually to snake its way over the scenic watershed of Ladies Brae, before it dips slowly towards Coolaney and the valley of the Owenboy River.

Just before the Ladies Brae stretch of the road begins you will see little Lough Achree tucked down in the valley to the right of the road. You should park your car carefully, to avoid blocking the road, which is narrow and also sometimes surprisingly busy in the summer months, with tourists 'doing' Ladies Brae, or visitors out from Sligo for a run on a fine day in spring or late summer. Better still, you may be able to park well off the road, if you ask first at Harte's House.

Lough Achree is also known as Harte's Lake, a name which may ring a distant bell if you remember Yeats's mysterious and haunting poem, 'The Host of the Air', for this is 'the drear Harte Lake'. You may still flush 'the wild duck and the drake', and perhaps a snipe or two, from among the 'tall and the tufted reeds' around its shores.

Happily for the fisherman, most of the shore is reed-free and easily fished from the bank or by shallow wading. Lough Achree is free fishing, but there are no boats and bank fishing is the custom. The trout are dark and with vivid crimson spots, typical products of a rather acidic hill lough fed by mountain streams flowing from blanket peat over a bedrock of schists. Half to ¾ lb (0.25–0.35 kg) is a good average weight, and bigger specimens running to over 1 lb (0.45 kg) are not uncommon.

This little lough is, like most of its kind, overpopulated with trout, the consequence of pure water and excellent spawning conditions combined with a limited food resource. Don't scorn to keep those 6-oz (0.15 kg) fish, but take them home and enjoy them for breakfast. They taste superb, and you can extinguish any twinges of misgivings by reminding yourself that you may be slightly improving the chances of someone catching bigger trout next season. It can be done, and Lough Achree yielded a trout of just under 4 lb (1.8 kg) in 1980. A visitor fishing from the south shore, underneath the shoulder of Knockachree, was skimming a large sedge pattern in the warmth of an August evening, when

> 'the reeds grew dark
> At the coming of night-tide . . .'.

This trout was large and dark but a perfectly proportioned, pink-fleshed specimen, evidence of the potential for growth of these wild trout of the hill loughs.

If you enjoy fishing Lough Achree and hill loughs like it, Sligo has a great deal to offer, and you do not need to drive on much further to find more fishing. Just up the road from Lough Achree, as you breast the top of the Ladies Brae and begin your descent into the Owenboy valley, a hill road turns off to the right. Leaving your car at the end of the road, just where it makes a swing to the left and begins to drop towards Longford House, Chapel Street and back to Dromard, little Lough Bree lies down to your right. It is only a short walk of a few hundred yards from the road to the water's edge.

Lough Bree is a free fishery, and its 6 or 7 acres (2.5–3 hectares) of dark water are full of sprightly little trout. Once again, these are the products of impoverished acidic waters, where food is at a premium. Bree trout are smaller and tend to be darker than the average fish from Lough Achree, but they are obligingly free-rising. This can be a significant bonus if you have fished and failed on other waters and want a boost to your spirits. And trout which are keen to rise to whatever fly you cast to them are a source of enormous encouragement to the young fly fisher, or to the beginner. However experienced you may be, and however inured to the disappointment of a dour day on a larger lough, in unrewarded pursuit of larger trout, your state of mind might be quickly redeemed by an hour's sport on little Lough Bree on your way back to supper.

Fly fishers using Sligo town as their base are ideally placed for quick access to some wonderful fishing within only a few miles of the town. Lough Gill is a big lough and an important game fishery of interest to salmon fishermen from the very start of the season, which begins on 1 January. Like the neighbouring Bundrowes River and Lough Melvin, which lie over the hills to the north, this river and lough system has a good early run of salmon. Average weights will probably be around 10–12 lb (4.5–5.5 kg), which is marginally higher than on the Drowes. In good years fresh-run fish in significant numbers start to enter the Garavogue River and ascend to the lough from late December onwards. This river was formerly part of the Wood-Martin estates, and in 1891 the then owner, Colonel Wood-Martin, was so intrigued by the early arrival of these 'spring' fish that he persuaded the Fisheries Board to agree to an experimental netting of some pools on the river in the month of November. This yielded forty-one fresh-run salmon at the first attempt. The early run was thus dramatically demonstrated, but the opening date was very properly left at 1 January.

A few years before the netting experiment confirmed the early Garavogue run, a dedicated game fisher named John J. Dunne had commended Lough Gill to the visiting salmon angler in his important book *How and Where to Fish in Ireland*. This is not the dull guide book and gazetteer its name suggests. Written under the pen-name of 'Hi-Regan' and first published in 1886, this was not only an excellent how-where-and-when-to-fish guide but also a delightful piece of fishing literature, full of fun and zest and irreverent remarks. Not every writer would have the flair, or the nerve, to write that a certain town 'has two hotels, and I have been tolerably comfortable in one of them'! One wonders what horrors awaited the guest in the other establishment. Dunne's book was hugely popular and was continually reissued in many editions between 1886 and 1914, with updated information about Irish fisheries. It kept two generations of Victorian and Edwardian game fishermen informed and amused, and it is still a fresh and amusing book. Happily, it is not rare or expensive, and any dealer in old fishing books should be able to find a copy quickly for under £10. Get a copy, savour Dunne's uninhibitedly candid writing, and compare the game fishing of Ireland in the 1890s with today's sport.

Dunne loved Lough Gill. 'Its beauty is entrancing, and its fishing is not unworthy its beauty', he wrote, and goes on to tell in an engaging turn of phrase of the bright freshness of the salmon caught directly after their brief passage up the short river – '. . . they are killed in the full dress of marine parade'.

Even in the mild west of Ireland the first weeks of the year are rarely a time of kindly fishing conditions. The water is cold and usually high, the weather often chill and blustery, and it is inevitable that most early salmon here are taken on the troll. As on the Drowes–Melvin system, the green-and-yellow metal Devon minnow – 'the Yellow Belly' – in 2 and 3-in (6.5 and 7.5 cm) sizes, is a local favourite, although the brown-and-gold version also accounts for its share of salmon.

By February and March Lough Gill should hold a good head of salmon, and although the majority of fish are caught by trolling, that is probably because almost all fishers use that method! There is undoubtedly good scope for the fly fisher on Lough Gill, especially if he is in the hands of a boatman who knows the lies and the taking sports, and can hold a boat over the right places. 'Hi-Regan' knew this in 1886, and wrote that 'the lodges [i.e. salmon lies] in Lough Gill can only be profitably described to an angler by a local expert, and of these Sligo has several honest and sporting . . .'. (Was he implying that the majority were dishonest rogues and poachers?) You can still find Sligo boatmen who know the lies and drifts, and who have local knowledge and boat handling skills of a high order, which you will need, especially if you fish the lough in a gusting March wind. In cold weather you should treat the lough as you would a salmon river under similar conditions, fishing deep and slow with a large fly. A Waddington of 3 in (7.5 cm) or even larger is not too big, and with a shortish (say 8 ft/2.5 m) leader on a fast-sinking line it will get down quickly. As on almost every salmon fishery in Ireland, shrimp and prawn-based patterns are popular here, including the Curry's Red Shrimp and the General Practitioner on size 4 and 6 trebles. Among the tube and Waddington patterns the Willie Gunn and the Yellow and Black do well.

But there is no doubt that the fly fisher for salmon on Lough Gill stands a much greater chance of success slightly later in the season. The system gets a second and usually slightly smaller run of fish in April, and then, if the spring weather is mild and the water temperature begins to warm up, salmon become much more responsive to a fly fished on a floating line and worked just below the surface. This is by far the most enjoyable and effective way to fish a fly for salmon on a lough, and when known lies are covered the results can be excellent. The Green Peter, dressed as a low-water pattern on a size 6 or 8 double hook is a proven recipe for Lough Gill in April and May, although the pattern was originally designed as a representation of a sedge pupa and with trout in mind. Suitably adapted, it has won its spurs as a salmon fly here, and it is also worth trying other comparatively sober patterns like the Brown Turkey and the Green Highlander, in similar sizes.

The salmon catches on Lough Gill are impressive and during the 1980s the annual averages were over 350 fish recorded. Undoubtedly others went unrecorded, not to mention the poachers' share, so the figures are high. Sadly, like so many other Irish fisheries, Lough Gill's salmon run suffers badly from the pressures of drift-netting, some of it legal but much of it illegal and unregulated. Many returning salmon never make it back to the river and the lough, and those that do are often net-marked, evidence of their narrow escape and a reminder of the netting menace. With three or four hundred salmon legally caught with rod and line each year, Lough Gill is nevertheless a considerable salmon fishery. The potential is enormous, for this catchment comprises almost 140 square miles (360 square km). One cannot help wondering what the runs and the rod-caught totals might be like if illegal coastal netting was stamped out. The prospect is mouthwatering.

Lough Gill's recent performance shows it to be a consistently reliable and productive salmon fishery, despite the pressures of drift-netting at sea. There is some consolation in comparing its present productivity with the sorry state of affairs which existed on the Garavogue and Lough Gill almost a century ago. In 1898 the Rods and also the legal nets noticed a sudden and serious falling-off in their catches. This went on for several seasons, and a distraught angler named Manley Palmer, who had forty seasons' experience of fishing on Lough Gill and the Bonet River, reported to the Fisheries Commissioners that '. . . as far as rod fishing is concerned they have gone to nothing. For six years I have not killed a fish in the lake or the river, while my keeper, who fishes much more often than I do, averages but two a year!' Thirteen years later the situation was seemingly no better, and Augustus Grimble wrote that 'since 1898 hardly a fish has fallen to the rod' on what he described as 'the ruined angling of Sligo'.

We can take some comfort from the fact that there has been a notable recovery since those days, which shows the vigour and powers of recovery of a migratory species like the salmon when the spawning habitat and the vital breeding stocks are not exploited beyond what they can sustain.

The early nature of the fishing on Lough Gill is underlined by the fact that few salmon are caught after the end of May, and unlike Lough Melvin there is no significant late-spring grilse run to prolong the salmon fisher's sport. But by that time a number of other north-western Irish salmon fisheries are in full swing, and the salmon fisher need not pack his tackle away, but should turn to other waters.

Lough Gill is also a brown trout fishery, although it is not often highly regarded by comparison with some of its neighbours. This reputation is not entirely unfair, because the trout do seem to be elusive. In part this may be attributable to their seeming dourness and a general reluctance to rise with the freedom you expect of trout on Irish loughs in limestone areas. But mayfly time can change all that, and the trout fishing in late May and June can be a lively and productive time for the trout fisher.

In most years the first mayfly appear on Lough Gill around 20 May, and there is a steady hatch for four or five weeks. A gradual tailing-off takes place in late June and by early July Lough Gill's mayfly season is over for another year. In this respect it differs from a number of other western loughs, where the first and liveliest of the mayfly hatches also takes place at that time, but on which good hatches of fly are likely to continue through July and August.

When the mayfly are up on Lough Gill the trout can respond with vigorous surface feeding, and good fish are taken each season by dapping the natural flies. In passing, it is interesting to note the local opinion, which experience seems to confirm, that Lough Gill trout can be 'struck' rather more quickly than the trout of many other loughs at mayfly time. Why this should be, and why the trout on one water should require a longer recitation of a rhyme or a catch-phrase than other trout on other mayfly waters, is a mystery. Is it fanciful to think there may be an opportunity here for a comparative scientific study of how trout take mayflies on different loughs?

Trout of 1–3 lb (0.45–1.35 kg) can be expected in a typical day's catch, and they are fine specimens, deep-bodied and heavy-shouldered. The pinkness of their flesh, and their general reluctance outside mayfly time to show on the surface or to rise to a fly, probably confirm the local belief that Lough Gill trout normally feed on the rich variety of invertebrate and crustacean foods available at lower depths and on the lough floor. If this is the case, a tendency to feed deep need not be an insuperable problem for the fly fisher, who must simply be prepared to fish deep and try to find the trout there. Lough Gill trout will feed in the rocky shallows, especially early and late in the season, and spooned fish have revealed eager feeding on shrimps and hog-lice.

This presents no problems in terms of tackle and technique for the fly fisher, who can cast right in among the shoreline boulders and along the shallows and work a mixed cast of wet-fly/nymph patterns in a few inches of water. But to manoeuvre correctly and safely so close to the shore requires the help of a capable person on the oars. Two anglers sharing a boat can take turns on the oars, or a boatman can do this while two Rods are busily searching the shallows. Needless to say, a good local boatman is always the best bet, especially as he is likely to know the lough, the best drifts, and the tricks of the wind. And since he probably spends a good part of each year on the lough, he can handle a good-sized lough boat with an effortless familiarity which does not come readily to the holiday fly fisher.

In deeper water, however, the traditional and generally successful techniques of Irish lough fishing, with a short line from a drifting boat, will not present flies at the depths necessary to connect with deep-feeding fish. On Lough Gill, and on many other Irish waters at various times of the year, there is undoubtedly scope for innovation and experimentation with some of the stillwater fly-fishing techniques developed on British waters.

On Lough Gill, like many Irish loughs, you can simply drive up trailing your own boat behind your car, and launch from one of several excellent public slipways and jetties. One of the favourites, and quickly accessible from Sligo town, is the jetty on the south shore, close to where the Garavogue River flows out. Here you are ideally placed for all the south shore drifts, especially if there is a westerly wind, which is usually the case. A short north-easterly spell of motoring will bring you across to a point along the Hazelwood shore, from where there are some well-known and productive drifts eastwards towards Church Island. Alternatively you may swing south from the pier, turning into Aughamore Bay, which is another good prospect with a short-lined wet-fly cast, around the shore and past the small island of Aughamore Rock.

The extreme eastern end of Lough Gill also has a jetty, at Scriff Pier, easily reached by taking the L16 road towards Manorhamilton from Sligo. This follows the northern shore, and from Scriff Pier you are then well placed to fish

A brown trout netted right among the shoreline rocks. Careful boat handling is necessary to fish the best drifts on Ireland's rocky western loughs.

the eastern end of the lough. At this end of Lough Gill you are actually over the county boundary and into County Leitrim. In the south-east corner of the lough the principal feeder of Lough Gill, the Bonet River, flows in and its course marks the Sligo–Leitrim boundary, which then takes an almost northerly line across the lough and over the peak of Keelogyboy mountain towards distant Glencar.

Salmon from Lough Gill run up the Bonet River, past Dromahaire and Manorhamilton, where the Owenmore tributary flows in, and there can be good salmon fishing in the lower reaches of the river and some excellent trouting in the upper waters towards Glenade.

On Lough Gill, as on virtually every Irish lough of any size, you will have better sport from a boat than from the bank. But if bank fishing is your preference, or if you only wish to wet a line for an hour or so, much of the shore is easily fishable, and especially along the northern shore where the road runs right along the edge of the lough. As with bank fishing everywhere, observe the courtesies and secure permission first.

For your tickets and permits, these are not normally required for the south shore, but are necessary for the north shore, and it is as well to have them if you take a boat out. Who knows what parts of the lough you may wish to fish during the day.

Lough Colgagh and Glencar

If you have been unlucky, and have found the salmon elusive and the trout dour on Lough Gill, or if your fancy runs to a day on a smaller lough and a change of scene, Sligo offers another fly fisher's delight, less than 4 miles (6.5 km) from the town and only a mile (1.6 km) north of Lough Gill. To find Lough Colgagh take the L16 towards Manorhamilton and turn left along a by-road. This takes you to a car park and the lough lies right in front of you. Cupped in a fold of land between the mountains and Lough Gill, Colgagh is a rich trout lough with a fine stock of good trout. It has always had a good reputation for the quality and size of its wild brown trout, which average well over 1 lb (0.45 kg), and may run very much larger. The natural feeding is abundant and the size of the fish reflects this.

This is a relatively shallow lough, with an alkaline environment which promotes sufficient growth of weed and bankside vegetation to encourage plenty of insect life, but not so much as to make it difficult to fish. But there are no boats, which seems a pity, since the full potential of this superb lough can only really be explored from a boat. Perhaps you might consider putting a portable boat on it for the day, and so far as I am aware there is nothing to prevent you doing this. A car-top pram-type dinghy or a wooden-framed collapsible boat would be ideal, especially if you can also manage to attach a little electric outboard – ideal for silent and pollution-free movement about the lough. But it will be wise, and a good piece of public relations, to inquire locally before you do so! Colgagh is a free fishery, but that does not necessarily mean the visitor is free to roll up and start putting boats on the water without a little local approval first.

Colgagh is fairly well sheltered and in normal conditions there should be no problems in getting even quite a small boat to behave properly and safely. Although no small boat, and especially a collapsible or inflatable one, is ever likely to give you the same sense of solid security and steadiness as a good big wooden lough boat, on Colgagh it will at least allow you to explore the northern and western shores, which are not so easily fished from the bank, and which receive much less attention from fishermen than the south and east shores.

Lough Colgagh's brown trout fishing begins on 15 February, and lasts until 30 September, in accordance with the general season for the Irish Republic's North-Western Fisheries District. The lough can fish well in almost every period of the season, with the duckfly and the duckfly nymph fairly certain killing patterns in the early weeks. Buzzer patterns do well from April onwards, and there can be some prolific hatches of olives almost any time during the spring and early summer, when a Greenwell's Glory is the proven local favourite.

If Colgagh produces a mayfly hatch I am not aware of it, probably because at mayfly time I am invariably occupied with fishing elsewhere. But it looks and feels as though it should, and the environment seems perfect. What is quite certain, however, is that Colgagh has some massive hatches of caenis –

the White Curse, or the Angler's Curse – in the late afternoons when the weather is warm, especially in July and August. When a hatch begins the whole surface of the lough can suddenly come alive, dimpled with the nymphing rises of trout. Not for nothing is the caenis known as the White Curse, and the minute nymphal, dun and spinner stages are notoriously difficult to imitate. A dark version of Goddard's Last Hope, on a size 18 or even a size 20 hook, is probably the best dry pattern on Colgagh. But on one occasion the best I could produce was a size 14 Sawyer Killer Bug, left in my box since a grayling expedition in Wiltshire the previous November, and this was fished very slowly and just below the surface, with all but the last 2 ft (0.6 m) of the leader greased. It seemed acceptable during the short but vigorous feeding spell, leaving me with three trout in the bag, almost identical at just about 1¼ lb (0.55 kg) each.

Colgagh seems to go off the boil in July and early August, a situation which is not uncommon with these western waters, but that is little consolation to the visiting fly fisher whose only holiday dates lie within that period. But the lough is always worth a visit, and the fishing in high summer can sometimes be excellent.

But the period of greatest excitement on this beautiful lough seems to begin in late August, with the first really good hatches of sedges. These are most evident towards late afternoon and on into the last light of evening, and they can stimulate a prolonged and exciting evening rise. Colgagh's biggest trout are lured up by the surface motor-boating movements of the big sedges, and will feed with a bold, slashing rise at the emergent nymph and the surface-scudding insect. Wet and dry patterns should both be tried, and the Invicta, the Fiery Brown, the Green Peter and the Wickham's Fancy are all reliable wet patterns on Colgagh.

The Murrough or Great Red Sedge is a favourite dry pattern, and some Colgagh enthusiasts also swear by a large Soldier Palmer, on an 8 or 10 hook and thoroughly oiled. For the special technique of skimming the sedge try a bushily dressed Murrough, perhaps incorporating a few strands of deer hair for added buoyancy. A Muddler Minnow also makes an excellent pattern for simulating a sedge and its floating, scuttling course across the water. Both can achieve good baskets of fish, whose size and power may surprise you.

I remember one August evening, when there had been a good sedge hatch and the feeding activity of big trout on Colgagh had been vigorous. Back at my car I met another fly fisher, who had come down to the lough late in the afternoon, and whom I had glimpsed from time to time in the gathering dusk as he fished along the south-eastern shore. He was a Sligo-born engineer, home on holiday from near Wolverhampton, and treating himself to an evening's fishing on a lough where he had caught trout since his boyhood. He had five big trout, all over 1 lb (0.45 kg) and the best almost 3 lb (1.35 kg). Hooked into the butt ring of his rod, damp and well chewed by several big fish, was a Soldier Palmer with a Muddler head of spun deer hair tied on a long-shanked size 10 hook. It was the perfect blend of old and new, local and imported – the Sligo exile returned to fish with a pattern combining a palmered dressing familiar on Irish loughs for generations and an Anglo-American deer-hair head.

Apropos skimming the sedge, do not forget the ferocity and energy of the take which may result. One regular visitor to Colgagh in early September now insists upon using a short length of Power Gum between leader and fly line, ever since he was broken by a smashing take while skimming with a Muddler on a 9-lb (4 kg) leader. Since wild trout of up to almost 8 lb (3.5 kg) have been taken from Colgagh in recent years, it seems wise to be prepared for something well above the lough's customary 1½ lb (0.7 kg) average.

On Lough Colgagh local experts have concluded that the full potential of the lough is limited not by the food supply, which is good, but by the spawning grounds, which are not. The little feeder stream which is the principal spawning area, enters the lough from the west. It has been cleared out and improved at the instigation of the Fisheries Board, and only time will tell whether this will bring about increased spawning success and recruitment to the trout population. If it works, it could turn this very good little lough into a really great one.

From Lough Colgagh the L16 road towards Manorhamilton takes you north-east, and at Shauvas crossroads you can swing westwards again on the N16, on a beautiful route which is one of the most scenic of many drives around Sligo and the Yeats Country. One of Ireland's many advantages for the fishing holidaymaker is that you need never feel guilty about your family trailing along in your wake. The scenery is one of the greatest delights, and even on wet days you are seldom far from somewhere of interest to visit. The disappointment of an occasional blank fishing day can be forgotten in the pleasure of watching the shifting patterns of light and shadow on the hills, or a soft twilight gathering after a shimmering sunset.

Travelling west again, the road takes you up over open moorland and then you begin the long descent into Glencar, the road following the foothills of the mountain slopes which lie to the south of the valley, while across to the north are the spectacular crags and waterfalls and wooded slopes of the sheer-sided King's Mountain. Below, cupped in the narrow valley, lies Glencar Lough.

There is something almost classic about this fishery. A long, deep lough lies in a deeply gouged valley, its waters fed by a major tributary, the Diffreen River, and by countless other hill streams and drains which tumble down from high, heather-clad hills on every side. The waters are acidic and there is excellent spawning for all three salmonids, but the availability of fly life and crustaceans is limited. Thus the resident brown trout are small, darkish and eager to take a cast of wet flies. Glencar Lough empties down to the sea through the Drumcliff River, which falls just over 120 ft (37 m) on its 5-mile (8 km) course to the sea at Drumcliff Bay, a northern inlet of Sligo Bay and the Atlantic. It is tailor-made for seatrout and small salmon, this classic combination of a short, west-flowing river leading from a large lough among the hills.

The Drumcliff–Glencar fishery is now looked after jointly by the Manorhamilton and Sligo Anglers Clubs. Although there seems always to have been a tradition of some free fishing on the lough, this fishery was formerly under the joint owership of two of the largest landowners in County Sligo, the Wynnes of Hazelwood, a demesne on the north-west shore of Lough Gill, and the Gore-Booth family of Lissadell, which stands with its 'great windows open to the south', just as Yeats described it, on the northern shore of Drumcliff Bay and the estuary of the river. Both families were keen on their sport, and some judicious management from the 1870s onwards was rewarded by increased runs of seatrout and especially salmon. We are still reaping the benefits of that effort more than a century later.

You may fish for salmon on the river and the lough from 1 February, as the District regulations permit, but it is interesting to note that this fishery receives its main run of salmon much later than the adjacent Garavogue–Lough Gill system to the south and the Bundrowes–Lough Melvin system to the north. While these have a big run of fish from December onwards, the Drumcliff–Glencar Lough salmon come in March and April, and there are some small runs of summer salmon and grilse during the period through to September, depending on water levels in the river and, inevitably, the pressures of the ever-present drift-netting offshore. Typically Glencar salmon run to 9–11 lb (4–5 kg), but there is always a fair chance of something much larger, and fish of over 20 lb (9 kg) have been recorded more regularly on Glencar than on neighbouring Loughs Gill and Melvin.

Happily for the fly fisher, and unlike on Lough Gill where most salmon are taken by trolling, the rules on Glencar are fly-only from boats, with spinning restricted to the shore fisher. Fly fishing for salmon from a boat is a pleasant activity, but it demands perseverance and is unlikely to succeed unless the fisher or his boatman have a thorough knowledge of the lough, its ways, its shore and the known lies of salmon in the lough, noted over many years. This makes it all the more important to dig a little deeper into your funds and make sure that you have a boatman. At the very least his company and his conversation will pass the time pleasantly even if the lough is dead and the fish dour and disobliging. And if all goes well he will manoeuvre you perfectly into position, holding the boat on the best drifts and over the known salmon lies, and thus giving you the very best chances of connecting with a fish – if they are in a taking mood!

In fact, if your fishing holiday takes you to Glencar any time from June onwards, it will probably be best if you take to the water with tackle and tactics which will be suitable for both salmon and seatrout. Glencar is a good salmon fishery, but seatrout are its real claim to the fly fisher's attentions, especially from June onwards. In this respect the river and the lough fulfil the hopes you might have when you look at Sheet 7 of the Irish half-inch Ordnance Survey and see that promising combination of a big western lough and a short, west-flowing river. And salmon can rise readily enough to a cast of flies intended primarily for seatrout. If your leader is strong enough and your touch is gently firm, there is no reason why a 10-lb (4.5 kg) salmon should not be brought to the net in due course, albeit a little less quickly than if you had hooked it on your 13-ft (395 cm) two-handed summer salmon rod with a 12-lb (5.5 kg) leader.

Of course, you will use lighter tackle for seatrout, but it is a mistake to go too light on these loughs. Few west of Ireland fly fishers will drop below 8-lb (3.5 kg) monofilament for their wet-fly casts, even if they are drifting for brown trout, and many will use 10-lb (4.5 kg) casts for preference. The fast, smashing take of a good lough trout can be devastatingly powerful, and where seatrout, grilse or salmon may be encountered a fine leader is even more likely to lead to lost fish and disappointment.

The need for adequate tackle can usefully be emphasised when talking about Glencar, for this is not only a prolific and productive seatrout fishery but it is also regarded as producing bigger seatrout than the average western Irish fishery. This is a proud local boast, and the average summer and early-autumn seatrout will be over 1½ lb (0.7 kg), which is above the ¾ lb/1 lb (0.35/0.45 kg) average for summer 'white trout' and 'harvesters' on western waters. Much heavier fish are common, and most seasons produce seatrout of 5 lb (2.25 kg) and over. It is therefore worth being prepared for something much heavier than the average, and you will be at no disadvantage when fishing in traditional wet-fly fashion.

The water levels in the Drumcliff River are influenced primarily by the lough in which it rises. If that were the whole story, you would find few sudden variations in the height and speed of the flow, for a big lough feeding a small river is usually a recipe for consistency. The Drumcliff River is different, however, because although it derives most of its water from the lough, it also receives the waters of at least half a dozen feeder streams which flow into the main river between the lough and the sea. Most of these are on the northern side, where rapid, tumbling waters rush down from the southern slopes of Ben Bulben.

This sheer wall of scree and cliffs rises abruptly from the rich, low coastal plain to heights of between 1500 and 1700 ft (460–520 m) on King's Mountain and Ben Bulben. These heights on the great limestone plateau are so placed and orientated that they get the full force of the rain-laden clouds which sweep in continually off the Atlantic on the steady south-westerly winds. A day of heavy rain or a sudden summer thunderstorm can turn dry, rocky hill drains into tumultuous torrents in a matter of an hour or two. The result is that the Drumcliff River can rise fast and colour quickly into a spate, fed by waters straight from the mountain above. The general tendency is for these floods to make the river unfishable for a brief period, and, more positively, to induce any seatrout and salmon waiting in the bay to run up into the river and, eventually, into the lough.

The Drumcliff River is unusually fortunate, from the fisherman's point of view, in enjoying the best of both worlds. It has a steady flow of waters from the lough, which maintain fishable water levels in all but the driest summers or during prolonged periods of strong westerly winds when the flow is 'backed up'; and it also gets the regular benefit of periodic floods caused by tributaries entering below the lough. The result is that the river enjoys something of the best characteristics of a spate river and of a lough-fed river, with few of the occasional disadvantages of either.

In normal years the first of the good runs of seatrout will have come up the river and into Glencar Lough by late May, and sometimes earlier. This is always welcomed, because Glencar enjoys a steady if unspectacular mayfly hatch from early June until well into July, and the seatrout are proverbially free risers to a hatch of mayfly.

Mayfly time on Glencar, as on most waters, can bring up some notable fish to feed on the surface, and it is at this time that you may see that Glencar's brown trout do not all stop growing when they are 10 in (25 cm) long. Big specimens are seen, and some are caught, every spring. Seatrout which may have been in the river and the lough for a week or two tend to stop rising to a surface fly as readily as fresh-run individuals, but at mayfly time they too will rise enthusiastically to the hatching insect and, more rarely, to an evening fall of spent gnat.

Glencar is a good dapping lough, and this is a highly productive method at mayfly time and again in the late summer and September when the dapped daddy-longlegs and the grasshopper will also take good baskets of seatrout. The lough's long shorelines and the west–east alignment of the water make it a pleasant lough to fish with the dap when there is a steady, warm westerly blowing. But that same orientation, combined with its position between two high mountain walls, can also conspire to frustrate the would-be dapper and to make boat fishing uncomfortable or dangerous when a strong westerly or south-westerly wind blows. This can be a stormy coast, and the western end of the Glencar valley lies open to collect and funnel the winds into gales of frightening power. Glencar's waters can be transformed in minutes from a rippling, rolling wave, ideal for short-lining on a broadside drift, into a scene of tossing, white-capped waves on which fishing is forgotten as you start the engine and run for the shore. Such things can happen even out of the clear blue of a summer's day, and the boat fisher on Glencar (and on any other big lough, anywhere) should be alert and prepared for it.

Dapping in mayfly time can be done with the natural insect, as on the great brown trout waters, but on Glencar there is an important difference. The main quarry is not brown trout but seatrout, and while seatrout will rise eagerly to a dapped natural mayfly, they will also respond keenly to the enticing movement of a well-fished artificial dapping pattern, or to the ripple-tripping movement of a bushy bobfly on a wet-fly cast. In this respect dapping on Glencar has more in common with dapping for seatrout on, say, Loch Maree in Wester Ross than with dapping for lough trout on Conn, Mask or the Corrib.

It is movement which provides the chief inducement for the seatrout to take, unlike the brown trout's discriminating quest for a natural insect or a clever imitation of it. Thus on lochs like Maree in Scotland and Currane in south-west Ireland you may have great success dapping a large, bushy and heavily palmered pattern, possibly with a tiny flying treble to ensnare short-taking fish, or, with more deference to the Irish tradition, a bumble of some sort. But here a balance must be struck. These Glencar seatrout are usually responsive and ready to rise when a fly is presented with an enticing movement, and so we need not be bound slavishly to precise mayfly imitations. But they are

The compleat mayfly fisher! The wet-fly boxes contain a selection of nymphs, wet-fly imitations and bushy bob flies, while the live-bait box is used to hold live drakes gathered from the bushes. A 17-foot telescopic rod is an additional tool for the dapping enthusiast.

undoubtedly attracted by the hatching mayflies, and so it seems best to use a pattern which in some degree imitates the insect which is interesting the fish and induces a taking mood among them.

Most of the various gosling patterns work well, oiled and fished as a tripping bob fly, and so too does the west of Ireland variant of the Grey Wulff Mayfly. This is heavily dressed in a bulk and size which would cause horror or gales of incredulous mirth if it was produced on the banks of the Test, where its smaller and finer version is favoured as a fine dry pattern in mayfly time. In Ireland it is used to create not only the impression of a hatching mayfly spinner but also to create a fish-enticing wake on the rolling, wave-broken surface of large loughs. This calls for size, bulk and buoyancy, and the Irish lough fisher's variant is usually on a size 10 or 8 hook, with two prominent and bushy forward-pointing tufts of hackle, which never fail to make me think of them as bristling and jaunty moustaches.

But the mayfly season on Glencar is fairly short and no one would claim that it is the only way to fish the lough successfully for seatrout. Indeed, the fish are obligingly willing to take a fly fished on a traditional type of wet-fly cast, especially if there has been a recent rise in the river levels and a fresh run of seatrout has come into the lough. These recent arrivals seem always to be keen and sprightly takers, while fish which have been in the lough for a time gradually become more difficult to rise, their zest and predatory energies seeming to fade as their tide-bright silver tarnishes and begins to colour in Glencar's peaty waters.

Glencar is a deep lough, which is not surprising in view of the abrupt steepness of the hills to north and south. But although the slopes of Crockauns to the south are rather gentler than the cliffs and waterfalls on the northern side, the shoreline on the south falls away into deep water much more quickly than the gentler, more shelving northern shore. This makes a difference to the way the north and south shores should be approached when fishing. For drifting the shoreline in the classic fashion, the north shore offers a greater area of comparatively shallow water, the kind of place in which seatrout can most readily be found. Here you can treat almost the entire northern shore as one immense drift, motoring up towards the western end of the lough and drifting back eastwards. On a day of warm, gentle westerly wind and good cloud cover the conditions for this will be perfect. The north shore is therefore a popular fishing area, and a productive one, and the majority of Glencar regulars prefer it, and also the short drifts around the east end of the lough, near where the Diffreen River flows in.

The south shore drops fairly steeply into deepish water, and this can present problems for the fly fisher in a boat. Too far out, and you are over deep water in which the chances of encountering a seatrout are slim. Too close, and you need to have a sharp eye open for rocks and a quick pair of hands on the oars to avoid them. But seatrout are noted for their readiness to lie in remarkably shallow water, and tight against the shore of a lough or the bank of a river, provided they are not disturbed. Consequently there are good fish to be found along Glencar's south shore if you can leave the management of the boat to a capable oarsman, and concentrate on casting your flies right in among the shoreline rocks. Another good reason for concentrating hard is that if a seatrout takes at this point, it is more than likely to make an instant and headlong lunge for the deeper water of the lough, dashing back towards and under the boat. The risks of line or leader fouling the keel, an oar or the propeller are obvious, and there may be a sudden and sad parting of fish and fisher. On such occasions, when I have managed to steer a plunging, depths-intent fish around the boat and keep it clear of snags and hazards, I am inclined to be grateful that I normally fish with a rod of 11 ft (350 cm) or 12 ft (365 cm) – and even then it may have meant jumping quickly to my feet to add further height and length, and to give additional command over the situation. (Perilous and unwise though it generally is, there are some occasions when you simply have to stand up in a boat.) A 10-ft (305 cm) rod might simply not have been long enough to stop a snag and the consequent loss of fish and temper.

The steeply shelving south shore is a better prospect for the bank fisherman than you might suppose. The shallow, fish-holding fringe is narrow but it is easily within reach of a short line cast from the shore. But a cardinal rule is to keep well back from the water's edge and resist the temptation to wade along the shore. Seatrout are shy and will vanish in a flash if they are disturbed. Splashy wading is a recipe for clearing every fish out of reach, and it is best to avoid casting any shadow on the water or allowing yourself to be silhouetted against the sky. This is especially important since, when fishing the south shore at any time during the period from the late morning to mid afternoon, you will have the sun at your back. Stand well back, and drop your flies into the shallows from a discreet and concealed distance.

Another successful strategy in fishing Glencar's southern shore when there is a gentle wind from the west is to cast a moderate length of line fairly square out from the shore and across the wind. Then, keeping your rod point well up and resisting the almost instinctive tendency we all have to work the line with our left hand, allow the wind to catch your line and to carry it round downwind. The movement imparted by the wind and the ripple on the water will be sufficient to impart all the movement your flies require. The wind and the water do all the work, and your only job is to be ready to tighten promptly when a slashing take occurs. The effect of casting across the wind is to allow your flies to swing in a steady arc, presenting themselves in full and visible profile to waiting fish. A bushy, buoyant pattern as a bob fly is useful here, for several reasons. It provides a prominent, wake-creating attractor, which may bring a fish up to look more closely, and if the attractor itself is not taken, one of the other flies which fish round slightly deeper in the water on the dropper or the point may well connect.

A good-sized bob fly also gives the wind and the ripple something more to work with, and helps to give additional life and movement to the whole team of flies. Not least, the bob fly acts like a float, providing you with a useful and visible marker as you follow the cast round. This can not only be valuable in poor light, but also when there is a gentle take, which you may not feel through the rod and the line, but which is signalled by the dipping of the bob fly.

As your cast comes round from its crosswind starting point a fish may follow it, swinging round below the flies and into very shallow water before it takes. This often happens when you have almost fished out the cast and your line has swung through a 90-degree arc downwind. The flies have almost come 'on the dangle', just as if you were fishing down a river pool, and if nothing happens, begin to recover line slowly and in a series of short, slow movements by retrieving with your left hand. This often does the trick.

4 West Sligo and Mayo

The Seatrout Streams of the Coast

Everyone turns his back with regret on Yeats Country, such is the scenery and the sport, and, at every turn of the road, fresh vistas of mountain, lough, sea, river and woodland.

Westwards from Ballysodare and Collooney lies the long and rising ridge of the Ox Mountains, beyond the 'drear Harte Lake' and the headwaters of the lively little Owenboy River. From the N59 trunk road you can see the hills off to your left rising higher and higher. Your westward course takes you across a succession of little streams, at least ten of them, between Sligo town and Easky. All are small, and some so well hidden by overhanging trees that you might easily miss them. All are short, drawing their waters from the northern slopes of the Ox range and flowing more or less straight down to the sea at the western end of Sligo Bay. Each gets its runs of seatrout, and also a few grilse and small salmon, when the conditions are right, but to be there at the critical time is the essential ingredient for successful fishing, jointly with that knowledge of the river and its ways which always guarantees that the local fisher will come away with the heaviest basket – and deservedly so. Such intimate familiarity with a river in all its moods, coupled with a near-instinctive knowledge of *when* to go fishing, *where* to try, and what tactics to use, is hard won, the result of years of trial and error, and deserves its rewards. The visitor may be lucky enough to chance on the right little river at the right time, in which case he should give thanks to whatever piscatorial providence brought it about.

But if you get the chance, especially if there are spates in late August or early September, do not on any account miss the chance to fish one or two of these little north Sligo rivers. That advice is as sound in the 1990s as it was in 1886 when 'Hi-Regan', typically brisk and to-the-point, urged his readers to 'fish out all the rivers from Killala Bay to Sligo Bay. White trout abound in all of them, after spates especially, and they are only fished by locals. August is perhaps the best month'. So small and undiscovered are these rivers that neither 'Hi-Regan' nor any subsequent writer has bothered to name them – perhaps because few are even named on the large-scale maps. A river without a name is not necessarily a river without fish. And these rivers do have names – familiar, local names which are woven into the living fabric of local speech, unaffected by the neglect of map-makers or fishing writers.

The little, local, obscure rivers of Ireland (and in every other country) are the unsung sources of an infinite amount of pleasure for the game fisher. All in all they provide more fun, and more fish, every year than all the great and famous rivers put together. They are a vital sporting and environmental asset, and yet their importance is continually underestimated, or overlooked altogether. And for migratory fish like seatrout and salmon these countless little western rivers are especially important. Who knows how many hundreds there are in total along the western coasts of Ireland, Scotland, Wales and the West Country of England? Seatrout, and to a lesser extent small salmon, will run and spawn in watercourses as little as 1 ft (0.3 m) in width, and their eggs will hatch and grow there, eventually developing into the smolts and migrant trout which drop down to the sea to begin the final and most dramatic stage of their growth.

Such little seatrout and salmon streams have many features in common, but one of the most obvious of these from the fisherman's point of view is their easy accessibility when the conditions are right. Many are only productively fishable for a few days each season, and then the sport may be confined to one or two prime hours, on one or two good pools in an otherwise unfishable little

Ireland has countless coastal spate streams, often small and under-fished. When summer and autumn water levels are right, sport with seatrout and occasional salmon can be excellent.

river. But fishers who live and work in rural communities often lead lives which are adaptable and in which a strict division of each day into hours of work and times of leisure is not so rigidly applied as in towns and cities. That is why you can see the village garage mechanic leaving the workshop for an hour or two, and slipping off with his rod when the river has come into fine form after a spate. That is why the country boys coming home from school will not alarm their parents if they are two or three hours late. Rural Ireland is still a safe environment for children, and parents know little of the anxieties which assail urban families when a child is out alone or late in coming home. The school bus probably drops them off in groups at crossroads and at road-ends. Eager faces peer over little bridges and see good prospects for fishing, and little spinning and worming rods materialise like magic from favourite hiding places among the bushes.

The potential of these precious fishing times on little rivers transcends barriers of age and occupation. A good flood and a river fining down in late summer or early autumn has a magnetic appeal for the bank manager, the priest, the cattle auctioneer, the solicitor and the local doctor – all able to slip away from their professional cares or pastoral ministrations for an hour or two when the river is just right.

And they catch fish. In the same pools and deep holes where they caught fish last year, and for many years past, and where their fathers and grandfathers caught fish long ago, they catch white trout and small salmon.

The visitor who joins them will find that a 9-ft (290 cm) fly rod fishing a #6 line will serve him adequately for anything he is likely to encounter on these waters. Ideally, perhaps, you might choose something smaller and more specialised, and my own favourite is a light brook rod of no more than 8 ft (245 cm). With a light reel and a #4 or #5 line it is perfect for tackling small streams where casting space is often cramped in the extreme, where overhanging trees and bushes are everywhere, and on which you are unlikely ever to find yourself needing to cast much more than a couple of rod-lengths of line. Bruce & Walker produce a superb range of short brook rods, and their 7-ft (230 cm) Hexagraph carbon model is a delight for this type of fishing in miniature.

I use a lightweight magnesium reel, the Ryobi 255MG, which weighs a mere 2 oz (60 g) and carries a #4 double-taper floating line, which I have cut in half and nail-knotted to sufficient backing to bulk it all out and fill the reel nicely. It will deliver a dry fly or a nymph with accuracy and delicacy when required, fishes a wet fly cast in typical down-and-across fashion, and has been used with good effect for worming, upstream or down, for fishing the seatrout fly-maggot combination, and even for dangling a prawn. Ultra-light and astonishingly powerful, it has chalked up a good tally of Irish 6-oz (0.15 kg) brownies, ¾ lb (0.35 kg) harvest seatrout, brown trout to almost 3 lb (1.35 kg) and (memorably) a 4-lb (1.8 kg) grilse. The latter took a moment or two longer to subdue than the others! All in all, the perfect set-up for exploring these little rivers, where you need to be mobile, unburdened by weight and unhampered by excessive rod length.

But when you get to your little spate river and find that sport is in progress, you should spare a few glances at the tackle the local experts use, as you meet them and stop for the inevitable exchange of courtesies and news. The variety of techniques and tackle you may see can be enormous, and a quick survey of the equipment and methods of the local fishers will reveal a good deal of individual preference, and an almost infinite capacity for improvisation and ingenuity. Worm and prawn, spinner and fly – all have their place and all account for fish, and the rods and reels can be wonderful in their limitless variety. One afternoon in mid September I worked my way along 2 miles (3.2 km) of stream in north-west Sligo and saw two fishers from the nearby village each fishing hard with hundreds of pounds' worth of rods and reels from Orvis and Hardy, alongside their friends with £5 spinning rods made in Taiwan. Above them another expert wielded a medium-weight boat rod which would have been more at home heaving ling and pollock from the sea, and was skilfully trotting a prawn down a fast pool, on heavy monofilament line drawn from an old but sound Allcock's salmon reel. Three good seatrout in his bag testified to his success.

Most unusual of all was a wand of about 11 ft (335 cm) of ancient greenheart, its two sections spliced together with whipped cord and plastic tape. Its owner had abandoned that day's task of stacking turf for his mother's winter fuel and headed for the river. He was a connoisseur of turf and a strict pragmatist in matters of fishing tackle. His high, pitched stack was built from uniform sods of the finest blackish-brown turf, cut with slow, rhythmic, loving, backbreaking care with a hand spade from the family's few acres of bog, a mile or two away on the northern slopes of the Ox Mountains. It had been well cut, well dried and well stacked, and its dark, ancient fibres would burn hot and slow, melting away into that saffron-golden ash which only the finest turf produces. But today the turf stack could wait, and instead his eyes and ears were on the river. He had unhooked his rod from its customary resting place on a line of nails beneath the low eaves of his cottage. It was an unorthodox concoction with an unusual history.

The rod had begun life as the middle two sections of a four-piece, 18-ft (550 cm) Castleconnell greenheart salmon rod, built for heavy Shannon salmon in the 1890s. In the troubled period after 1920 a British army officer on leave and fishing the River Erne at Ballyshannon had been urgently recalled to his regiment in India, leaving the rod behind with his ghillie. He had never returned for it. Now, with its slender top section long shattered and the butt portion unmanageably heavy, what better use for the remnants than to be put to work worming for salmon here in County Sligo, reincarnated with new chromium rings roughly whipped on and a bright new Japanese-made fixed-spool spinning reel wired and taped to the thick end of the greenheart? At dusk I passed him on the road, and he seemed to be walking home with a spring in his step. The headlights caught the silver glint of a fish, and I would guess it weighted about 5 lb (2.25 kg).

The excellent series of Irish half-inch Ordnance Survey maps reveal the whereabouts of these little rivers wherever you go in Ireland. And as you drive from Sligo towards the village of Dromore West, you cross the lower reaches of one of the larger of these north-west Sligo rivers. The Dunneill River is a bright spate stream which rises as the Owenduff River high in the western slopes of Knockalongy and flows almost due north, changing its name from Owenduff to Dunneill at some unspecified point about halfway along its course. Like so many western rivers it is short, rocky, acidic, moody and given to dramatic fluctuations in flow in response to the rainfall in the mountains. It also receives a good summer and early-autumn run of seatrout, ¾-lb (0.35 kg) harvesters mostly, and a few grilse and salmon. The runs come when the water is boosted by a spate, and to be there at the right time is vital. Then your choice of flies will probably be immaterial – you will simply catch fish and have a lot of fun. If this or any of these rivers looks in good fishing condition stop and ask locally, ensuring that you have the requisite permission and tickets (if the latter are required, which is unusual), and then put up your rod quickly and lose time in getting into action.

But when the streams are low and clear you had better not waste your time looking for fresh seatrout or a salmon. The best you can hope for is to creep stealthily up the stream with a brook rod, fishing what pools and holes you can find, or perhaps marking down a rising fish and stalking him with a dry fly. You might find a seatrout or two which came up on the last spate, and there are always the little resident brownies. Especially in bright, summer conditions this is the sort of fishing for which you need stealth, a good deal of fish-craft and the ability to travel quickly over rough ground, unburdened by anything more than a short, light rod, a spool of spare leader monofilament, a box of assorted flies and some floatant. Sandwiches and a pocket camera complete your simple equipment for the day, and with luck you may have a pocketful of delicious little brown trout for tomorrow's breakfast. (This is even more likely if you also pack an old tobacco tin of worms! Skilfully fished upstream in low-water conditions, the worm is not to be scorned.)

Easky Lough and the Ox Mountain Waters

But if you are disinclined to spend a day on the Dunneill in the solitary pursuit of miniature fish on small tackle, drive on for a mile (1.6 km) or so beyond the Dunneill Bridge and then turn left up the long, straight road which runs over the northern Ox Mountains towards Mullany's Cross and Aclare to the south. From Dromore West it is a long, steady climb up 8 miles (13 km) or more of rising ground, but take time for the occasional backward glance at the wide vistas down towards Sligo Bay. Then the gradient eases, and you find you are driving along close by the eastern shore of a large and inviting hill lough.

Easky Lough is sizeable, well over 100 acres (40 hectares) in extent, and it is cupped in a hollow on the top of the watershed, at just over 600 ft (180 m) above the sea you left behind you at Dromore West. Its biggest feeder streams flow in from the high ground to the east, from off the blanket peat which covers these hills. At the northern end the lough tapers to a narrow point, where the

Easky River flows out on its 12-mile (19 km) descent to the sea, gathering the flows of several hill streams and other small rivers en route.

Easky might appear to have in miniature some of the essential qualities of the classic river-and-lough migratory salmonid fishery. But the lough is too small in proportion to the comparatively long river and the fall to the sea is too steep to make this a textbook example. The waters of Easky Lough, extensive though they are by the standards of hill loughs, are insufficient to give the buffering, flow-sustaining benefits which a large lough can confer on a small, short river. In addition, the Easky River receives so much additional water from other feeders and tributaries on its way from the lough to the sea that the whole Easky system must be regarded as essentially a spate fishery, and should be fished as such.

The brown trout fishing here is what you might expect from a sizeable hill lough, with a large population of small and free-rising brown trout which proliferate in waters which provide ideal spawning grounds and a pure environment. But the trout are more abundant than the food supply, and so the average size remains small, about 6 oz (0.15 kg) and anything over ½ lb (0.25 kg) is large. These are attractive little fish, dark overall and with the bright, blood-red spotting of typical hill-lough trout. Their white flesh makes delicate eating, especially if you put them in the traditional wrapping of wet newspaper and broil them over the glowing embers of a fire of heather stalks, gorse furze and bog fir. (Remember to light such fires with care and never to

Judith McKelvie tightens into a summer seatrout, risen and hooked on a lively ripple in early June.

leave them until the last sparks have been extinguished and every scrap of litter gathered up and taken home!)

In addition to these diminutive and very toothsome trout, there have been accounts for many generations, firmly supported by local wisdom, of large *ferox* or cannibal trout in Easky Lough. The challenge is to find someone who has actually caught one, or seen one at close quarters. The presence of a race or subspecies of *ferox* in the lough is difficult to prove or disprove, especially for the visiting fly fisher whose tackle and methods are unlikely to entice any massive, deep-living trout, and whose stay is usually too short to allow a thorough investigation of the lough and its fish. Netting and electric fishing, with the proper authority, of course, might be the answer, or a thorough series of sweeps of the lough with an efficient echo-sounder. These are now readily available at a price and compact size which puts them within the bounds of the angler's budget and his carrying capacity for equipment and gadgetry.

If an echo-sounder revealed the mid-water presence of objects the size of large trout the next stage would be to troll with a deep-fished lure, perhaps on a downrigger system. But echo-sounding and downrigging presuppose the use of a boat, and there are no boats for public use on Easky. If you want to fish from a boat here you have always had to bring your own. In 1886 the Irish angling writer 'Hi-Regan' wrote of coming with a 'pony and collapsible boat'. In the 1990s you have four wheels instead of four hooves to carry you and your boat – but it is still an important courtesy to ask permission locally before you launch it.

The question of Easky's alleged *ferox* therefore remains doubtful. In fact, what many fishers may have thought were huge trout may actually have been grilse or salmon, which can often be seen head-and-tailing in the lough, especially in late summer. By then the spates should have brought them up into the lough, and recently arrived fish tend to lie close to the shallow bar at the north end of the lough near to where the river flows out. For salmon August and September are usually the best months, but Easky is not primarily a salmon fishery and to connect with one there is a bonus.

What really draws the fly fisher to Easky Lough, and to the river, from late July onwards, is the prospect of seatrout. The main run of seatrout along this coast is always late, with a small number of big fish appearing in April. However, the bulk of the fish come up on suitably high waters in August, and in the lough they can give excellent sport. Typically these fish average under the pound (0.45 kg), bright little fish which come as summer ends and the harvest is gathered – 'harvest trout' or 'harvesters', as they are known.

Most of the fishing on Easky Lough is done from the eastern shore, probably because it is only a few paces from the road, and some fishers show a distinct reluctance to walk an inch further from their cars than is absolutely essential. From the road near the north end it is only a couple of hundred yards (180 m) over the heathery grass to reach the point where the lough narrows at the mouth of the Easky River, usually a likely spot for seatrout and the occasional salmon. But the lough is fishable all around the shore, and unless you are in a great hurry it is worth working your way around to the west and south-west sides. This gives you an opportunity to cover much of the likeliest fish-holding water, including corners which may have been undisturbed by anyone else's fishing for ages. A complete circuit of the lough makes a very pleasant day's outing, but it amounts to about 4 miles (6.5 km) of very broken walking over sometimes difficult ground, and this should be taken into account before you attempt it.

But if you do decide to take a really full day's fishing here, try to allow time to fish the two smaller waters which lie just to the south of Easky Lough. Lough Rumduff is barely five minutes' walk from the south shore of Easky and a similar distance from the road. It is small, full of free-rising little brown trout, and its high banks of peaty grass may call for some ingenuity in casting compared to the open environs of the bigger lough. It is unlikely to produce anything of exciting size, but it deserves half an hour's fishing before you move on, and it is well worth seeing the zest and vigour with which its little trout respond to insect life on the water. Terrestrials blow off the banks and are eagerly gulped, and I remember watching the dark water boiling with all the energy of a fish farm at feeding time when a scattering of thousands of heather flies was blown onto Rumduff by the warm breeze of an August evening. I had been fishing with wet flies all day, indeed all week, but I managed to find a tiny reddish-hackled Ginger Quill size 16 stuck in my hat, put there and forgotten from weeks previously. Every time it alighted on the water there was 4 or 5 oz (0.1 or 0.14 kg) of Rumduff brownie waiting to grab it like a flash.

I cannot say I have been so lucky on the neighbouring waters of Lough Gal. A few minutes' walk over the heather from Rumduff, Gal is a tiny lough, but it is known to hold trout out of all proportion to its small size. For no immediately apparent reason there are big trout in this glorified bog-hole – and I call it that advisedly, for its approaches are a mass of soggy sphagnum flushes, ready to engulf you thigh deep. In such an essentially peaty, acidic environment it seems amazing that Lough Gal's trout grow to 1 lb (0.45 kg) and more, with reliable reports of individual fish up to 4 lb (1.8 kg) and over. The water appears dark, deep and decidedly uninviting, and the trout are dour and difficult to catch. Perhaps the spawning success and recruitment rate are very poor and the meagre natural foods are sufficient to allow a few trout to grow big and heavy, in contrast to many hill loughs which have wonderful spawning conditions but gross overcrowding, with countless Lilliputian trout competing furiously for food.

I would never have known of the Brobdingnagian size of the Lough Gal trout if I had not chanced to meet a solitary fisherman on the Easky mountain road one September evening. He was trudging up the hill back to his car when I was putting my rod in the roof clips and getting ready for the drive home after a day's seatrouting on Easky Lough. We stopped for a chat and an exchange of news, as fishers do the world over, and he shyly but proudly opened his bag to reveal a magnificent trout from Lough Gal. Deep in the flank, dark and ruby-speckled, it was firm and thick in the shoulder and weighed just under 2 lb (0.9 kg). He had spooned it and found no identifiable stomach contents. But it had still taken his fly, a heavily dressed variation on a

Watson's Fancy, with prominent jungle cock sides. He had tied it himself, principally for seatrout, and had been fishing it deep and slow on a sinking line when this Lough Gal thumper had taken it, apparently with the gentlest of pulls before the line tightened and the inevitable explosion occurred. 'I always knew they were in there,' he said, 'but it's taken me years to get one.' I was lost in admiration of this lovely fish extracted from the unlikeliest of waters. 'My brother-in-law had two in a day about twelve years ago', he added. 'They were both over 2 lb.' And he smiled and turned away up the hill. And that is why Lough Gal should not be missed: it might be your lucky day!

From Easky Lough and its smaller neighbours the road descends south-wards towards the L133 Tobercurry to Ballina road. For the last few miles you might glimpse the Owenboy River down below the road to your right, and you can see from your map that this is one of the upper tributaries of the Moy. The main river rises back towards Collooney and the Owenboy joins it near Mullany's Cross. Since the 1960s the Moy has been probably the finest and most productive salmon river in Ireland, but here you are far upstream and the river takes a south-westerly course before it swings around the end of the Ox Mountains near Foxford and turns northwards on its winding lower course towards Ballina and the sea.

Lough Talt and the Hill Loughs

Take the Ballina road westwards for about 4 miles (6.5 km) and you will find Lough Talt (its name is pronounced like '*alt*itude', not like 'salt'). This is a large, attractive lough which lies in a deep valley right in the heart of the Ox range. It is not only a wonderfully situated lough but it is also noted for the beautiful colouring and conformation of its abundant little brown trout. 'Hi-Regan', writing in 1886, mentioned the 'exceeding beauty (they don't run large) of the trout of this rock-bound little lake', whose brown trout he preferred to those of Easky Lough. Like Easky, Lough Talt is fed by the acidic waters which drain down from the high blanket peat of the hills, and conditions are right for abundant spawning, far more than the food supply in this acidic water can sustain beyond a tiny size. Short of netting out 90 percent of Talt's countless trout to give the remainder more food, or finding some miraculous way of enriching its waters, the beautifully marked trout are for ever destined to remain little gems. Six ounces (0.15 kg) is a good average size, and you might find a monstrous half-pounder (0.25 kg), but the sport is almost guaranteed.

If you are trailing your own boat behind the car you can launch it here at the little slipway, and an alternative is to hire a boat from the Lough Talt Inn which is close to the road which runs along the lough's north-eastern shore. Talt is a beautiful spot, a fact which is not lost on tourists and coach parties heading to and from Ballina, and on a sunny summer's day the area can become a little crowded. However, in this part of Ireland crowding is a relative term, and you can still find complete peace and quiet once you are afloat on the lough, or, on foot, if you fish around the northern end of the lough and down the south-western shore.

Lough Talt is such a pleasant spot that it is a pity not to stop here. A family party will enjoy a picnic along the lough side, and it is as good a lough as any on which to put a fly rod into the hands of a beginner or a complete novice and begin to get fairly immediate results from small but lively trout. On a bright summer's day the fishing may suffer, but the scenery is magnificent and it is worth having an hour or two out in a boat on the lough for the simple pleasure of the experience. On a day of warm breezes from the west and good cloud cover, conditions will be ideal for making a fine basket of small trout, especially if you chance upon such conditions in the early part of the season, in April and May. But at all times Lough Talt can be a tricky lough if a strong wind gets up. The lough is in a deep cleft in the mountains, and its north-west/south-east orientation causes some sudden and awkward swirling and gusting of the winds. This can make boat handling uncomfortable and casting maddeningly difficult, and in anything more than a stiff breeze it can become alarming and almost unfishable. If this happens, do the sensible thing, reel in and head for the shore.

The trout in Lough Talt are free-rising and will take the classic western wet-fly patterns, size 12 or 14 for preference, and the Black Pennell, the Connemara Black, the Mallard & Claret, the Sooty Olive, Black & Peacock Spider and Invicta are all successful here.

This is a delightful fishery, and a good place to spend a day as one of a family party. But the game fisher will inevitably regret the lack of large trout, and especially the absence of any connection with the sea, which would bring seatrout and salmon up into the lough system. If ever a lough looked as though Nature had designed it for classic summer seatrout and grilse fishing it is Lough Talt. Unhappily, you would need to have the faith to move mountains (literally) to bring this about, for the swelling mass of 1400-ft (430 m) Meenaglogh lies between Lough Talt and the nearest northward-flowing river, the Gowlan. This and the Owenwee River rise just over the watershed and flow due north, eventually joining together and later merging with the Easky River system. These get runs of seatrout and salmon, although the majority of the fish follow the main river up to Easky Lough, and the headwaters of the Gowlan and the Owenwee only hold fish in autumn when spawning time is near. To the south the Lough Talt river trickles out to merge eventually with the upper parts of the Moy system, but few seatrout come this far, and none have access to the lough.

But if your faith and fishing aspirations cannot move mountains, perhaps your enthusiasm to fish somewhere really exciting will be able to persuade your legs and lungs to find the energy to tramp over the mountains. Some fairly energetic and dedicated hill walking is called for if you want to sample the real delights of fishing the remote little hill loughs of the Ox Mountains. More than a dozen of them are littered across the south-western spur of the hills which runs from the Lough Talt gap across towards Foxford and the low river plain of the Moy, Lough Cullin and Lough Conn. On the half-inch

The great loughs of the west of Ireland are rich in game fish, and have a uniquely spacious grandeur.

A typically reliable selection of summer fly patterns for Irish seatrout and grilse.

The pontoon at the southern end of Lough Conn is one of Europe's most celebrated game-fishing centres.

Ordnance Survey map they show up like a scattering of little sapphires against the terracotta browns of the long Slieve Gamph ridge. Some lie within the western extremities of County Sligo, while others are just across the county boundary in Mayo, that vast and wild tract of western land which has always had so much to offer the fly fisher and anyone with a feeling for wild, open, beautiful places. On the map you can see the dotted line of the county boundary snaking south along the ridge of Meenaglogh, across the gap west of Lough Talt and along the spine of the hills.

All these hill loughs hold brown trout. All can provide excellent sport, especially in May and June and again in late August until the end of the season on 30 September. Almost all are acidic, with the deep, dark, peat-stained waters typical of loughs fed by streams out of blanket peat or the steady soaking of rainwater which has percolated through saturated peat and collected in these pots and troughs. The trout tend to reflect this environment, and for the most part they are small, dark-backed and olive-hued below, with blunt, rounded, bullet heads and a spangling of vivid blood-red spots along their flanks. Their flesh is firm but pale, sweet to the taste, and never better than when it is eaten alfresco, preferably baked in the ashes of a fire made from the woody, fibrous stalks of old, rank heather.

There are several good reasons for not missing a chance to fish these loughs. One is the knowledge that you will be wetting your line on waters which seldom see another fisher throughout a whole season, or even for years on end. There is a special pleasure in feeling that this is your very own private lough, as near as can be without actual ownership. The fishing is free, there are no bag limits or by-laws, you can come and go entirely as you please. Your only restraints are the fisheries district open season and the reasonable courtesies and commonsense practices of the countryside. Go where you will, camp by the loughs, light fires and take your dogs with you – but avoid litter, prevent runaway fires, and do not allow your dog to err so much as even to look sideways at sheep, let alone chase them.

Another good reason is the scenery, which is wonderful. Clarity of sky and brightness of sunshine are not the ideal conditions for successful fishing, but if you get a chance to walk the heights of these hills in such weather you can see memorable views and enjoy a sense of spacious peace. On top of this long, wide ridge you can feel that the whole of western Ireland is laid out below you. To the west the land falls away to the heathery bogs and, beyond them, to the greenness of north-east Mayo, with its great loughs and rivers. To the east lie the plains of north Sligo and the distant profiles of the Bricklieve Mountains and, to the north-east, the huge limestone escarpments around Ben Bulben. To the north, beyond Meenaglogh and Easky, you have a sense of sea beyond the land, a hazy presentiment of the western ocean.

Finally, there is the quality of the fishing you may find. There is superb fishing, and some very big fish, to be found here, but it is not the kind of sport you can look up in any guidebook. The loughs are named, there are notes and hints to guide you, but it still remains largely a matter of personal discovery. The great inducement is the mystery of the hills and the fact that some of these loughs have produced brown trout of 2, 4, 6, and even 8 lb (0.9–3.5 kg). Great, well-conditioned, firm-bodied, pink-fleshed trout, deep in the flank and elegant in conformation have been brought down the hill from some of these loughs. Not the ugly, heavy-headed *ferox*, the so-called cannibal trout of the big loughs of Ireland, but prime specimens of *Salmo trutta*, which have grown and thrived in certain well-favoured waters where the local conditions provide abundant natural foods and allow the trout to achieve their full potential for growth. It is immaterial that these loughs seldom extend to more than a few acres in extent: small loughs do not necessarily mean small trout. If the trout population is small and the food supply is good, the fish will be big.

'The Wee Lough'

To take a wild brown trout of 3–4 lb (1.35–1.8 kg) from the vast expanses of alkaline waters in Lough Mask or Lough Derg is something to be proud of. How much more remarkable to take a similar fish, or something even bigger, from the close confines of what might look like an unproductive Mayo bog-hole!

One special little lough comes to mind. It is not a very big lough, even by the standards of these generally small upland waters. Indeed, its little speck of blue seems like a pinhead on the half-inch map. It is easily overlooked, even when you are scrutinising the map carefully with fishing in mind. Even when you do locate it this is not the lough to choose if your idea is to fit in a couple of hours' fishing on a spring evening. This lough requires effort and dedication to reach it and then to extract fish from it. It lies about two hours' walk from the nearest hill road, where you must leave your car and take to the soft heather and moss of the hills. It is not an easy approach, for your way lies over soggy bog and broken peat hags, every step requiring a sharp eye if you are not to be ensnared in one of the innumerable hill drains, sphagnum pools and the turf cutters' banks and ditches. The gradient is not steep but it is relentless, and the broken ground prevents you from getting into that easy, swinging stride which can make hill walking so rhythmically exhilarating. Here you stumble and trip and puff up every yard of the way.

It has been the salvation of this little lough that it is so inconspicuous, and, once identified, so difficult to reach. That remoteness and obscurity ensure that its waters are seldom disturbed by anyone's line. Nor does it yield its fish readily, even after you have tramped up those long boggy slopes. But the lough, its setting and its fish are so beautiful that the successful fisher will never forget them.

The top of the long ridge which comprises the Ox Mountains is a wild and lonely place, vistas of blanket bog over a bedrock of granite and schists. Here the loughs are dark and acid, their sombre waters are stained by the peat and their trout are the abundant, lively little dwarfs typical of hill loughs every-where. But this lough is different. Almost alone among this spangled scattering of waters, this is a rich fishery. Its water is quite exceptionally alkaline, and there is a profusion and diversity of plant growth, weeds, insects and crustaceans which would do credit to a Hampshire chalk stream. And with all this wealth of food items, its trout are very big. They are not numerous, and the average size is large, because for all its richness the lough has limited spawning and nursery areas. The population grows slowly, the annual recruitment of young fish is not large, and there is ample food for all of them. This makes them big, powerful – and discriminating.

You might think that trout in a remote, seldom-fished little lough would have a naivety and guilelessness which would make them easier to catch than the fish in other, more frequented loughs. Not so on this lough. Barely a mile (0.8 km) away there is another lough where a beginner might catch a score or more of suicidally obliging little fish, and raise and lose twice as many more. But here on 'the wee lough' the united talents of a dozen professional trout fishers might fail to tempt a fish for days on end. They feed as they please, with a superabundance of food all around them, and unlike the hungry little bog-hole trout they are not waiting to fling themselves obligingly upon your fly as soon as it hits the water. This is its maddening charm, this combination of the extreme difficulty of the fishing and the magnificence of the fish, if you are fortunate enough to connect with one.

In 1969 I was initiated into the small band of fishers who know 'the wee lough', a freemasonry of enthusiasts, while I was on holiday with friends in Mayo. That first visit, the first of probably not more than a dozen made over a period of almost twenty years, was an unforgettable revelation.

It was on a warm August day of cloudless sunshine. Hopelessly low water and the brassy, stale look of the shrunken pools sent us home from the river where we had hoped for a summer salmon or a grilse. It was dog-day weather of the most extreme kind, and there was no relief in prospect, for the weather forecast stubbornly reported yet more sun and drought for days to come.

'We'll go to the wee lough,' said my friend and mentor, and we exchanged salmon rods for trout tackle and set off on the short car journey and the long uphill tramp. There was a freshness in the air on the hills, and a rangy Irish setter quartered ahead of us. All three of us revelled in the freedom of the hills, and the dog paused in his quarterings only to indulge in the occasional brief but evidently blissful wallow in one of the innumerable sphagnum bogs, to cool his heaving mahogany-coloured flanks and to refresh what seemed like yards of pink tongue. Several times on our outward walk the experienced old dog froze in a classically statuesque set, rock-steady on the grouse which lay upwind of that infallible black nose, and only roading-in and flushing them when he heard the commanding click of his master's fingers. It was good to see them and hear them, those whirring brown coveys with their gruff *Go-back, go-back!* cries, and it is sad to reflect how scarce grouse have since become on these and other Irish hills since the mysterious and countrywide decline of the early 1970s, from which grouse numbers have never recovered.

At first glance the lough seemed small and unremarkable enough, a tiny patch of cobalt blue nestling in a fold of the hills and reflecting the cloudless sky. But our final approach and the opportunity of a closer look revealed that this was something very special. The shores of the other hill loughs we had passed had been rocky and bare, or overhung with tussocks of rank heather growing on high and undercut banks. Here there was a fine fringe of reeds and weeds and water plants of many species. Everywhere there were insects, in the water, among the reeds and plants and in larval form in the shallows. I took a step into the water where it lay perhaps 3 in (7.5 cm) deep over a pale, sandy-looking bottom, and at the pressure of my foot the sand seemed to bulge up and burst like the slow, viscous plop of a hot mud spring. A white cloudiness turned the water opaque, and I bent down and scooped out what looked and felt like pure china clay.

A slow and fascinated progress around the margins of the little lough was like a voyage of discovery in miniature, every step revealing new insects, more crustacea, a profusion of freshwater shrimps. We became so utterly absorbed that we almost forgot about our rods and the business of fishing.

It would be nice to report that we went back down the hill a few hours later with a brace of four-pounders (1.8 kg) each, but it was not to be. In any case, the wee lough does not yield up its fish quite so easily. But we had tried our best, in what seemed like reasonable conditions. Despite the bright sunshine there had been sufficient breeze at that height to give a lively ripple to the water. We had deployed every combination of flies which our boxes could produce, fishing fast and in the surface film, deep and slow, and every other tactic we could think of. But we failed to move even a single trout, although we fished on deep into the gloaming of that summer evening. The first stars had begun to appear as we reluctantly took down our rods, regretting we had not brought a tent and prepared to spend a day or two by the lough. We made our way by moonlight back to the car parked at the end of the turf cutters' road, and fell ravenously on the picnic lunch we had forgotten to take with us. The food tasted very good, but our appetites for a return visit to the wee lough were even keener.

A few days later we were back. Conditions for salmon on the river were as low and dour as ever, but by now the Twelfth of August had come and gone, and grouse were in season. (Grouse numbers have declined seriously since the early 1970s, a consequence of habitat deterioration and excessive predation and not over-shooting. Nevertheless, grouse are now fair game in the Republic of Ireland only for the thirty days of September.) We planned to shoot our way up to the lough, in anticipation of finding a few of those well grown coveys we had seen the previous week. Once at the lough, rods would replace guns, we would have a full day's fishing, and we would shoot our way back to the cars. This seemed to be the best way of ensuring the maximum combination of exercise and sport, with a fair prospect of having something, feathered or finned, for the larder on our return.

It was pleasantly warm and overcast, altogether better weather for fishing, and for shooting too. The setter was as staunch as ever, the birds were there and lay well to the dog's set. Neither of us had fired a shot since the last woodcock shoot of previous winter, so it was a good omen when we found we were shooting fairly straight, managing to pick the old birds out of two coveys and account for a geriatric single cock grouse which had squatted among some peat hags. The score was two and a half brace of old birds and a single young grouse by the time we breasted the ridge and sighted the wee lough.

How to begin? There was no sign of a hatch of fly, nor of fish moving. Why should they, with such a feast of bottom feeding available? I opted for a shrimp pattern on a size 14 hook, fishing slow and deep on a longish leader. More daringly, my companion put up a small and heavily chewed General Practitioner salmon fly, dressed on a little double hook and a veteran of several successful grilse expeditions. We fished steadily and with an absorbed, silent concentration. A hatch of olives and sedges began, slowly at first and then in profusion all over the few acres of the lough's surface. And still nothing moved.

Then my deep-fished shrimp was taken with a long, slow pull which quickly turned into a screamingly fast run as I tightened on the take and set the hook. Something big and powerful was making a dash for the far shore, the sunken line and leader slicing through the water like a cheese wire. He fought hard and deep, reluctant to come anywhere near the surface. There were three more deep, fast runs before he turned on his side and showed a deep, buttery-yellow flank as I drew him over the net. Heavy-shouldered, neat and small in the head, his flanks deep and perfect with a speckled golden sheen, he pulled the pointer of the spring balance to just a shade under 3 lb (1.35 kg). That was the only trout I moved or touched all day – but a fish to remember all my life.

The wee lough was in a generous mood that day, for it eventually gave each of us a fish. The other was magnificent, exactly 4 lb (1.8 kg) and as beautifully formed as any trout could be. He came to that well munched little prawn pattern just as the light began to fade – a doughty, powerful fighter in the same golden livery, deep-bodied and with a firm flesh of salmon pink.

It was getting too late to stay and fish, and too dark to shoot on our twilight tramp back to the car, although we could hear cock grouse crowing their challenges into the western sunset. After his long hours of expectant waiting the setter gave us one of those meaningful, reproachful looks as only an Irish setter can, but his was the only downcast spirit as we set off down the hillside. No grouse-and-trout expedition could ever have brought more pleasure and total satisfaction.

In thinking back to that visit, and others since, I must remind myself that this was not a matter of pure self-indulgence in secret sport. There was an element of scientific interest in our expedition, too. Remembering those crustaceans, the snails, the profuse weed growth and that bursting bubble of china clay we had seen on our first visit, we took a few bottles and little glass jars with us, to collect and bring back samples of the water, the lake bottom and the invertebrate life of our amazing little lough. A few days later I took them to a scientist friend who worked in the biology department at Trinity College, Dublin and asked him to cast an expert's eye over them. He – and his colleagues in the now-defunct Inland Fisheries Trust – were staggered. The water was possibly the most alkaline they had ever tested from an Irish lough, the china clay was indeed an almost pure chalky matter, and they were bursting to know more about this lough. Where was it? Could they go there and do more tests? Could they try netting it or electro-fishing it, to see what the trout population was like?

Politely but firmly, we declined to disclose its name or its location. And twenty years on, I am not going to name it now. All I will tell you is that it is within the Ox Mountains, and if you want to find it and experience its joys and challenges for yourself you will have to hunt for it. Discovery, publicity and over-exploitation would destroy a little bit of piscatorial Heaven for ever.

Trout and Salmon on the Moy

But there is no secret about our next fishery, the River Moy. No account of game fishing in this corner of Ireland could omit some reference to the excellence of the Moy, one of the most consistently productive game fisheries anywhere in Ireland. It rises on the north-eastern slopes of the Ox Mountains, just a few miles to the east of Easky Lough, and its headwaters are shown on the map as a tracery of little hill streams just to the south of the main watershed. Only a mile or two (1.6–3.2 km) to the north rise the northward flowing waters of the Owenboy River, part of the Owenmore and Ballysadere river catchment. But the Moy's course is south-westerly, and it collects the tributary flow of the Owenaher River from the north and the Owengarve River from the east before its winding course takes it around the southern flanks of the Ox Mountains, past the towns of Swinford and Foxford. From there its

One day's catch for two Rods on the Ridge Pool of the River Moy at Ballina, comprising seatrout, grilse and summer salmon.

final twelve or fifteen rather sinuous miles (9.6–12 km) take it due north towards Ballina and the sea at Killala Bay.

The Moy therefore drains a wide U-shaped sweep of counties Sligo and Mayo, and the character of the river is also influenced by an important connection with the wide waters of Lough Cullin and its immediate neighbour, Lough Conn. This occurs just south of Foxford town, and it ensures that the salmon which enter the Moy system in such profusion have access not only to the upper parts of the Moy river and its tributaries, but also to these inter-connected loughs and their tributaries.

The Moy has been a notable spring and summer salmon fishery since Irish angling records began. Augustus Grimble, in his comprehensive *The Salmon Rivers of Ireland* (1903), referred to the 'far-famed Moy river . . .', while his predecessors like Walter Peard declared the Moy to be 'the best open water in the three kingdoms', and 'Hi-Regan' (with typically dry understatement) reckoned this fishery as among Ireland's very best.

The estuary fishing in the long, narrow inner reaches of Killala Bay is of top quality, with good prospects for seatrout and also the occasional salmon, while the most productive single pool on the Moy (and perhaps the most heavily fished pool in any Irish or British water) is the Bridge or Town pool in Ballina town itself. Some prodigious catches of sizeable seatrout and good summer salmon have been made here, and upstream there is some superb water between Ballina and Foxford. Mount Falcon Castle, once a private house and now a delightful sporting guest house, is close to some of the very best pools, and Salmon & Woodcock Game Holidays Ltd., based at Foxford, also have access to some excellent fishing on the upper and lower stretches of the Moy, and on the adjacent loughs of Conn and Cullin.

5 The Galway Fishery

The waters of Lough Corrib, which permeate under the bridges of the town, go rushing and roaring to the sea with a noise and eagerness only known in Galway . . .

William Makepeace Thackeray, *Irish Sketch Book* (1843)

The Galway Fishery is the name often given to the outflow of the short Corrib River from the southern end of Lough Corrib into Galway Bay. Indeed, this is actually the outflow of the waters from a very big catchment comprising three sizeable loughs: Corrib, Mask, further to the north, and Carra, the smallest and most northerly of the three, though at around 4000 acres (1600 hectares) it is still a sizeable lough by any reckoning. All three loughs, and their complex systems of tributaries and interconnecting rivers, converge and empty to the sea through this one short stretch of river. Its brief and dramatic course flows through the city of Galway itself, and the history of the river and the city are inextricably bound together.

In 1270 a royal charter of Edward I confirmed the status of a city upon the settlement at Galway, which had been established and developed steadily there for at least the previous four hundred years. At any rate, the marauding Danes in 835 had regarded it as worth raiding. But with the later development of Galway as a thriving centre for trade, shipping and manufacturing, it was inevitable that the presence and the power of the Galway River should be exploited by the city. Weirs were constructed, and water-leads and mill races diverted small portions of the flow to give the power necessary for driving machinery. Galway was a walled city, buttressed and bulwarked by ramparts of grey and red Connaught granite and Munster limestone against the encroachment of the Irish tribes of Gaelic Connemara to the west, against the risks of attacks from the sea, and against the twin forces of the sea and the river. And the same skills which built the city's stout walls also created a weir, sluices and systems of flood gates and other water-regulating mechanisms.

In time the Galway River was channelled and directed with new pace and vigour, giving power to the city for its workshops, wealth to the people from the harvest of salmon, and an income to the municipal authorities from taxes levied on fish caught. In 1362 the city needed extra funds for maintaining and strengthening the protective walls, and the wealth created by the port and the fisheries were obvious targets for the tax gatherers' attentions. A levy of four pence was paid on every tun of wine imported, and this was no small source of revenue for a port which had a busy wine trade with Spain and Bordeaux. The Irish–Spanish link remains strong, and you will find sherry shippers with names like O'Neill and Garvey, Hispano-Irish families descended from the old Catholic trading and soldiering dynasties which fled from Ireland in the aftermath of the routing of the Jacobite cause in 1690 and the final ignominy of the Treaty of Limerick in the following year. A century later claret, that dry red wine of Bordeaux which has always been so attractive to British palates, used to be referred to as 'Irish wine', so great was the trade between Galway and Bordeaux when the Napoleonic wars had halted normal and more legitimate trade between Britain and France.

And if your trade was not wine shipping but salmon netting you paid one farthing per fish as your customs levy at Galway. Sixteen salmon therefore equalled a tun of wine, which makes salmon look cheap, until you delve further into the schedule of levied taxes and see that one salmon paid the same duty as a hundred eels or as much seafish as one man could carry. A whole community at Galway was founded on the area's wonderfully prolific sea fishing, and the cottages of the Claddagh were rich repositories of the Gaelic language and culture. The Claddagh fisherfolk had a life which was largely separate from that of Galway City, and they enjoyed an unusual degree of quasi-autonomy in local government, having their own semi-official mayor, and distinct by-laws and customs.

Sadly, and despite the romanticised portrayals of the place and the people by visiting Victorian artists and writers, the Claddagh was also riddled with all the evils and diseases that overcrowding, poverty and demoralisation can bring upon a community. The cholera epidemic of 1832 was especially devastating, and the Claddagh community suffered a blow from which it never recovered. Little of the Claddagh remains today, but the name of the place and memories of some of its traditions and customs are perpetuated by the Claddagh ring, the traditional gold wedding ring of the Claddagh fisherfolk, which was passed from a mother to her eldest daughter on her marriage. Its distinctive design shows a crowned heart clasped between two hands.

Just as the mill wheels of Galway drew their motive power from the river from medieval times until the 1900s, it was inevitable that more modern developments should have capitalised on this source of huge and unfailing natural energy. Today you can go to Galway and see the massive flood gates which regulate the river's flow. Below them is the bridge, and only a few hundred yards further down the turbulent, rushing stream is the upper limit of the tidal water. Salmon which run up here are only moments away from the saline environment in which they have lived and grown massively since they first dropped downstream as silvery smolts, and they move up with all the fresh vigour of fish straight from the tide. And their incoming energy is matched by the outflowing power of a river which 'goes under the bridge like a pack of white hounds'. That is the vivid description of this river you can find in the incomparable *Irish R.M.* stories of Edith Somerville and Martin Ross. The latter, whose real name was Violet Martin, belonged to an old-established Anglo-Irish family of Galway, and the river at Galway must have been a familiar sight to her. And what better metaphor for a hunting authoress to choose than the image of pale hounds hurtling along at full tilt and in full cry?

Before looking at the Galway River and the sport it provides today, it is worth reminding ourselves of some aspects of the enormous historical importance of this fishery. Its formal status as a salmon fishery stems from undertakings given in Magna Carta and in a grant of Henry III in 1221. Six centuries later the first Irish salmon hatchery was established here, in 1853. Thomas Ashworth and his brother, of Cheadle in Cheshire, bought the Galway fishery and immediately launched into an enthusiastic campaign of fishery improvement and expansion. They were also lucky enough to have the help and advice of one of the most knowledgeable and celebrated fisheries experts in the history of aquaculture, the lively and eccentric Frank Buckland. In his important book *Fish Hatching* (1863) Frank Buckland describes in some detail the work carried on at the Oughterard hatchery on Lough Corrib's western shore, which resulted in the placing of hundreds of thousands of eyed salmon ova each year in many rivers and streams on this massive and elaborate loughs-and-rivers catchment.

By the early 1860s the numbers of salmon ran into millions, and almost £700 – a huge sum at that period – was spent on creating a fish passage across the short strip of land separating Lough Corrib and Lough Mask, its near neighbour further up the catchment. The eagerly anticipated prospect was of salmon running through the entire system, spawning in the higher tributary streams of Mask and even Carra, and massively improving the productivity of the entire fishery. Sadly this exciting project did not succeed, and today Loughs Mask and Carra remain primarily brown trout fisheries – though few sportsmen will complain about that, for they afford some of the finest fishing for wild brown trout in the world. We will be looking at these and other waters in the upper Galway catchment shortly, but what of the main Galway river and its runs of migratory fish?

The Galway salmon fishery gets a notable run of good salmon in the spring, followed by grilse in summer, and the catches are consistently good. The fish running up from the sea do so in full view of passers-by, and the salmon weir at Galway has been on the tourists' list of 'sights worth seeing' since the 1800s. Under the pen-name 'Cosmopolite', one John Allen wrote a two-volume book entitled *The Sportsman in Ireland*. This is probably the most useless book ever to purport to describe sport in Ireland. It contains virtually nothing worthwhile about sport or wildlife, and is really a long and tedious diatribe about Irish politics and religion. But even Allen, in his avid search for social and religious problems in Galway, could not help noticing the amazing spectacle of the salmon run. In 1840 he described how he looked over Galway bridge and saw that 'masses of black, here and there, covered the bottom, forming the appearance of seaweed, gently moved by the course of the waters, till occasionally by a silvery flash, here and there, was seen the delicate white of the

The iniquity of illegal off-shore drift netting for salmon and seatrout intrudes on the otherwise perfect tranquillity of a western Irish sunset.

salmon; those masses were constituted of fresh-run fish, congregated in preparation for their annual voyage to the vast lake'.

It was this very density of salmon, lying in serried ranks and queuing for their chance to move on upstream, which led to the hateful but unfortunately very common Galway practice at that era of taking salmon by 'snatching', 'stroke-hauling', or – in simpler modern terms – deliberate foul-hooking. This was easy, requiring little more than the casting of a heavily weighted hook or series of hooks over the throng of fish and retrieving line until resistance on the line indicated that the hooks had found a hold. Then the salmon was hauled unceremoniously out of the river, so unsportingly strong were the rods and lines used for this form of salmon catching – for it certainly cannot be described as salmon fishing in any sporting sense. It was almost a required event for the holidaymaker or tourist to Galway in Victorian times to visit the fishery and try his or her hand at pulling out a fish in this shameful way.

Even among the genuine game fishers who went about their business with the conventional tackle of a normal fly rod, line and gut cast, and who caught most of their salmon by fair means, it was sometimes said that a foul-hooked salmon gave the best sport, owing to the unusually powerful performance which a fish hooked in the body can put up. Happily, definitions of what constitutes 'sport' have changed, and deliberate snatching and stroke-hauling on Irish rivers is now confined to the poaching fraternity, against whom the fisheries authorities and riparian owners wage a constant battle. Like every other nation with rich salmon fisheries, Ireland has a major poaching problem, although it must be acknowledged that the minor iniquities of the riverside villains are trifling and unimportant when compared to the enormities of the illegal off-shore drift-netters. It is these criminals, who scoop tens of thousands of returning salmon and seatrout out of the sea, who represent the main poaching threat to migratory fish around the shores of Ireland and many other north Atlantic countries. Responsible governments and judiciaries everywhere should crack down ruthlessly on this rape of a precious natural resource.

A generation or two ago, the salmon fisher enjoying his sport between 'the cribs' and the bridge below often became an object of intense public interest, especially if he happened to be locked in prolonged combat with a big fish. This was common at Galway, and also at Ballyshannon, on the lower beats of the Erne River. One passer-by would see that a Rod was into a fish and would stop to watch the fish being played. Others would join him, and if the proceedings went on for anything more than a few minutes a considerable crowd might gather, cheering on the fisher – and sometimes the fish – and shouting plenty of gratuitous advice. Two of the favourite cries were 'Easy now!' or 'Give him the butt!' depending on whether the fish needed careful handling or some powerful strain at that particular moment.

The hapless fisherman, who already had quite enough to contend with in playing a big fresh fish in a torrent of fast water, simply had to try to close his ears and eyes to the distracting shouts and gestures of his audience, at least until the fish had been gaffed or netted – or lost. To lose a good fish is a moment of intense and personal grief, which the afflicted fisher should be allowed to endure as a private misery. A crown of onlookers deprives him of that small courtesy. Little wonder that many Galway salmon fishermen lost their fish and then their tempers because of unsolicited advice and unwanted commiseration. It takes great self-control to lose a big fish publicly and still keep smiling. But it is a hazard on every salmon river in Britain and Ireland which has a 'town water' beat. Sadly, Ballyshannon Bridge is no longer a grandstand from which a crowd can watch an Erne angler and an Erne salmon in contention, but at Galway it still happens.

To fish in such an environment is not to everyone's taste, however good the sport may be. In the 1880s 'Hi-Regan' was not much taken with the idea of fishing from a gravel path alongside the wall of Galway gaol, and remarked that it 'lacks the poetry of sport on a wild lough or river', but he could not deny its potential for 'excellent sport'.

The Galway fishery is a short beat on which the angler's approach and tactics will be largely dictated by the water level. Those who know the fishery well take it as a rule of thumb that when five or more of the weir gates are open, the depth and power of water is such that fly fishing is best forgotten. Spinning and shrimping come into their own under these conditions, and tackle must be capable of dealing with big fish in fresh fighting trim in a mighty torrent of water. A salmon spinning rod of 11 or even 12 ft (335 or 365 cm) is best, and it is inviting disaster to use line of less than 25–30 lb (11.5–14 kg) breaking strain. A multiplier with braided line would perhaps be ideal, but most fishers use a large fixed-spool reel with heavy monofilament.

The green-and-yellow metal Devon minnow is the almost universal favourite in spring conditions, at least 2–3 in (6.5–7.5 cm) long, and it is interesting to note how very popular and successful the 'Yellow Belly' is on almost all Irish spring salmon fisheries. The brown-and-gold Devon and also the Kynoch Killer have their devotees at Galway, but they are in the minority. It is interesting to speculate whether the Yellow Belly has indeed some special attraction for these fish, or whether more are caught on them simply because more fishers use them.

With this robust tackle you can fish with some confidence and the same combination of rod, reel and line is also suitable for bait fishing with a shrimp. For this a bubble float, preferably the easy-to-see, dayglow-red type rather than a clear plastic one, is used to work the shrimp down the main flow or along the slacker waters of the run-outs and the eddying pools out of the full force of the water. The bright float is easy to follow as the bait fishes down, while the float can be filled with whatever water is necessary to give the optimum combination of casting weight and buoyancy.

When the flow is reduced and the water level drops lower, which is likely to happen when not more than three or four of the weir gates are open, the water is normally in suitable condition for fishing with a fly. The spring tackle is much the same as you would use on any fishery, a powerful rod of at least 14 or 15 ft (425 or 455 cm), a slow-sinking line, and large, long Waddington or tube-type flies. The Galway experts have a special fondness for the Garry Dog as a spring fly, usually dressed on a heavy long-shank treble. But the superior hooking qualities and reduced fly leverage of Brora-type Waddington and tube flies, using the most modern types of out-pointed, needle-sharp hooks, are ousting the older flies. Nor is there anything especially magical about the killing qualities of the Garry Dog, although most successful spring patterns do tend to share something of its predominantly yellow colouring. The Silver Wilkinson and the Silver Doctor, for example, have provided the basic patterns for proven Galway spring flies. It is interesting to note that although the specifically prawn-like patterns such as the General Practitioner, the Curry Red Shrimp, the Parson and the Torrish are popular with most Irish salmon fishers on most Irish waters, they are not much used at Galway in the spring.

Despite their unbalanced and unpleasant casting characteristics, sink-tip lines are favoured by some Galway regulars, and with good results too, but a slow-to-medium sinking line will achieve the same effective depth in fly presentation. And now that modern rod design has made salmon rods of 16 ft (490 cm) and longer available in manageable weights, some of these are beginning to appear. Effective coverage of the water, which rod length confers, is important and productive on the Galway fishery, but until fairly recently few rods have had the combination of length and light weight which makes this comfortable for the fisher. In the 1890s the Shannon-side workshops of rodmakers like Enright and Burke produced their 18 and 20-ft (550 and 610 cm) rods, and they were once as popular on the Galway River and other big Irish fisheries as carbon-fibre is today. But the titanic strength and stamina necessary to fish effectively with such rods for long periods was a penance for the angler, and the dour, dogged, backbreaking dedication of those turn-of-the-century salmon fishers has vanished, just as the ageing greenheart of those massive old rods has gradually lost its strength and resilience with the years.

One senior sportsman of my acquaintance, who had been brought up to fish for salmon with those massive, heavy Castleconnell rods, remarked to me that he thought all modern rods and modern fishers were lightweight and spineless! As we say in Ireland, 'I passed no remark', but quietly thought of my lovely light salmon rods and my tendency to recurrent back trouble. If I now suffer odd twinges after a day's fishing with a 15-ft (455 cm) Hexagraph, what would be the agonies after a few hours wielding my grandfather's massive steel-cored cane rod and its huge reel, which together must have weighed several pounds?

Since the late 1980s the very biggest and most powerful carbon rods have become more evident each spring at Galway. One recent visitor actually turned out with 20 ft (610 cm) of carbon rod, which attracted some curious glances and a few pithy comments. Even for a fishery like Galway with biggish fish and heavy water conditions, this individual had definitely over-rodded himself. More realistically, Bruce & Walker's recently developed Hexagraph range have done especially well, particularly the stiff-actioned 'Walker' models and the other rods specially designed for fishing a heavy fly and a sunk line in heavy water conditions, in lengths of 15 ft (455 cm), 15 ft 4 in (465 cm) and 16 ft (490 cm). It is an eloquent comment on the power of the water and the strength of the fish at Galway that such tackle is used, for few western Irish fisheries require these powerful rods and heavy lines and flies, however customary they may be on the great rivers of Scotland and on some of Ireland's east-coast rivers, where the pools are wide and deep and the fish are big.

One of the perennial challenges of the Galway salmon fisher has been to hold a strong fish which is hooked just above the tide. These are massively strong fish, as fresh as it is possible to find, which have come straight from the sea. They have not had to negotiate any falls, rapids or other energy-consuming obstacles, and their reaction to the pressure of hook and line is powerful. Invariably a Galway 'runaway' turns back downstream towards the sea, a violent and instinctive lunge back towards the familiar, safe, salty environment. The urgent challenge is to stop him and turn him before he reaches the bridge. Once he has gone under and through one of the arches he is almost sure to be lost. (The same problem bedevilled many previous genera-tions of salmon fishers on the Erne, where the head of the Falls pool was fished from the Ballyshannon bridge. A fresh fish dashing back to sea simply had to be held and turned if he was not to be lost instantly over the falls and into the sea pool. And another excitement lay in store if the fish, once turned, came back upstream and carried the line up through another arch on that many-spanned bridge. A fish which 'threaded the arches' at Ballyshannon was as good as lost.)

When a fresh fish is hooked and runs downstream at Galway the line is stripped off the reel in a fast run, the fighting strength of the fish aided by the force of the current. A faulty slipping clutch on a reel, loops of fly line or backing which do not run absolutely freely, a momentary faltering of the spool or the gearing, and the line cracks like a pistol shot as it parts. Every season there are woeful tales of fish which have broken 30-lb (14 kg) monofilament or 25-lb (11.5 kg) leaders, and in many cases this must have been due to some defect of the reel or some entanglement or unevenness in the winding of the line.

It is an important part of every fisherman's preparatory drill that he should strip off the line and rewind it onto his reel carefully each day before he goes to the river. It is fatally easy to find that during the previous day's fishing the line has been unevenly wound back and become awkwardly doubled over, with a coil caught fast under other turns of line. When a fish runs and strips off line fast, that snag will almost certainly cause a sufficiently abrupt check to be fatal, and a break will be inevitable. Far better to take a few short minutes in preparation to find and correct that flaw by unwinding all your line and backing in your garden or across the lawn at your hotel, and rewind every inch carefully, than to lose a fish.

In the turmoil of high water in spring or when the flood hatches are open you will do well to fish from the banks. But in late spring, when the Galway grilse run and the water is in fine condition for the fly, you will want to wade, especially if you fish from the left (i.e. east) bank. Chest waders are essential, as also is a good wading staff and the combination of confidence and care necessary for deep wading and effective fishing in heavy water. No one wants to lose their footing and take a ducking in this dangerously powerful flow.

The Galway grilse runs come from May onwards and the fishing peaks in June. The heavy lines, big flies and stout leaders of the spring can be changed for summer equipment. Shorter rods are not recommended, and many Galway fishers stick to their fifteen-footers (455 cm) throughout the year. But a floating line is now appropriate, and the flies should be low-water sizes, usually 10s and 12s, on suitable doubles and trebles. If the smaller fly is to fish with a suitably attractive liveliness it must be tied to a lighter leader, of course, but it is courting disaster to go too light. Grilse and summer salmon in this water are powerful contenders, and it is a brave man who will drop below a 15-lb (7 kg) leader, or 12 lb (5.5 kg) as an absolute minimum. The ubiquitous Stoat's Tail accounts for as many summer fish on the Galway fishery as it does everywhere else, and many regulars here use nothing else. Popular alternatives are the low-water dressings of those spring favourites, the Silver Wilkinson and the Garry Dog.

The Galway fishery is a popular and highly organised fishery, and the fisher has to conform to a simple but rigidly enforced set of regulations. In the late spring, from 21 May to 4 July, when the grilse fishing is at its height, the management divides each day's fishing into two seven-hour periods, from 6 am to 1.00 pm and from 1.30 pm to 8.30 pm respectively. The maximum number of Rods who may fish during any one session is six, and no individual may fish both sessions. Thus the fishery can cater for twelve people in the course of a fourteen-hour fishing day. This represents a good compromise, and shares out the maximum amount of fishing opportunity among the maximum number of visitors without causing overcrowding of this short stretch of river. Because of the lunchtime changeover, no team or Rod is seen to hog the water for too long, and with other superb waters within easy reach, most notably Lough Corrib, it is perfectly possible to have a satisfying seven hours' salmon fishing before or after a good evening or morning's trout fishing. No one could ask for more, and few fishers have the reserves of physical or mental stamina to fish effectively throughout a longer day. Fishing should be a pleasure and not an extended demonstration of staying power, whatever my old friend may say about the spinelessness of the modern angler!

At Galway in June you will almost certainly find that the water is low and that the management will apply a fly-only rule for the first five hours of your seven-hour fishing session, with a wider choice of methods for the last two hours. Whatever the day, make sure you know the rules which apply on that day.

The Galway salmon fishery is superbly run and a wonderful experience to fish. Its fame dates from the earliest oral and written records of the Gaelic Irish and their Norman settlers, and it has deservedly gained a worldwide reputation. It remains one of the most remarkable fisheries in Ireland. Therefore do not imagine that you can simply drive over to Galway and stop off for a day's salmon fishing when you feel so inclined. You must plan and book well in advance – and you are unlikely to be disappointed.

6 The Wild Fisheries of the West

Western Seatrout and Brown Trout

Westwards from Galway city and over the Galway River you move into a different landscape and a new environment. The limestone of the Corrib catchment and of the north-west of Munster, with its rich loughs and alkaline rivers, gives way to a rough-and-tumble scattering of granite boulders amid wide expanses of blanket bog, where the water seeps coloured out of the peat or runs like frothing beer down tumbling, rocky courses. The lush greenness of rich Munster pastureland famous for its prime cattle and its heavy-boned bloodstock, and the stone wall country beloved by generations of hunting people in the country of the Blazers, are proverbial.

The move from limestone to granite, from pasture to rock and heather, also marks an important shift in the style of fisheries and the types of fishing we find. The big, sometimes massive lake trout of Corrib and the heavy spring-run salmon are left behind, and we move into an area where summer salmon and late-run seatrout dominate the game-fishing scene. This is not to imply that we are moving from top-quality fishing to anything poorer or less desirable. On the contrary, the westward move from Galway takes us to some of the most important, exciting and sought-after game fishing in Europe – the celebrated fisheries of Connemara and the west. Kingsmill Moore described the northern shore of Galway Bay as 'a succession of one famous white trout fishery after another', and it was among these barren hills, sparkling loughs and tumbling rivers that he found a lifetime's sport and much of the inspiration for that most celebrated of Irish fishing books, *A Man May Fish*. Anyone who puts pen to paper on the subject of the fisheries of west Galway knows he stands in the shadow of that great and kindly man, and of his wise and wonderful book. It remains holy writ for anyone who loves fishing, wild places, or fine writing, and it will always be required reading for anyone planning a fishing holiday west of Galway city.

Although the seatrout and salmon of summer and autumn dominate the fishing scene in Connemara, it is always perilous to generalise, especially about the ways of wild creatures or about a subject as complex as fishing. There are some small runs of early salmon in some Connemara waters, and as is usually the case these early fish tend to be heavier than the average for summer salmon, and on examination of the scales it will be found they have usually spent an additional winter at sea. There are also a few early-run seatrout, which can also be significantly larger than their summer and autumn cousins. However, it must be said that no one who goes fishing for salmon or seatrout in Connemara in March or April, or even in May, can realistically expect to see or catch very much. These fisheries are quintessentially summer and early-autumn waters.

The seeker after good-sized brown trout will also do well not to concentrate his attentions on Connemara. That is another generalisation which requires some qualification, because there are a few fisheries in this part of Ireland which have exceptionally fine brown trout, but they are very much in the minority. It is worth considering them for a moment, not only because they are delightful waters which may bring you good sport and memorable fish, but because their distinctive characteristics are different from the generality of local fisheries. Sometimes we can learn the rules by studying the exceptions.

There are three particularly good brown trout fisheries in Connemara, and as you drive west from Galway the first you come to is on the island of Gorumna. This is the largest of a scattering of more than a score of islands which lie at the north-western end of Galway Bay, where the coastline begins to turn the corner and swing towards Clifden and the western extremity of the province of Connaught. Gorumna and its smaller neighbour Lettermore are linked to the mainland by a series of bridges and causeways, and you can drive out on the L100 road from the village of Costelloe. The road takes you right alongside three loughs, Awallia, Nagowan and Hibbert, and a little further on you come to a fourth, Ballynakill Lough. Here you find yourself confronted with one of the puzzles of Connemara fishing.

These four loughs hold really good, wild brown trout, many wet-fly baskets producing fish to well over 1 lb (0.45 kg) and occasionally much more, particularly from Ballynakill, where trout of 3–4 lb (1.35–1.8 kg) are not uncommon, and five-pounders (2.25 kg) have been encountered. Yet these loughs are small, they lie over poor, acidic rocks and soils, and they are all within a mile (1.6 km) or less of the sea, to which the system is linked by a river. Seatrout are seldom seen or caught here, except occasionally in Lough Nagowan, and yet everything appears perfect for the existence of a fine seatrout fishery. All around to the north and east are countless lough-and-river systems, some of them world renowned, where the seatrout run in their thousands, and where any brown trout caught are unlikely to make more than 5 or 6 oz (0.1–0.15 kg). Why are the Gorumna loughs so very different?

To find the answer let us look at two more fisheries. First we must drive back again to Costelloe, turn north towards Screebe and turn left at Screebe. From where you park your car it is only a short walk (but usually a difficult and boggy one) down to the Camus loughs, a network of loughs which link together and form the Camuseighter fishery. Like the Gorumna loughs, the setting is typically western, with dark waters in an acidic environment. And yet these loughs are full of surprisingly big, finely conditioned brown trout. The fly fisher is likely to find the Camus trout quick to rise to the fly, and one celebrated catch in the early 1980s comprised no fewer than seventy fish. Furthermore, you will also find the average size here is around 12 oz (0.35 kg) and a good day's catch may comprise a dozen fish and perhaps many more, some of which are likely to be well over 1 lb (0.45 kg). Yet there are no signs of seatrout, despite the proximity of the sea at Camus Bay only a mile or two (1.6–3.2 km) to the south.

The Gorumna loughs and the Camuseighter system each comprise a network of loughs which are connected to the sea by a short river. The conditions are ideal, one might think, for migratory trout to run up from the sea and spawn, and for the eggs to develop as alevins, fry, parr and eventually smolts within the waters of the loughs and their feeder streams, before they migrate downstream to feed and grow in the richer marine environment. And yet it does not happen.

Nor does it occur on the third major Connemara brown trout fishery, which lies far to the north-west beyond Clifden and the village of Claddaghduff, where Aughrus Point juts out into the Atlantic just south of the remote islands of Inishbofin and Inishark. Your long journey to Aughrusbeg Lough, which lies on the uttermost fringe of western Europe, may be rewarded by brown trout fishing of astonishing quality. Within less than a mile (1.6 km) of the Atlantic surge and often within clear earshot of it you will find superb trout averaging almost 1½ lb (0.7 kg), with fish of 2–3 lb (0.9–1.35 kg) common enough. Trout of 6 and 7 lb (2.7–3 kg) have been taken from Aughrusbeg each year by the few enthusiasts who know the lough and who are prepared to forego the main Connemara attractions of seatrout and salmon. In this respect Aughrusbeg has something in common with the Durness lochs of north-west Scotland, where large and beautiful trout can be found by those who do not regard the far north as a place for the salmon and seatrout fisher only. But the acidic environment of Aughrusbeg and the other Connemara brown trout loughs is in marked contrast to the pellucid clarity and alkaline richness of those limestone loughs of Cape Wrath, so the comparisons have strict limits. But the remoteness of the locations and the quality of the fish and the sport provide interesting parallels.

There is a particular pleasure in taking good baskets of sizeable wild brown trout from these western waters, especially since there are realistic prospects of catching something really memorably big on Camuseighter and Aughrusbeg. The killing flies here, and on the Gorumna and Camuseighter loughs, are the Connemara Black (appropriately enough), the Black Pennell, the Invicta, the Bibio, Watson's Fancy, the Kingsmill and the Greenwell, with the sedge patterns like the Murrough and the Green Peter also advisable for Aughrusbeg from late July onwards, especially at dusk.

But what about our main piscatorial puzzle, the size of those brown trout and the virtual absence of seatrout in an area where almost every other river and lough has big runs of them?

Without entering into a long consideration of trout biology and ecology, it is now widely accepted that brown trout and seatrout are in fact the same species. However, the brown trout is resident in fresh water, making local migrations into the headwaters of rivers and the feeder streams of loughs to spawn, but otherwise living a fairly sedentary existence. The seatrout is hatched and grows in fresh water, as does the salmon, until it has reached a size and achieved an appetite for food which the resources of the river or the lough of its birth and early life cannot supply. Then come the pressures of territorial claims and competition for food and space in which to live and grow.

Wild trout, even when very small, are fiercely territorial, for the securing of a territory within the stream or lough also means the securing of a supply of food. To fail to find and hold such a territory, or to have insufficient food within a territory, means displacement and possible starvation. This situation forces the growing trout to migrate downstream and there it may find more food and more room. If it does not, as is the case on many western river-lough systems, its ultimate destination is the sea, where the rich feeding creates fast growth and heavy body weights, and where overcrowding is not a problem. Eventually the trout which has undertaken this enforced migration returns to its natal water to spawn, and so the cycle of birth and reproduction comes full circle.

This concept of the seatrout as a fish which is forced to migrate owing to a paucity of food and space fits well with the ecology of most fisheries which have runs of seatrout. Usually there are excellent spawning and nursery streams, which produce young trout in numbers far above what the main rivers and loughs can accommodate and feed. Thus there is an important imbalance between the system's ability to produce young trout and its capacity to support them as they grow bigger. It is this imbalance which forces the growing trout to migrate in search of food and *lebensraum*.

In Ireland, and especially here in the bleak moorland and granite lands of the west, there are clear streams which provide prime spawning conditions and good environments for growing salmonids, but whose impov. ished acid waters have limited amounts of the insects and other invertebrate food items that growing trout require. Acid waters are also lacking in the dissolved calcium elements which build bone in the growing fish, and the result is that those trout which do not migrate tend to remain small. In Connemara rivers and loughs few brown trout will grow beyond ½ lb (0.25 kg) and many will never achieve even that modest size.

But in the excellent brown trout fisheries of Gorumna, Camuseighter and Aughrusbeg the local conditions are different, and that is why they are notable for their brown trout but have little or nothing to offer the seatrout enthusiast. All three fisheries have very limited spawning areas, and therefore the reproductive rates of the trout are much lower than in river-lough systems with plenty of well-oxygenated feeder streams with good spawning gravel. The rate of recruitment of young trout to the total population is therefore much lower than normal in Connemara, there is much less competition for the available food and space, and all the signs are that these systems are in states of equilibrium, with sufficient food and space to allow the resident fish to grow to a good size.

There are no pressures on the young fish to migrate, and so they do not. At any rate, this seems to be the logical environmental explanation, if you subscribe to the 'seatrout-are-made-not-born' school of thinking, which regards the sea-going trout as a brownie which has been forced into migration by local conditions. It seems more than likely that there is also at least some genetic component in this equation, an innate disposition among some trout to migrate to sea while others remain behind. But the dividing line between the practical and pragmatic business of competition, lack of food, lack of space and restrictions on growth on the one hand, and genetic migratory impulses on the other, is something best left to the fisheries biologists to study and resolve. It certainly lies outside the scope of this book.

As I suggested earlier, these few excellent brown trout fisheries, which have unimpeded river links with the sea and yet do not enjoy significant runs of seatrout, are exceptions to the general rule in west Galway. And since most game fishers are drawn to Connemara by prospects of seatrout and salmon it is to the more typical western fisheries that we must give our main attention.

Whatever your eventual route when you leave Galway city on a fishing tour of the west, it is unlikely that it will follow a predictable pattern. The fishing and the weather will usually see to that, and one of the pleasures of any fishing holiday comes from being able to fish where and when you please.

Spiddle, Boliska and the hill loughs

But in attempting a survey of the game fisheries of Galway and Connemara it seems logical to begin at Galway city and work our way clockwise around this wild, indented coastline to the north of Galway Bay. If you were in a hurry to get from Galway to Clifden, deep in western Connemara, you would take the main N59, a fine trunk road which will take you as quickly and directly across the county as the geography permits. But that would mean missing the coastline and the best of the fisheries. Instead our route will follow the lesser roads, the L100 which leads due west from Galway to Spiddle and Costelloe, and eventually links up with the L102, which winds around the complex contours of the south-west of this region, from Screebe Lodge through Carna and Cashel to Derryclare and northwards to Clifden.

The first important fishery you will come to is at Spiddle, where the River Spiddle slips into Galway Bay at the end of its 15 miles (24 km) or so of southward flow, from its source high in the hills of south Galway. It is the first of what Walter Peard, writing in 1867, described as the 'small streams of exceeding goodness' of west Galway. The river widens out at several points along its course and forms a chain of important seatrout loughs, a river-and-linked-loughs type of system which, as we shall see, is characteristic of this part of Ireland. Also fairly typical is the fact that the Spiddle system does not receive any worthwhile runs of seatrout or salmon before mid June, with sport picking up throughout the summer and fish gradually moving up the system as the season progresses.

The Spiddle is an interesting example of a fishery which benefited greatly from the improving zeal of earlier generations of fishermen. Up to the 1850s the river had a series of waterfalls which, though they were spectacular and picturesque, were an impassable barrier to migratory fish. Seatrout and salmon could not negotiate them, even when the water was high and the flow fast. Above the falls the river and its chain of loughs was strictly a brown trout fishery, and not a very exciting one. All that changed after some judicious blasting and the creation of a semi-natural fish ladder, which gave the fish access for the first time to 8 or 9 miles (13–14 km) of the upper system. This enlightened and successful move was accompanied by some careful river management and keepering. Eight full-time bailiffs were employed, each with his beat of 1½ miles (2.5 km) or so to watch and guard, especially when the big runs of fish arrived, and later at spawning time. This was not an unusually large staff for a fishery in Victorian Ireland, with an abundance of cheap labour available in the countryside, but it was evidently successful in helping the newly extended Spiddle fishery to consolidate and become established as a successful salmon and seatrout system throughout its length. The quality of its sport and its reputation for bracing air, good food and friendly hospitality made Spiddle in the 1870s a popular fishing and health resort.

Spiddle is the home of the Morris family, one of a number of important old Anglo-Irish families in the county of Galway. The head of the family, Lord Kilannin, takes his title from the parish of the same name, and his two sons have achieved notable sporting successes, one as a falconer and sporting photographer, the other as a national hunt jockey, which is in keeping with the best sporting traditions of Irish county families. But there are other sporting links which are perhaps more widely known, for Lord Kilannin is a past President of the International Olympic Committee, whose activities he co-ordinated with masterly skill and universally popular affability during the troubles faced by the Olympics in the 1970s.

Lough Boliska is the first lough you will encounter on this fishery, and as the lowest on the system above the sea it receives the first runs of salmon and seatrout. This is a sizeable lough, well over 100 acres (40 hectares) in extent, but it is not deep, being little more than a widening of the river's course as it passes through a shallow depression before it gathers its waters together and enters the sea. Boliska is a pleasant lough, with something to offer every fly fisher. There is a large and lively stock of small brown trout, which come to the fly with gratifying enthusiasm. It is perfectly possible to make a basket of a dozen or twenty fine pan-size brownies here in a short day's fishing, and the sport is brisk and exciting, although nothing over ½ lb (0.25 kg) is likely to figure in the basket. The beginner should find on Boliska all the instant results and encouragement which are so psychologically important at the start of a fly-fishing career. There is ample time for disappointments and blank days in later years!

But the enthusiast will have seatrout and salmon in mind here. The seatrout – 'white trout' on this and most western fisheries in Ireland – are not the big, deep-bodied sewin of the Welsh rivers or of Ireland's east-coast waters.

The typical size on Boliska is around 1 lb (0.45 kg). The fish are bright and silvery, and with a verve and energy which belies their modest weight. But bigger fish are taken, and there is usually a fair showing of two-pounders (0.9 kg) through the season, with the occasional much bigger specimen. With its north-south orientation Boliska's many drifts fish well in the westerly or south-westerly winds which prevail here, and with its generally shallow characteristics there are few places on the lough which will not yield a fish if it is in a taking mood.

Much of the rocky shore is fishable too, and you can drive your car to the very edge of the water at many points around the lough. But on every sizeable lough, and on the majority of smaller ones too, the fly fisher will do best to fish from a boat. This means you have total command of the water, and on Boliska you may either make inquiries locally to hire a boat and engine, or launch your own – having first observed the courtesies and spoken to one of the riparian farmers. You will never be refused, but your thoughtfulness in asking will not go unnoticed.

The seatrout fisher on Boliska cannot do better than to adopt the classic western lough tactics – three flies fished on a shortish line with a longish rod, your boat beam-on to the breeze and drifting steadily. The proven local patterns are the Connemara Black, the Sooty Olive, the Black Pennell, the Bibio and the different Butcher variants, not forgetting those western fisheries specials, the Bumbles. The palmered pattern of the Claret Bumble, with its natural buoyancy and the subtle play of light through its fibres, makes it a favourite fly for the top dropper on your leader. Tripped over the wavelets of a good ripple, on Boliska and almost every other western seatrout lough, it can be deadly. And its use is not only practical but also symbolic. It will catch fish for you, and using it is a small ritual acknowledgement of the abiding presence of Kingsmill Moore, the presiding *genius loci* of these western waters. The spirit and the influence of 'K.M.' are always at your side, and he devised and developed the Bumbles with wonderful success.

For salmon the flies need not differ so much, though the tactics require some changes. All these seatrout patterns can and will entice a salmon, but a larger hook size and a stronger leader are advisable, and your fly-box should contain the ever-reliable Green Peter and also a selection of salmon patterns with prominent yellow in their dressing. Try the Logie, the Garry and the Silver Doctor, all tied on up-eyed, low-water single or double hooks.

Salmon have their accustomed lies or 'lodges', and these are ancient and well-established spots which are familiar to the local fishers and boatmen. An unaided visitor might spend ten seasons finding out such vital information for himself. A knowledgeable boatman or ghillie is therefore a sound investment, and will vastly increase your chances of coming home with a fish at the end of the day. Skilful manipulation of the oars will hold your boat in the ideal position over known lies one after another, more efficiently than you could ever manage single-handed, even if you knew where the lies were in the first place. And if your day is a blank one, its disappointments will be amply mitigated by the company of a kindred spirit who will teach you more about the lough and the countryside in a few hours than you would otherwise discover in a lifetime.

Before leaving Boliska and looking briefly at the other loughs of the Spiddle system, it is worth noting that this lough has a reputation for giving good sport to a daddy-longlegs, either dapped as a natural or fished dry as an artificial. 'Dapping the daddy', like other blow-line methods using the natural mayfly and the grasshopper, is a classic Irish technique, part of the local repertoire and ritual on these waters. It takes advantage of the avidity with which trout will rise to these large, conspicuous terrestrials which occur so abundantly in the reeds and rough grasses along the shore, and which are blown in large numbers onto the lough. The little brownies of Boliska will hurl themselves with glee at a 'daddy', which can be a nuisance if seatrout are your quarry. Take plenty of naturals with you in your live-bait box, and change to a fresh insect as soon as your bait shows signs of becoming bedraggled and sodden. Each year some of Boliska's best baskets of seatrout fall to the 'daddy', and it also accounts for a significant number of grilse and salmon.

Boliska is generally regarded as a free fishery, but further up the Spiddle system the situation becomes more complex. Local tradition and custom has it that 'the Galway shore' (i.e. the eastern banks of the river and the eastern shores of the loughs) is free to all comers, but the western shores are under the control of the Crumlin Lodge Fishery. This holds true for the main loughs which lie upstream of Boliska, Natawneighter and Loughanillaunmore, both get good numbers of seatrout by September, and earlier if the weather in August is wet, while the chain of loughs which comprise Lough Fadda, Lough Naweelan, Lough Ardderroo and Derryherk Lough all offer good seatrout prospects late in the season. Each and every one of these can give lively fishing for breakfast-sized brownies at almost any point in the season, but for seatrout they are rarely fished seriously until after the end of August. Then, if the 'Lammas floods' have come and brought the fish up, the sport can be memorable.

No one would claim that the Spiddle system is in the first flight of Galway's western seatrout and salmon waters. Other, more famous names and more productive waters lie in wait for us to the west and north-west. But Boliska and the other little loughs to the north have a charm of their own, and when conditions are good they can all give excellent fishing. It would be foolish not to give them a try before you move on, an opinion I share with 'Hi-Regan'. Writing a century ago, he said 'they should certainly be fished before starting on the north-west', that is, before you succumb to the magnetic lure of those other, more famous waters.

Fermoyle and Costelloe

But succumb you will. Succumb you must, for you have come this far west and it is only a few more miles until you reach Costelloe and Fermoyle, twin seatrout fisheries of world renown and the first classic waters we meet on our westward progress from Galway.

If you look at a good relief map of this area – the half-inch Ordnance Survey is the best, as always – you will see just how richly endowed this part of Ireland is with loughs and rivers. A closer glance shows that most of the loughs are linked by common rivers, and combine to form quite complex systems. The full complexity then emerges when you try to establish what lough is fed or drained by which river; which lough is higher or lower on the system than the others; and which fishery controls the sport on which water. Happily, local advice is readily given; the tourist authorities are also well informed; and no intending visitor to Ireland's loughs should even consider planning his trip without making repeated reference to Peter O'Reilly's incomparably useful *The Trout and Salmon Loughs of Ireland* (1987). This compendious guide is the work of a dedicated and experienced fly fisher and a professional fisheries expert, and it has filled a yawning gap in the factual literature of modern Irish fishing.

Gathering all your maps, leaflets and books around you, it soon becomes apparent that Costelloe and Fermoyle actually comprise two separate fisheries. This seems to make confusion worse confounded, but it is rather more straightforward than you might fear. The Costelloe fishery used to be known as the Lower Costelloe, while what is now known as the Fermoyle fishery was then the Upper Costelloe, and it is perhaps a pity that this more self-explanatory nomenclature was later abandoned. However, today the Costelloe system is taken to mean Costelloe Lake (usually referred to as Glenicmurrin Lough) and its outflowing river, the Cashla, which slips down a short and direct course of about 3 miles (5 km) to the sea at Cashla Bay. This is the point at which the northern shore of Galway Bay begins to turn the corner, swinging north-west among a chaotic mass of bays, inlets, coves and an archipelago of islands large and small.

Glenicmurrin Lough is accessible, fairly large by western standards, sheltered and readily fishable in all but the most extreme weather. Add to this its well-deserved reputation for producing consistently good sport with summer and autumn seatrout and salmon, and you have the recipe for a popular and productive fishery. It gives a great deal of sport to many Rods from June onwards.

Glenicmurrin and the Cashla River are not heavily dependent upon rain to bring the runs of fish upstream. The lough and the river maintain good levels in all but the very driest summers, such is the steady seepage of water from the saturated blanket peat which envelops so much of the upland landscape of these western regions. The gradient of the Cashla is slight and devoid of falls or other obstacles, and the fish can run as they please. But it appears that it does not please them to run until late May at the earliest. Consequently the Costelloe and Fermoyle fisheries do not open until 1 June and then enjoy a four-month season, with angling finishing on 30 September.

It is interesting to note that while many salmon and seatrout fisheries in Scotland and England have seen the gradual dwindling to near-extinction of their spring runs of fish, with summer and autumn runs now predominating, these fisheries of the west of Ireland appear never to have had significant spring runs of either salmon or seatrout. Scanty though it is by comparison with the well-documented history of Scottish fishing, the literature of these seatrout and salmon waters of west Connaught tends to show that they have always been summer and autumn fisheries. This has often caused comment and speculation among fishers in Galway, especially as the Galway river and the Corrib system was noted for its good run of big spring salmon in February, March and April, fish which presumably had to run into Galway Bay and past the innumerable estuaries of the more westerly fisheries. And yet, for whatever reason, the Galway fishery was unique in having a sizeable spring run.

In taking a glance at the history of fishing in these parts, it is also worth noting that in Victorian and Edwardian times it was apparently commonplace for salmon to be fished for and caught with some regularity on fly in the salt water of the estuary at Cashla Bay. Fly fishing for seatrout in estuaries is nothing unusual, and is a specialised branch of the seatrout enthusiast's art, but taking salmon on a fly in salt water is another matter. Since no one seems to do so nowadays in the Cashla estuary, perhaps it is merely an historical oddity. Even so, someone might like to have a try!

Local recollections of fly-caught salmon in the sea appear to be sketchy, to put it mildly, but it appears that whatever pattern of fly or lure may have been used, the key to success was that it should be bright blue in colour! The 'killing lies', if that is the appropriate term, were apparently found where the Cashla estuary forms a narrow cut near the top of the bay. Salmon waiting to run upstream gathered here, especially when dry weather had reduced the river's flow and they had to wait for a flood to let them run up. Quite a build-up of waiting fish could occur in a dry spell, and it was at such times that frustrated river fishers apparently resorted to the estuary. But it is interesting to speculate on how many of these fly-caught salmon had taken a lure and been fairly caught, and how many had actually been foul-hooked. In view of the amount of deliberate foul-hooking which took place on the Galway fishery in late Victorian and Edwardian times, in full view of the management and with apparently general acceptance as a fair angling method, the Cashla estuary salmon may not have been truly fly-caught fish. But perhaps we shall never know.

On the upper part of the Cashla catchment, on the Fermoyle fishery, the fishing comprises the river and a chain of eight loughs. The uppermost of these is Shannawona, which takes its name from the mountain on whose slopes it is cupped. It is worth the effort to tramp and scramble to the top of Shannawona on a clear day, for it affords probably the finest views of the landscape and the fisheries of south-west Galway. Here, at just under 1200 ft (366 m), you can see back down the Cashla system and also glimpse the scattering of loughs and the silver threads of the rivers which form the neighbouring fisheries at Screebe, Furnace, Inver, Gowla and beyond to Ballynahinch and the mountain peaks of Connemara.

Shannawona is different from the other loughs on the Fermoyle fishery for two main reasons. As the highest and last it is inevitably the latest to receive the runs of fish, which have first to negotiate the miles of river and the other, lower loughs. Glenicmurrin may yield good baskets of seatrout in the first week of June, but it may be July or August before this lough at the top of the catchment has been reached by worthwhile numbers of fish. And secondly, it is at Shannawona and in the river above and below it that the running fish find their eventual destination, the vital and sole reason why they have come here. This is where they spawn, among the granite gravel of the headwaters, with seatrout in their thousands and salmon in their hundreds.

If your enthusiasm and energy have taken you to the top of Shannawona mountain, this is the ideal spot from which to trace the development of the Cashla system as it descends through the network of loughs and short river beats. Below Shannawona Lough, and next on your downward route, lies Clogher (or Aclogher) Lough. This lough is something of a legend in itself, with a longstanding reputation for giving some of the best sport on the entire fishery when conditions are right. The seatrout here are often considered to be consistently bigger than elsewhere on this fishery, but it is difficult to know if this is a conclusion based on a careful comparison of weights or simply on the anecdotal impressions of the fishers! But it would be a bold commentator who would gainsay the opinion of Kingsmill Moore, who knew Fermoyle and loved Clogher above all. He was convinced that the Clogher trout were on the large side, and was sure that the record basket from Clogher, believed to have been thirty-six fish to two Rods, would have equalled fifty from any other part of this fishery.

Clogher should certainly not be missed by the visitor to Fermoyle, and there is little excuse for doing so nowadays. It was not always thus, and until recent years it was a difficult lough to reach. The old approaches to it called for some dedicated foot-slogging, and lay across deep and boot-sucking blanket bog or up and down over a jumbled chaos of tumbled granite boulders. Either was a disagreeable alternative at the beginning or end of a day's fishing. In recent years much of this landscape, once so open and spacious and vast, has been afforested, and already the blanket of conifers, laid out in serried ranks, is encroaching darkly on the loughs and the river. The broad vistas that earlier generations of fishers knew have gone now. But afforestation has at least brought one advantage – roads. Clogher, formerly so demanding to reach, is now barely ½ mile (0.8 km) of easy walking from where you park your car on the forest road.

The layout of the lough, and your tactics in fishing it, are dictated by a large, long island, and this has the effect of creating two principal beats on the lough, in the north-eastern and south-western sectors respectively. Seatrout can be taken on drifts at almost any point on the lough, although the western parts of Clogher have a reputation for dourness. Most Fermoyle regulars seem to favour the eastern side, and this is certainly the sector on which to concentrate your efforts if you aspire to catch a Fermoyle salmon, as well as the seatrout for which it is chiefly famous. A number of feeder streams enter Clogher along its eastern shore, and these are the traditional and proven 'lodges' where the salmon have moved up into the lough.

Western Connemara

In exploring the wonderful white trout and salmon fisheries of Connemara and the west, your planning and your enjoyment in anticipation will be greatly enhanced by the really excellent *Angler's Guide to Game Fishing for the Western Fisheries Region*, published by the Western Regional Fisheries Board in Galway. This splendid guide, in the form of a handy paper-back book, first appeared in 1987, and it provides not only an excellent general introduction to the area and its game fishing waters, but also a wonderfully detailed series of maps and diagrams, each linked to a thoroughly informative section about the individual rivers, loughs and catchments which comprise this important Fisheries Region. There are 100 pages of clear and well illustrated information, and some of the photographs of fine catches made in this area, and on the adjacent Corrib system, are truly mouthwatering. This guide should be a constant source of reference for every game fisher, local or visitor, who wets a line within the Western Region, for it is one of the finest and most comprehensive regional game fishing guides available anywhere in the world.

Continuing our tour of the fisheries of Connemara and the far west, *Angler's Guide* in hand, we move on from the Fermoyle and Costelloe fishery to the nearby villages of Maam Cross and Recess. These are excellent centres from which to explore a number of the best seatrout and summer salmon waters of

Once owned by Test cricketer Prince Ranjitsinghi, and fished by the eminent W. G. Grace, Ballynahinch Castle is both a fine salmon fishery and a superb seatrout water.

these parts, which include Screebe, Cashel and Gowla, the Inver and Inagh fisheries, and a whole scattering of loughs large and small, with an intricate tracery of interconnecting rivers. As always, a good relief map such as the Irish Ordnance Survey's Sheet 10 in their excellent half-inch series, is the best way to form a general impression of the wonderful complexity and diversity of the waters of this part of Ireland. Then when you settle down to detailed planning, that same map will be your best guide to the principal roads, the by-roads and the mountain tracks by which to approach your chosen lough or river.

One of the fisheries in these parts which you should not miss is Ballynahinch Castle, a world-famous fishery which comprises a typical western loughs-and-river combination. Ballynahinch is not only a superb fishery, but its attraction is enhanced by the grandeur of Ballynahinch Castle itself, one of the more splendid sporting lodges to have been built in the west of Ireland. It has had distinguished guests since the mid-nineteenth century, and has passed through the hands of a number of proprietors. These included a brief tenure of Ballynahinch by the Indian Maharajah and eminent international test cricketer, Prince Ranjitsinghi.

Ballynahinch fishery includes the Ballyahinch River and the Lower Ballynahinch Lough, and this fishery achieved a well deserved reputation for excellent salmon fishing, in spring and especially in late summer. But this prime interest in salmon among earlier generations of Ballynahinch aficionados tended to overlook the fishery's wonderful potential as a seatrout fisher's paradise. Yes, salmon remain important, especially if you are fortunate enough to connect with one of the small run of biggish spring fish which move into the system early in the season. But, as always in the west, it is the coming of late spring and summer and the arrival of the seatrout and the grilse and summer salmon that really brings this fishery to life.

There is superb fishing here both by boat and from the bank, and an individual basket comprising a dozen or eighteen good seatrout averaging around 2 lb (0.9 kg) is a fairly commonplace event here when conditions are right. That generally means a good, steady flow of water and a balmy westerly or south-westerly breeze, and these conditions are prevalent throughout most of the season. August and early September may provide the visitor with perfect conditions to take fine baskets of mixed grilse, small summer salmon and good seatrout, the equal of anything available on any Irish or British fishery.

Upstream on this river-and-lough system, and set in wonderful mountain scenery to the north-west of Ballynahinch are the loughs of Derryclare and Inagh, two more names to conjure with in any discussion of Irish seatrout fishing. These loughs give good sport throughout the season, for there is a fair chance of a spring salmon before the arrival of the summer grilse in June and the main runs of countless thousands of seatrout from late June onwards, accompanied by summer salmon and late-running fish until the very end of the season.

There is nothing very specialised about the tactics or the tackle required for success on these loughs and rivers, for a traditional selection of proven seatrout patterns continues to take an excellent annual toll of many seatrout, and

Summer and autumn salmon abound on western waters when water levels are suitable, especially after the traditional August 'Lammas floods'.

salmon too. All the classic western patterns succeed here, including the Connemara Black, the Black Pennell, the Bibio, the Peter Ross, the various Butcher patterns, and the Bumbles. Dapping can be deadly too, in which case the best flies will be large and bushily buoyant versions of these patterns, perhaps with the addition of a tiny flying treble at the tail as an insurance policy against the occasional fish which may come short.

Delphi and Erriff

Further on from the villages of Maam Cross, Recess and Clifden the western-most part of Connemara swings around to the north and east, the coastline leading on to the deep indentation of Killary Harbour, a long and wonderfully sheltered natural anchorage which is probably one of the world's most perfect havens for any vessel, however large, which might require a sheltered anchorage from ocean storms. At its western end Killary Harbour receives the waters of two beautiful and notable fisheries, the Delphi and the Erriff.

The Delphi system begins in the high hills to the north, where the Bundorragha river begins at its outflow from Lough Cunnel. This is a small and little-fished lough, although it is perhaps unfairly neglected, and can provide good sport with some very obligingly free-rising brown trout averaging perhaps a shade under ½ lb (0.25 kg). It also provides a hill walk to get there, but the exercise, the views and the sport are all part of the total experience of exploring and enjoying this wonderful western wilderness.

Delightful though the mountain environs of Lough Cunnel are, the Delphi fishery proper, at least as regards migratory fish, is generally considered to begin with the next lough lower down the river, at Glencullin. Not surprisingly, Glencullin has a reputation for giving its best sport in the latter part of the season, for it is quite high up in the hills, and there are two biggish and attractive loughs just below it, in which seatrout and salmon may linger for some time after they have run up from the sea. But in late August and September Glencullin be outstandingly productive, especially if there has been sufficient rainfall in the right quantities and at the right time to keep the fish moving up, and to maintain reasonable conditions for fly fishing.

Boats are available on this lough, and are usually moored at the southern end of the lough close to the point at which the rivers flows out and down to Dhu Lough. But its high position on the system can make this important lough a little vulnerable to windy weather, when the management of a boat is not easy, and fishing can lose a lot of its pleasure. Another factor to bear in mind, especially for the fisher with thoughts of a salmon, is that the lies and 'lodges'

On the Delphi Fishery, Doo Lough in its precipitous glaciated trench is one of the most celebrated and dramatic of Ireland's western game-fishing loughs.

are really only known to Glencullin regulars, so it will be best to fish in the company of someone who knows the right spots to aim for. The northern and north-eastern portions of the lough seem to yield most of Glencullin's salmon, but the seatrout are obliging enough to rise almost anywhere over the lough, and when fishing conditions are good it is difficult to pick a bad drift.

Just a short distance downstream from Glencullin is Dhu Lough, surely one of the most spectacular and productive seatrout and salmon loughs to be found anywhere. As its name in Irish implies this is indeed 'the dark lough', for it lies in a deep cleft in the mountains and from early afternoon onwards you will probably find the sun has begun to dip below the crest of Mweelreagh Mountain which towers above the lough on the south-western side. Good-sized spring salmon and a small run of heavier than average seatrout move into this lough in April and May, and June sees the seatrout season at its height. The southern and western parts of the lough have a reputation as the best taking places, and although this can be a dour and unproductive lough at times, it is also capable of producing some stunning catches. In the 1970s I had several baskets of over a dozen good seatrout to my own rod in the course of a fishing day lasting no more than five or six hours; and there are truly mouthwatering accounts of one or two seatrout bonanzas in recent years, with catches of two and three dozen fish to a single boat in a few hours.

Dhu Lough was a favourite of the late Justice Kingsmill Moore, who wrote about this and other western fisheries with such engaging authority in his classic *A Man May Fish*, a book which, together with the local *Angler's Guide* must be compulsory (and compulsive) reading for everyone who visits these waters. But Dhu Lough is moody and unpredictable, and its steep-sided valley is a natural funnel for the winds which sweep in from the Atlantic. Even on warm and balmy days in mid-summer or early autumn, a sudden squall or a mountain storm can descend on the lough, churning its waters into a mini-maelstrom of misty, turbulent waves and a chaos of white-capped rollers. It is not a lough on which to embark without a sound boat beneath you, a good supply of warm and weather-proof clothing, and an ever-open eye for the onset of a sudden storm. Any ominous darkening of the skies, any sudden strengthening of the wind, and it may be prudent to reel in and run for cover, rather than risk being caught in Dhu Lough's natural wind tunnel.

Fin Lough is the next and lowest of the loughs on this fishery, and is considerably smaller in size than the sometimes awesome loneliness of Dhu Lough in its great glaciated trench amid the high hills. There is a pleasant intimacy about this lough, which is barely ½ mile (0.8 km) wide and a ¼ mile (0.4 km) across. It is shallow, too, and there is good light penetration which tends to promote some vigorous weedy growth in summer, which can sometimes interfere with the fishing. It is possible to fish from the shore, but most fishers prefer the greater freedom and flexibility of a boat, and two boats are allowed on this lough at any one time. When the seatrout are in – and that is almost a certainty from late June onwards – almost any drift you care to choose will produce good fish.

But salmon are more particular, having their traditionally favoured lies and

Summer seatrout, a bright little 'harvester', comes from a spate river in north Sligo.

Late season salmon and grilse from the Ballynahinch Castle fishery in Connemara, a favourite resort for visiting game fishers.

Three plump, fresh-run seatrout from Lough Fern in north Donegal.

Tranquillity, space and the prospect of good sport: a fish-rich lough in southern County Clare.

haunts. In Fin Lough, like most loughs of these western fisheries, a favoured spot is where the Bundorragha River enters the lough from the upper parts of the system, from Dhu Lough and higher up. This can be regarded as rather like the lough equivalent of the throat or head of a pool on a salmon river, where a fish may lie for hours or days in fairly gentle, slack water before it decides to move onwards and upwards on its relentless return journey to its natal headwater stream. This type of salmon lie – known as a 'butt' on most western Irish loughs – is often very productive, and can be fished steadily throughout the season without apparent detriment to the sport. As soon as one or two occupants of these lies have been hooked and removed, other fish quickly move in to take their place, and 'fishing the butts' provides steady and reliable sport on many a western lough throughout the season, and especially in late summer and early autumn.

The Delphi fishery bears a romantic and decidedly un-Irish name, which is attributed to the fashionably whimsical enthusiasm of one of the Marquesses of Sligo in the early nineteenth century. The Grand Tour of Europe was all the rage for young persons of high birth, good education and with aspirations to the cultivation of good taste. Scenes made famous in the literature of classical antiquity, and especially the remains of Greek civilisation, were high on the list of desirable places to visit. And so it came about that one of the Marquesses of Sligo went on his tour to Italy and Greece, and returned to give the famous name of Delphi to one of the most beautiful and romantically scenic places on his vast estates in the west of Ireland. 'Everyone has heard of Delphi,' proclaimed Walter Peard in his *A Year of Liberty*, that classic account of a fishing tour of Ireland, published in 1867, and went on to call it an *Elysium piscatorum*. Nothing has changed to diminish that reputation in the century and more that has passed, and the fly fisher who comes off the Delphi waters with a good basket of seatrout, and perhaps a summer salmon for extra good measure, might well think he had indeed found the perfect fishing paradise.

Delphi is magnificent, but how invidious it is to make one's choice among so many superb fisheries in this corner of Ireland! If you are a salmon or a seatrout nosing back along the sinuous length of Killary Harbour, a sharp left turn at the mouth of the Bundorragha River takes you up to Fin Lough and so upwards through the succession of Delphi Loughs and short river stretches. But if your subtle and mysterious senses home in on another chemical message in the taste or smell of the water, you may be drawn further up the innermost recesses of the Harbour, past Leenane and into the Erriff River.

The Erriff and its associated loughs comprise yet another superb western salmon and seatrout fishery. The river has its headwaters high in the hills to the north-east and north-west, in little Lugcolliwee Lough and Lough Glenawough. These loughs each discharge a hill stream, and these join near Shralea Bridge and are further augmented by another tributary which flows in from the west, from Tawnyard Lough. The united flow of all these upper waters comprises several miles of excellent river fishing for salmon and seatrout as the river tumbles and glides south-westwards to its estuary downstream of Aasleagh Lodge. Walter Peard described this as 'one of the most comfortable in

Ireland' and extolled the beauty of its surroundings and the excellence of the hospitality and the sport to be found there.

The Erriff and the Delphi fisheries were at one time equally famous, and also equally inaccessible to the fishing visitor, for both were in private ownership and strictly reserved for the pleasure of their proprietors and the long-term tenants who rented the fishing and other sporting rights. But times change, and nowadays the Delphi fishery is in the hands of a private owner, Peter Mantle, who is an enthusiastic and dedicated game fisher who has done his utmost to make Delphi an attractive and accessible fishery for visitors from many parts of Ireland, from Britain and further afield as well. The loughs and the river retain their sporting reputation, with the added attractions of comfort, good food and warm hospitality in the recently restored lodge, which successfully combines the character and charm of the 1830s with the amenities and comforts of modern luxury.

In an average year Delphi can produce over 100 salmon and well in excess of 1000 good seatrout. These figures, based on averages over the 1970s and 1980s, seem likely to improve under the new regime of dedicated, year-round management of the fishery and the understandable interest of those who have acquired shares in the 30-year rod syndication scheme – a modified form of time-share fishing – which was introduced in the late 1980s. Careful surveillance of the rivers and loughs and their protection from poaching during the season is allied to assiduous management and protection of the spawning areas. All of this bodes well for the gradual improvement of what is already a superb fishery.

Delphi's neighbour, the Erriff, has undergone recent changes too, and is now owned by the Irish state. Its management is overseen by the Western Fisheries Board, and what was once a strictly private fishery is now available at modest cost to enthusiastic game fishers from all over Ireland and much further afield.

But on Delphi and Erriff, and on every other salmon and seatrout fishery, no management of the fresh-water haunts of migratory salmonids will bear fruit if it is not matched by rigorous measures taken at national and international level to protect and conserve this wonderful and renewable natural resource of wild game fish. For the future of these and all salmon and seatrout fisheries to be assured, the actions and concern of individual proprietors must be accompanied and supported by concerted action for fisheries protection on the part of the Irish government, which in its turn must be part of an internationally concerted drive to eliminate the unacceptable high-seas exploitation of migratory fish. Our responsibility for the future of our wild game fish extends from the tiniest upland trickles of spawning streams to the uttermost parts of the ocean. Effective conservation must extend to every part of the fishes' range and cover every stage of their lives, from fertilised eggs in the spawning redds to their eventual return as mature fish to their natal rivers.

From the thrilling scenery and the fine summer and early autumn sport of Killary Harbour and its fisheries we move on northwards around the coast of Connaught, across the rounded Murrisk peninsula and past the pilgrims' mountain of Croagh Patrick, via Louisburg and around the deep bight of Clew

Bay, with its scattering of islands. At the town of Newport we end this clockwise tour of the western fisheries with a glimpse of two of the most interesting and contrasting of all the fine game fisheries of Ireland.

Lough Beltra and the Burrishoole Fishery

At Newport you have a choice of some excellent fishing within easy reach, from tiny hill loughs and little spate rivers to excellent sport with salmon, grilse and seatrout on sizeable rivers and loughs. But your choice may well be dictated by the season of the year. A visit to the far west in spring means a limited range of productive waters, and the first of these spring-run salmon will be your quarry. For this, take the road north-eastwards from Westport which roughly follows the course of the Newport River for about 7 miles (11 km) to Lough Beltra.

Beltra lies within clear view of the spectacular peak of Nephin, soaring to over 2500 ft (763 m) to the north, and its 1500 acres (608 hectares) represent some of the very best and most consistent salmon and seatrout fishing to be found in the west of Ireland. The precise dates of the fishing seasons in the various parts of this large and important North-Western Fisheries Region vary from one area to another, but here on Beltra salmon fishing starts on 20 March and ends on 30 September. The special thrill of this fishery is that there is a fine run of big, powerful spring fish to give wonderful fishing from the very first day. The average weights are good, around 12–13 lb (5.5–6 kg) and significantly higher than on many other early west-coast rivers. On the Bundrowes and Lough Melvin, for instance, the spring run is good and the fish are splendidly conditioned, but the average weight is probably closer to 9 lb (4 kg), which is also typical of Lough Gill.

Beltra enthusiasts can look forward confidently to some good early sport, but they also fervently hope for tolerable weather conditions. St Patrick's Day falls on 17 March, just three days before Beltra opens for the new season, and proverbially the patron saint of Ireland is said to herald the coming of improved spring weather, by 'turning up the warm side of the stone'. This pious hope is often in vain, and early conditions on Beltra can be wintry and stormy in the extreme.

Boat handling and the effective use of a powerful rod and biggish flies in rough water and a gale of wind are not easy, so a division of labour is usually called for. Salmon in loughs take up traditional lies or 'lodges' just as surely as they do in rivers, and unless the boat and the fly fisher are steered carefully over the likely taking spots a blank day is a near certainty. That is why effective and productive early fly fishing for Beltra's early salmon really calls for the help of a boatman who knows the lough and the 'lodges' and can hold his anglers over the right spots despite rough wind and a rolling wave. Two fishers who know the lough thoroughly might take turn about on the oars, but the visitor really must ensure that he has the services of a local boatman. And it is noteworthy that Beltra salmon in spring and seatrout in summer tend to lie in quite different parts of the lough, with seatrout catches tending to be best around the bays and islands towards the southern end of the lough, so it is especially important to ensure that you have the necessary expertise on board before you cast off for a day on this excellent fishery.

The fishing on Beltra is divided into two sectors, the western side being managed by Newport House Hotel and the eastern portion by the Glenisland Anglers' Co-operative. The hotel provides boats and experienced boatmen, and there is a notable reputation for a high success rate for early salmon enthusiasts fishing on the western side of the lough. On the eastern side there are boats for hire, with or without engines, and a total of fifteen boats is the maximum permitted on the entire lough at any one time, usually comprising five from the hotel and ten from the eastern fishery.

Inevitably kelts are in evidence when the fishing starts and may still be encountered in early April, but the visitor who is well guided by an experienced boatman has an excellent chance of connecting with a good spring fish at almost any time up to mid-May, when the first flush of Beltra's season begins to decline.

But the excitement and the challenge of early spring is soon followed by the additional pleasures of some really excellent summer fishing for seatrout and grilse, both of which run up the Newport River and into the lough in good numbers. Grilse can be present from late May onwards, but they have an uncharacteristic tendency to be rather dour and elusive on Beltra. Considering how lively and sprightly grilse tend to be on most waters, their comparative unwillingness to come to the fly on Beltra is rather odd, but the game fisher does not have long to wait before almost guaranteed sport comes along, in the form of Beltra's summer seatrout. These have always had a reputation as free risers, and some run to a good size, with a sprinkling of seatrout of 5 lb (2.25 kg) and over being taken each season. The general run of fish from July to the season's end in September is usually around the 1½ lb (0.7 kg) mark.

All the classic flies work well on this superb fishery. The early salmon devotee can fare well with patterns like the Jock Scott, the Thunder & Lightning and the Hairy Mary, while seatrout come readily to the Bibio, the various Bumble patterns and trusted flies like the Black Pennell, the Invicta and the Peter Ross. In those early days after spring salmon you will probably be wise to choose stout tackle, a powerful two-handed rod of 13–14 ft (395–425 cm) casting a slow-sinking line or, if you do not mind its rather unbalanced casting characteristics, a sink-tip line. As the season progresses you will observe a general trend to single-handed wet-fly rods of 10–11 ft (305–335 cm), fishing a shortish floating line on a drift in the familiar lough style. But the position, direction and speed of that drift are all-important for a good basket of fish, so it is back to local knowledge and the guidance of an experienced boatman if you are to make the best of Beltra.

As a final note, and to whet the appetite of anyone who has not already decided that Beltra is well worth a visit, it should be mentioned that the Newport House Rods take an annual average catch of approximately 180–200 salmon and 1200–1400 seatrout, with the eastern side probably accounting for nearly as many again. All this from a medium-sized lough, with excellent accommodation readily available locally, and with good sport for the visitor at almost any time during the 6-month fishing season.

We have mentioned that the fisheries of the Newport area have contrasting characteristics, and this is best demonstrated by comparing the spring sport on Beltra with the conditions which are found only a few miles away to the west, on the twin loughs of Furnace and Feeagh.

These loughs together comprise the Burrishoole fishery, and they are managed by the Salmon Research Trust of Ireland with the twin objects of providing sport for the game fisher and increasing our understanding of migratory salmonids by careful study. The recent history of this fishery stems from its acquisition by the Guinness brewing group in the 1950s, when the then managing director, Sir Hugh Beaver, joined forces with the fishery owner, Major C. W. Roberts, to use Burrishoole as a test-bed for various forms of salmon and seatrout management. Guinness eventually bought the fishery in 1965 and handed over control to S.R.T.I. in 1980.

Within this Fisheries Region the statutory season opens in February and runs through to the last day of September. But Burrishoole is different, because the management policy is to defer the start of angling until 15 June. This reflects the fact that these loughs do not receive worthwhile runs of seatrout or salmon until well into late spring, in sharp contrast to the situation on Beltra, where good numbers of biggish spring salmon are up the river and into the lough by mid-March. And yet the access to Lough Furnace, which is tidal and

After salmon and grilse in the far west. There is seldom any need for a rod longer than 12 or 13 feet.

links directly to the sea, is only a few miles west of the Newport River mouth, and every Beltra salmon has to swim past it. Further proof, if any was required, of the firm fidelity of salmon and seatrout to the rivers of their birth.

Beltra's success is measured principally by the evidence of the rod catches, which are superb. But because Burrishoole is primarily a scientific fish study area, there is data aplenty from other sources, including the counters which record every sizeable fish which enters the fishery. The recent records, so meticulously maintained, are complemented by the excellent records of rod catches which were kept in earlier years by the former proprietors, and a complete record of all rod-caught salmon exists from 1933 onwards. It is always difficult to know quite how heavily a fishery was fished in decades gone by, when rod-days (including the statistically significant blank days) were often not entered in the records, but the figures from Burrishoole nevertheless make up an interesting profile over more than half a century.

In the period from 1933 to 1940 the annual salmon catch averaged about 15 fish, and this rather modest figure jumped to an average of 62 fish per season in the decade 1941 to 1950. By the 1960s results had soared to almost ten times that original average, with 146 salmon as the average catch over that decade and there were two really notable high spots in the early 1970s. In 1970 a superb total of 354 salmon were caught here, and in 1972 the season ended with 335.

Alas, the 1970s was also the era in which there emerged that iniquitous menace to all migratory fish, the widespread netting of salmon and seatrout on the high seas and off-shore, often illegally and using nets of a mesh size far below what could be justified on any pretext. The counters at Burrishoole indicated that something like 1500 grilse ran into this system each season during the late 1960s and the early 1970s. By 1984 the S.R.T.I. reported that this had been lamentably reduced to around 270 fish in total, a decline of well over eighty percent. Everything pointed to illegal and over-exploitative netting as the culprit, with whole runs of Burrishoole-bound grilse and salmon intercepted and scooped up out at sea.

The Burrishoole fishery incorporates a hatchery and a smolt-rearing unit, and this was seen as a possible means of saving the fishery. Smolts – young salmon which have matured to a silvery-hued 6 or 7 in (15–18 cm) – are ready to go to sea and begin the marine stage of their lives, exploiting the rich feeding of the Atlantic and putting on the muscular, pink-fleshed plumpness we expect in a mature salmon or a lively maiden grilse. Smolts are released in very large numbers from Burrishoole each year, and the results have been pleasing, with good numbers returning despite the continuing depredations of seemingly unchecked illegal netting off Ireland's west coast and further out on the high seas. Natural mortality is quite high, but that is part and parcel of the way of life of wild creatures. What is utterly unnecessary and totally inexcusable is the greedy over-exploitation of wild fish, which if unchecked could push the wild salmon of the Atlantic basin to extinction.

Fishing on Burrishoole can be arranged by contacting the S.R.T.I. offices at Newport (Tel: 098-41107) and every facility is made available to the visitor.

There are good boats, experienced boatmen and Lough Furnace, lower of the twin loughs and brackish, has some delightful sport to offer, in pleasant scenery and with the prospects of good baskets of lively little seatrout averaging around the 1 lb (0.45 kg) mark. In addition to the classic flies of the west, it is an act of courtesy and piscatorial piety to tie on a Green Peter when you fish this water. It was here that the late Rev. Canon Patrick Gargan, doyen of Irish clerical anglers, developed and proved the killing qualities of this fly when it is suitably dressed for salmon. It is now very popular on many Irish waters.

Further up the system you come to Lough Feeagh, which is only a short distance to the north but lies in altogether wilder and grander scenery. This has none of the tidal and sometimes brackish qualities of Furnace, and the road leading north from Newport hugs its eastern shore, giving you some superb views over the whole length of the lough. Boats and boatmen can be arranged here through the management offices, and the period from late June to the end of July can offer excellent sport, especially along the eastern side of the lough and close to the southern end. Both seatrout and salmon tend to lie close in near the feeder streams and in the marginal shallows, and they are obligingly free to rise and roll at your fly, although there is a rule-of-thumb on Feeagh that you will do well to net one fish in five. These fish have a maddening habit of coming short to the fly, and your day afloat on the lough may be a succession of emotional ups and downs as fish rise and are lost.

7 'Twixt Galway and Limerick

A glance at the map will show you that Ireland's western coastline swings around the great bight of Galway Bay, with its innumerable islands, bays and inlets, before turning south-westwards in a long peninsula which is curiously similar in outline to the English counties of Devon and Cornwall. But here the land ends not at Lands End but at Loop Point, before the coastline turns sharply eastwards to form the northern shore of the long and winding estuary of the Shannon, longest of all the rivers of Ireland and Britain.

This is the culmination of a vast river catchment which has its headwaters far to the north on the borders of counties Fermanagh and Cavan, near where Northern Ireland and the Irish Republic meet, and its course encompasses a great sweep of central Ireland in its long progress through the great trio of Loughs – Allen, Ree and Derg – before it meets the sea beyond Limerick. Small wonder that the local Shannon Region Fisheries Board, managed from offices in Limerick City, is named after this great 240-mile (384 km) waterway.

But if your piscatorial progress around Ireland takes you south from Galway your first introduction to the Shannon system will probably be in County Clare. Lisdoonvarna is not to be missed by any tourist, and you must also make time to see the mighty cliffs of Moher and to explore the bizarre and fascinating landscape of the Burren. This is a karst rock formation, amounting in total to almost 100 square miles (259 square km) of bare limestone pavements cloven with cracks and fissures in which a profusion of wild flowers and many rare plants thrive in luxurious abundance, especially in the months of late spring. Tucked out of the wind and fostered by unique micro-climates in these limestone clefts is to be found such a wealth of plants that even the most dedicated botanist will only be able to scratch the surface of its potential, finding species after species which is rare or quite unknown elsewhere in the British Isles.

But just as there is more to a fishing holiday than fishing, so we must not let sightseeing, however delightful, distract us from our exploration of the game fishing potential of this corner of Ireland. From the coast at Lehinch your best bet is to drive westwards by Ennistimon and Kilfenora, heading for the town of Corrofin. Here is the perfect centre to choose as your base for an exploration of one of the most attractive and rewarding areas of the Shannon catchment, the River Fergus and its many associated loughs. With its source in the limestone lands of northern County Clare the Fergus follows a gentle southerly course and eventually flows into the Shannon estuary to the south of the town of Ennis – sometimes fondly referred to as 'Ennis of the hundred pubs'. The river and most of the loughs are cradled in a gentle landscape of low heathery hills, where blanket peat and an acidic environment dominates the higher ground. But the river and the principal loughs are set in a lower, lusher landscape where the water flows over limestone and is filtered through it. The waters therefore have many of the characteristic qualities of an alkaline river system, being clear, rich in fly life and many other invertebrates, and providing an ideal environment to produce sizeable brown trout in abundance. In some parts of west and southwest Clare you may find the poorer feeding and the acid conditions which mean limited growth for brown trout and excellent conditions for their seagoing cousins; but on the Fergus system you are first and foremost in a top quality brown trout fishery.

Inevitably, every shiny coin has its other side, and the principal drawback of the Fergus system with its limestone bedrock is the likelihood of very low water levels in summer, and with them the possibility of de-oxygenation of the water and some build-up of algal bloom. The water levels are at their optimum, and the fishing usually at its best, from the beginning of the season in March to the end of May and early June. July and August can be disappointing in all but the wettest summers, which is unfortunate for the visiting game fisher who finds himself tied to school holiday dates for his visit. By September, however, the rains of late summer – the 'Lammas floods' – have normally refreshed the river and the loughs, and sport enjoys a brief revival before the season's end.

On the road from Ennistimon to Corrofin you will pass close to Lickeen Lough, and this should not be neglected, especially if you have just had a day or two without much success and your morale could benefit from the reviving effects of some lively, free-rising little trout. Lickeen is a free fishery, for which you require only your State Rod Licence, and it is a mixed fishery which includes large numbers of rudd alongside the abundant little brown trout. There are also char in Lickeen, but as is the way with char they tend to keep to the deeper water and are only seldom taken by a fly fished on or near the surface. Access to the lough is very easy, and you can drive your car almost to the water's edge at two points. It is then only a few steps to the shore, which is sound and easy to fish, and if your preference is to fish from a boat you can hire one from Bill O'Brien who lives close to the lough.

Delightful though Lickeen Lough is, you must press on to Corrofin along the L53. Westwards, to the right of the road, lies the 260 acres (105 hectares) of Inchiquin Lough, which is barely a mile (1.6 km) from Corrofin. This is another lough with excellent access by car, with thoughtfully placed car parking and an excellent pier and slipway at the southern end, where, as in so many Irish loughs, you may simply drive up and enjoy the pleasures of launching your own boat without charge on a first-class trout water. But unless you are dedicated to trailing your favourite boat around Ireland behind your car, it is better to hire one of the excellent local boats, and your best contact is through Burke's shop which is in the main street of Corrofin town.

A glance at the map and a spot of local reconnaissance are well worth while, and from just outside Corrofin you can do a complete circuit of Inchiquin. If you take a clockwise course you will find the road crosses the river Fergus just below its outflow from the lough at the southernmost point, and the road carries on northwards with the waters of the lough and its islands spread out on your right and the slopes of Clifden Hill rising to your left. Turn right at the next crossroads and after little more than another 2 miles (3.2 km) you will again cross the Fergus, this time some 2 miles (3.2 km) upstream of the lough. This stretch of the river, from the road bridge down to where it enters the lough near a spot known as the Swan's Nest (for reasons which will be obvious to you when you see it) is especially attractive, and well worth the gentle couple of miles walk involved. Inquire locally about river access and fishing rights from the farmers and riparian landowners.

Inchiquin Lough is a trout fisher's delight, but it can also be a frustrating nightmare if conditions are not good. The environment could scarcely better for promoting the growth of wonderful trout, solid and well-fleshed and amply nourished on the wonderful richness and diversity of the fly and invertebrate life which emerges from this limestone environment. Indeed, Inchiquin disputes with the Midland lakes of Owel, Ennel and Sheelin the claim to holding the highest density of wild brown trout to be found in any of Ireland's loughs – a proud boast which each lough's aficionados are pleased to claim for themselves, and which, happily, will probably never be accurately resolved, however careful the fishery censuses may be. We have already noted how the Fergus system can be plagued by low water levels in summer because of the limestone hydrology, and this in turn has a definite limiting effect on the spawning productivity of this lough and the nursery streams in which the young trout develop before moving into the main waters. On Inchiquin the general rule of thumb has alway been that a dry year will result in fewer fish the following season, but of bigger size and heavier average weight, while there are more abundant, smaller fish in the season following a wet year – all of which seems perfectly logical.

You may find Inchiquin's water levels good, and its trout obliging, in high summer, but the lough is at its peak in early spring and again in September. The ever-reliable duckfly, without which no Irish game fisher's fly box would be complete, produces excellent backets of fish from the opening day in March through to late April and early May, and both nymph and wetfly versions should be in your fly box, in the usual range of sizes from 10 to 14. There is also the customary progression from the duckfly fishing of the early season into buzzer time through late April and May, and Inchiquin can also produce some plentiful and consistent hatches of mayfly. A mayfly nymph, perhaps on the point of a three-fly cast with a Grey Wulff or a Gosling or French Partridge Straddlebug pattern tripped over the wavelets as your bobfly can be highly productive, as also can dapping with artificials and the natural insect; and when the spent gnat is on the water in the evening there can be some

130

Seconds after it hatched from the limestone waters of a small County Clare stream, this mayfly came and alighted on my Bruce & Walker fly rod.

breathtaking sport as you try to stalk and intercept big trout cruising purposefully and feeding intently along the shore and around the islands.

Inchiquin also offers some excellent sedge fishing from late August onwards, always provided that the water levels are right. Most of the innumerable permutations of dry, wet and nymphal sedge patterns can work well when the fish are on the take, but every fly-fishing visitor to a new water would do well to take local patterns into account. Invariably they account for the majority of the fish, and there is also a pleasing element of courtesy in adopting the patterns which your hosts – and perhaps their forefathers for many generations past – have used successfully. On Inchiquin the local confection is the attractive little Cock Robin, which was devised by the Egan family of Corrofin. This pretty little fly has a bi-coloured body comprising a front section of scarlet or crimson seal's sur and a rear section coloured a subtle golden-olive, the body ribbed with gold and with a wing and tail of bronze mallard, finished off with a red cock hackle.

Also on the Fergus system and almost half as big again as Inchiquin is Dromore Lough, 375 acres (194 hectares) of fine limestone fishery close to the village of Ruan. Access to this lovely lough (which, interestingly, is often referred to as a 'lake' rather than a 'lough') is not quite as good as that to

Inchiquin, and your best approach will be along the forestry road which leads southwards to an excellent car park by the lough shore. But it is worth warning the first-time visitor to Dromore to have his Ordnance Survey map handy in the car, for the approaches to the lake are through an unbelievably intricate network of small country roads, and you may find yourself playing a frustrating game of 'hunt the lake' for some time before you find it.

Broadly speaking, Dromore trout are of a slightly smaller average size than those of Inchiquin, but they are equally numerous and early in the season they can be enormously obliging, especially when a good duckfly hatch is in progress. You may finish the day with a heavy basket of fine brown trout averaging almost 2 lb (0.9 kg), and there is a very good chance of connecting with something a good deal heavier. This is not an easy lough to fish from the bank, but you can arrange to hire a boat by contacting Michael Clearly at Corrofin (Tel: 065-27675). The boat gives you the freedom of the whole lough, which is comparatively shallow and almost any drift you choose is likely to produce a fish or two. But as always there is great advantage in having the complete freedom and flexibility which a boat confers on the lough fly fisher; and an added bonus on Dromore is that you can use the boat to travel the mile (1.6 km) or so up-river and through the little Black Lake to Ballyline Lake, which is another top quality limestone lough.

These three loughs on the Fergus system all provide excellent sport, always provided you remember the possibility of problems resulting from fluctuating water levels. Although these loughs have so much in common, each nevertheless has its own distinctive charms and personality, and if the fishing is good and you can spare the time it is well worth investigating all three in turn. Inchiquin is a broad and generous expanse of trout water, while Dromore is long, narrow and sinuous, a characteristic which means it is often referred to by the locals as 'the Long Lough'. This was the name adopted by one English-based fisher who first visited this part of County Clare before the First World War and began a lifelong love affair with the uniquely attractive Fergus system. F. D. Barker was born and brought up in the United States, later settling in England and holidaying with his fishing rod in County Clare. There, over eighty years ago, he discovered a fishery which was virtually unknown to English visitors, who tended to be drawn to the famous mayfly loughs of the Irish Midlands or the celebrated western Loughs such as Mask, Corrib and Derg. Like many another fisherman, before and since, he was torn between the desire to share his discovery and his sporting pleasures with his fellow anglers, and also to conceal its whereabouts and so prevent an influx of other anglers, with all the disadvantages of overcrowding and over-fishing which that might entail. In the end he compromised and wrote a book which described the river and the loughs, large and small, in intimate and affectionate detail, but without betraying their geographical position or their correct names. *An Angler's Paradise*, published in 1929 by the now-defunct publishing house of Faber & Gwyer of London, is a scarce and delightful little book, its end-papers decorated with subtly altered maps of the river and loughs, each with its fictitious name. If you can lay hands on a copy before you visit the Fergus system it will give you an enjoyable and useful introduction to waters which have not changed significantly since Barker's day; and after your visit you will get constant pleasure from taking it down off your bookshelves for a bit of armchair fishing by the fireside on a winter's evening, when you can revisit the Fergus and its loughs in your imagination.

8 The Midland Lakes

Lough Gowna and Lough Sheelin

It is unfortunate that when an article appears in a British fishing magazine about the sport on loughs like Corrib, Mask, Conn or Derg, these large limestone loughs are often described as though they are the principal limestone loughs of central Ireland. This is a mistake which stems from a misunderstanding of geography and also a failure to recognise the changes which have taken place in Irish lough fishing in recent times.

In fact, although all the loughs just named are wholly or largely over limestone, they are all in the western or south-western parts of Ireland. These are not the 'classic limestone loughs' of central Ireland in the sense in which earlier generations of fishers would have understood the phrase.

The Irish Midlands, and especially the counties of Meath, Westmeath and Cavan, are the rich heartland of Ireland, and it is here that you will find a number of large loughs with names which have always been famous in angling history. Lough Gowna, Lough Sheelin, Lough Derravarragh, Lough Owel, Lough Ennell – all are big, all are attractive, and all have produced huge trout and generations of consistently good sport. In the heyday of Irish mayfly fishing, up to the 1950s, there is little doubt that the finest of the fishing, and the greatest amount of sport for the greatest number of fly fishers, residents and visitors, was on the Midland loughs. Since then the Midland fisheries of Ireland have had to endure a succession of environmental vicissitudes and piscatorial disasters, from which they have emerged in remarkably good heart. They have not emerged unscathed however, and on several of the lakes the nature and style of the fishery and the fish have undergone important and possibly permanent changes.

It is significant that we tend to talk about the *lakes* of the Midlands, rather than *loughs*. This subtle but significant change in terminology is itself revealing. The Gaelic word *lough* or *loch* is wholly appropriate for the lakes of the wilder, remoter parts of the western and northern parts of Ireland, and of the hills and islands of Scotland. The very sound of the word carries with it something of the essence of the wild quality of these waters and their settings, among the bogs and rocks and mountains. The English word *lake* has altogether gentler connotations, evocative of softer, richer landscapes. In the manicured, well-tended parkland around a great mansion you might well find a lake, but never a lough or a loch.

So it is with the Midland lakes, which are set not among high, heathery hills, or below sheer slopes of scree and tumbled boulders, but amid the lushness of some of the richest pastureland in Europe. The glacial clays and the general bedrock of limestone have been formed here and there into wide, shallow basins, in which are collected the waters of natural springs and of the slow rivers which drain this landscape of low, fertile meadows. The bottom of the lake is composed of muddy clay, in contrast to the boulders, gravels and marls of the big western loughs, and the depth is rarely more than 20 ft (6 m). There is none of the profound glacial gouging which can take the waters plummeting to dark depths, such as you find on Lough Melvin or on the loughs of Connemara.

On a relief map of central Ireland you can see the Midland lakes quite clearly. They lie in a long north-to-south string from just below Cavan town to just south of Mullingar, with Lough Gowna lying at the north-western end of the chain and Lough Ennell at the south.

Lough Gowna is a large but straggling lake, its waters spreading in a spidery, intricate complex of bays and narrows. At no point on this lake are you ever far out from the shore, and the amount of shoreline in proportion to the area of water is enormous, probably unequalled by any other Irish stillwater. This is good for the fly fisher, of course, because it means that the lough enjoys a large extent of shallow shoreline water through which the sunlight can penetrate easily, and in which trout can be found feeding on the abundant invertebrate foods which proliferate in shallow, rich waters.

Gowna has suffered in a variety of ways since the end of the last century. It used to offer excellent fishing for trout, but it always suffered from being too close to Lough Sheelin and the other Midland trout lakes, where the trouting was so consistently superb that they inevitably tended to attract all the attention. Lough Gowna had its fans, and deservedly so, but Sheelin, Owel, Derravarragh and Ennell got the full spotlight of attention. The result was that there was little local benefit from the fishery in terms of income and trade generated by visiting fishers. The fishery was therefore not accorded any great importance, and in the Victorian guides for sporting visitors it barely gets a mention. To underrate a fishery is the first step towards its neglect and eventual deterioration.

Like almost every one of the Midland lakes, Gowna fell victim to progressive enrichment of the waters during the 1960s and 1970s. The intensification of farming, the widespread use of silage with its attendant risks of effluent leakage, and the heavy use of nitrogenous fertilisers to promote grass growth all contributed to the enrichment of the waters of Lough Gowna, to the point where the insect life of the lough began to suffer, the trout began to decline in quality and numbers, and there were recurrent problems with algal bloom and dirtying of the water in warm summers, to compound the problems of the de-oxygenation of the water. The effects of this eutrophication are always grave on any fishery, but fishers and fisheries biologists never fail to be astonished at the powers of recovery which such fisheries can display when the sources of pollution and enrichment are contained and brought under control. Although Gowna's problems with nitrogenous run-off, silage seepage and slurry leaks have not been overcome, they do at least appear to have got no worse.

The mayfly hatch, which was once as spectacularly prolific as that of any Irish lake, still continues, although on a greatly diminished scale. The disappearance of the mayfly usually sets the seal of disaster on such a fishery, but Gowna can still show pleasing hatches and good rises of large trout from late May to early June. When the big trout are tempted up to feed on the hatching drakes or the spent gnat you may see some very big fish on the move, and it will surprise no one locally if you take trout to 5 and 6 lb (2.25 and 2.7 kg) at mayfly time. But the really big trout of this sort are usually taken on Gowna by trolling, which goes on extensively all season. In such enriched conditions the bottom feeding is excellent, and most of the large trout do not come readily to the surface to feed.

Where Gowna still shows excellent sport for the fly fisher is during the early weeks of the spring when the duckfly hatch is in progress. This seems to be a peculiarly Irish affair, or at any rate the term 'duckfly' is rarely heard among fly fishers elsewhere, except perhaps on certain waters in Wales and Scotland. On the loughs of the west and south-west of Ireland 'duckfly' can be a useful umbrella term to cover a number of insects belonging to the large family of the chironomids or non-biting midges. On Gowna and the Midland loughs, however, the water-borne varieties of midge are effectively confined to one principal species, the so-called black midge or *Chironomus anthracinus*. When considering Lough Gowna it therefore seems appropriate at this point to say something about the duckfly and the ways in which the rise to this insect can be approached by the fly fisher.

Although the duckfly hatches are usually heaviest and most productive from the fly fisher's point of view in late March and April, these important little insects can produce useful hatches through to July or later. For the fly fisher they offer three important opportunities, or three significant difficulties, depending upon your point of view. Trout taking duckfly will readily feed on the ascending insects at the pupal stage, or on the emerging insects in the very topmost layer of the water, or on the fully developed insect when it is on or just above the surface, having hatched fully, or when the females have returned to lay their eggs or are lying spent and dying on the water. It is uncommon to find trout which are feeding on all three stages of the duckfly at any given time, and part of the challenge and the secret of success at duckfly time is to watch the rise form and determine which of these three types of feeding is in progress. This in turn will dictate whether you should use nymph patterns, fish a wet-fly imitation in the surface film of the water, or, more uncommon in Ireland, try to match the hatch with a dry pattern.

Often the fly fisher's tactics will involve a wise compromise. Trout rising to the duckfly can change from taking the pupal stage to feeding on the suspended, emergent insects. A three-fly, wet-fly cast with a nymph pattern on the point and soft-hackled wet flies on dropper and bob may be used; or two nymph patterns on point and dropper and a wet fly on the top; or perhaps a nymph on the point, a buoyant or suspender-type pattern on the dropper and a fuller pattern on the bob. There are a number of such possible permutations.

The classic wet-fly imitation of the *anthracinus* duckfly in its emergent form is the Blae and Black, and an excellent second string is the Sooty Olive. The Duckfly Nymph represents the ascending pupa, and the black body ribbed with silver gives a good representation of the segmented body of the natural nymph. Other similar patterns which can be used are the various Buzzer, Hatching Buzzer and Hatching Midge nymphs, which are largely variations on a common black-bodied theme, differing chiefly in the hints of colour at tail and head. The suspender-type patterns, incorporating polystyrene or similar beads, are also useful, and can do especially well when there is a good rise to emergent nymphs close to the surface in a lively ripple or bigger waves.

On Lough Gowna, as on all lakes where the duckfly hatches in good numbers, success depends on observation and on getting into position at the right spot. It is common to see duckfly hatching in localised patches rather than at a more uniform distribution across the water. Often this is caused by some variation in local conditions on a particular area of the lake bottom, which triggers off a hatch. When this occurs trout which would otherwise live and feed independently tend to converge and form temporary feeding shoals, which can sometimes be big. If the fly fisher can mark down such groups of feeding fish and then position himself on the best drift or, in calm conditions, simply float above the hatching hot-spot, he can have fast and frenzied sport.

Gowna is best fished from the villages of Granard, Arvagh or Lough Gowna village itself, all of which are within easy reach of the lake and the various access points, where you may launch your own boat if you wish.

Lough Sheelin

Lough Sheelin lies to the south-east of Gowna and its waters straddle the boundaries of counties Cavan, Meath and Westmeath, although the largest proportion of the lough lies within County Cavan. Sheelin is not a large lough by Irish standards, but its 4500-plus acres (1820 hectares) have possibly given as much sport and produced as many trout per acre – and words of fishing literature per acre, too – as any Irish fishery. Sheelin is oval in shape, orientated from south-west to north-east, and it is interesting to note that this is actually part of the vast Shannon system, although we tend to think of the Shannon as that great waterway over towards the west of Ireland. But the Shannon's huge and intricate network of tributary streams should not be overestimated, and the headwaters of the great river itself are high up in the Cuilcagh mountains of north Cavan, close to the border with County Fermanagh and Northern Ireland. But Sheelin is actually a broadening out of the waters of the Inny River, which flows in at the lough's south-eastern end and emerges again as a bigger, stronger flow at the western end. The Inny below

Sheelin near the town of Finnea is a wonderful trout stream, as fine a water for nymphing or dry-fly fishing as you could wish for.

Lough Sheelin is a naturally rich lake. It lies over a limestone bedrock and it is a highly alkaline water, with a natural pH of about 8.7. That alkalinity promotes plenty of trout food, and plenty of trout, and Sheelin always used to have a fine reputation as a lough with excellent spawning and nursery areas, which means that recruitment of new generations of fish should be in balance with the rich supply of invertebrate food to make them grow big and powerful. I say 'used to have', because Sheelin's qualities as a spawning and nursery lough for trout are not what they used to be. But more of this shortly.

Set in low, rich farmland, Sheelin is fringed with trees which shelter the shoreline and provide constant supplies of terrestrial insects. This lake is set in a broad, shallow basin, and the water is nowhere very deep. And when there is shallow water over limestone this is a natural recipe for abundant plant growth and the development of large quantities of invertebrate creatures. Where the life-promoting light of the sun can penetrate, it encourages weed growth and with the weeds come the insects, the shrimps and the other forms of crustaceans which trout love. On Sheelin you can row or drift for most of the day over a shallow bottom with abundant weeded areas and waters rich in trout and trout foods. You might almost imagine you were afloat on a vast chalk stream. In this important respect Sheelin is at the opposite end of the stillwater spectrum from the large man-made waters which consist of deep, concrete-lined bowls where the water falls away quickly into great depths.

On reservoirs not only is the nature of the bottom quite different, but there is only a narrow margin of water which enjoys full penetration of sunlight and the benefits which that brings for the fish and the fisherman. Shallow lakes like Sheelin are also very different from the deep, rocky loughs gouged and scooped by glacial action from among the granites and old sandstones of the western and north-western parts of Scotland and Ireland, and from the great glacial troughs of the lakes of Cumbria. There the underwater contours are a continuation of the surrounding landscape, and the shorelines fall away abruptly into deep trenches and troughs. On such lochs, loughs and mountain lakes, and on the fringes of deep reservoirs, there is only a narrow peripheral band of shallow water through which the light can reach to promote plant and insect life. A further feature of deep glaciated loughs is the invariably acidic nature of the water, derived from hill streams and springs flowing from deep peat over acid rocks, and the water is frequently coloured by the peat or dirtied by suspended peaty particles, which make it more difficult for sunlight to penetrate. Such waters produce seatrout and salmon, often in large numbers, but they are not conducive to the growth of large specimens of resident brown trout.

It is as a natural paradise for big brown trout that Lough Sheelin gained her reputation. Its beautiful setting is matched by the incredible richness of its aquatic life. Small wonder that it has always been highly regarded since the earliest times. Its name in Irish is 'sidhe linn' or 'sileann', which is usually taken to mean 'the fairies' pool' or 'the lake of the fairy islands' – and there is something magical about the lough and its environs. Sheelin is also a girl's name – and all the Sheelins I know are pretty girls, which is appropriate. They are named after a beautiful lake!

Sheelin's beauty and the supreme quality of its brown trout fishing appeared to have sustained two catastrophic body blows in quick succession, one in the 1960s and another a decade later. A large and over-enthusiastic drainage scheme was undertaken in the lake's catchment. In this part of Ireland the soils are rich but heavy, and farmers understandably wanted to make their rich pastures drier and more manageable. Agriculture everywhere was becoming more cost-conscious and competitive, and the predominantly dairy-farming community of the Irish Midlands was no exception to this general trend. But large-scale drainage work was begun without a full appreciation of the environmental consequences, and for Sheelin these were to mean the degradation and destruction of many important spawning and nursery areas for the trout.

When this takes place on any fishery its immediate consequences are likely to be a disruption of the balance between the ability of the waters to feed the adult trout and the fishes' ability to reproduce and create future generations. Other things being equal, reduced spawning and recruitment would tend to reduce competition for food among the remaining trout, which would grow larger and heavier in consequence. But Sheelin was always rich in food of many kinds, and it was noted for the consistently large size of its trout. Every mayfly season it produced a sprinkling of 6 and 7-lb (2.7 and 3 kg) fish, and specimens of 11 lb (5 kg) and over were not unknown when the big, bottom-feeding trout were tempted up to join in the short-lived annual bonanza of 'the drake'. Thus the Sheelin trout were in no sense suffering from retarded growth owing to excessive competition for limited food! And thus poorer spawning simply meant fewer fish, with the eventual dismal prospect of Sheelin turning into a lake dominated by massive quantities of coarse fish, with only a few huge but uncatchable trout.

That appeared to be the outlook for Sheelin from the late 1960s, although the lake still attracted numbers of fly fishers at mayfly time, for however poor the spawning and reproduction rates were in the 1960s, the mayfly hatch was still a spectacular sight, and sport could still be superb. But without new generations of fish coming on for the future, what chances of sport in the long term?

And the first signs of another catastrophe for the fishery were already becoming evident. Sheelin was beginning to suffer badly from eutrophication, the organic enrichment of the lake by elements carried in by the rivers or washed off the surrounding land. The principal agents appeared to be silage effluent, the inadvertent and sometimes downright negligent escape of toxins from pits and clamps used to store silage; the washing-off of nitrogenous fertilisers used for dressing pastureland; and slurry effluent from farms with large piggeries and in-wintering quarters for cattle. All three destructive forces stemmed from the radical changes which were taking place in Irish agricultural practices, as small, traditionally managed family farms gave way to larger

139

and intensive units, seemingly bent upon profit and productivity regardless of the environmental consequences.

Sheelin rapidly became a disaster area. The former crystal clarity of the water was replaced by a murky, greenish-brown opacity, especially after periods of high wind stirred up turbid conditions, and in summer when the warming up of the shallow water created massive algal bloom. The fly life was vanishing, the fish were few, and their flesh tasted foul, redolent of the tainted waters of the lake. On a warm day in summer the 'fairies' pool' smelt more like an open sewer. Sheelin appeared to be dying before the helpless eyes of the loyal local fly fishers, and the ultimate *coup de grâce* appeared to have fallen when almost a month of high winds and continuous chill rain hit the mayfly hatch in May and June 1971. The hatch was ruined, what flies did emerge were blown or chilled into oblivion, and the legendary Lough Sheelin mayfly hatch has never recovered from the 1971 destruction. The enrichment of the lake and the contamination of the lake bottom with foul sediment created conditions in which the mayfly population could not readily recover, and those flies which did hatch had a poor reproductive success. The hatching drakes and the spent females were unpalatable to the trout, like any insects hatched from an unclean environment.

And that was that – or so you might think. But help was at hand through the twin agencies of enthusiastic local anglers and the Central Fisheries Board. Pollution and enrichment were checked, partly by improved standards of husbandry and partly through firm action against offenders. Massive re-stocking boosted the trout population, and the niche which had once been so spectacularly occupied by the big, yellowish-green mayflies was taken over by other insects, especially the chironomid midges and buzzers. The stocked fish thrived, and the lake was repopulated quickly. Happily for visiting fly fishers the newly stocked trout were obligingly easy to catch, as is normal with stockies, but with succeeding seasons the fish became more difficult to catch, more wary and attuned to a wild existence in the lake – and bigger. Average weights of catches made during the late 1970s and early 1980s showed a steady increase, and by 1987 the average Lough Sheelin fish was well over 2 lb (0.9 kg).

The saving of Sheelin has been a triumph for local enthusiasm aided by centrally funded expertise, a famous victory for local and national sporting and environmental concern against the massively powerful vested interests of commercial agriculture. The near-death of the lough has led to some of the most thorough fisheries research anywhere in Ireland, to establish the best ways of rehabilitating the lake and restoring its trout population to a successful and balanced level. It is ironic to reflect that such detailed work would never have been carried out if the lough had not been on the verge of extinction as a trout fishery, and if local sportsmen had not forced the authorities to take action to try and restore a lake which was a national disgrace and a reproach to Irish agriculture.

Detailed fisheries research has shown that Sheelin's potential as a brown trout fishery is greater than any other Irish water of comparable size. Acre for acre, its waters can maintain more trout, and more big trout, than anywhere else. Putting this statement into round figures, the Central Fisheries Board have stated that the lake can support over 100,000 adult trout, at least forty percent of which can be of the order of 2–4 lb (0.9–1.8 kg).

The story of Lough Sheelin is a combination of calamity and a happy ending. It must be said, however, that the lake will never be quite the same again for those of us who knew it when the mayfly hatched in clouds and the big, powerful, truly wild Sheelin trout came up to hatching drake or spent gnat. The water clarity of old seems also to have gone for ever, with recurrent algal blooms and an unsightly tendency for the water to vary greatly in clarity from time to time, often starting the season bright and clear and gradually becoming clouded and soup-like from summer onwards. But there is no denying the resilience and natural powers of recovery of a lake which many wise heads had declared was irreversibly ruined. The restored lake is not the Sheelin we knew in the 1960s, but a different type of fishery requiring a different approach in tactics and fishing mentality. It is within 60 miles (96 km) of Dublin, with its large and growing demand for good trout fishing, and there are signs that the revived Sheelin has encouraged a new generation of young, urban-based trout fishers who have come to Sheelin with open minds, uninfluenced by memories of the old days.

A gentle drift on trout-rich waters enfolded in some of Ireland's lushest pastures. The Midland lakes are some of Europe's finest game fisheries, provided enrichment and pollution are kept at bay.

I remember an evening in 1986 when I came in to Kilnahard jetty after a few hours' drifting the northern shores of Sheelin. In the half-light I spotted another angler tying up his boat and gathering his gear together. He was an old friend, a priest whom I had regularly met on Sheelin in the 1960s. We fell to reminiscing, as all fly fishers will, and he contrasted the old times with this new, different Sheelin of the 1980s. 'And there rose up a new Pharaoh which knew not Joseph.' The biblical quotation he tossed into our conversation stopped me in my tracks for a moment, until I realised how apt it was. A new breed of Sheelin fly fisher, young, keen, adaptable, pragmatic and skilful, had come along, for whom the old talk of mayflies, drakes and spents was incomprehensible, and for whom the reality was the succession of duckfly, buzzer, caenis and murrough hatches.

Sheelin is a different lough, but the beauty of the setting is unchanged, the trout are as big and bold as you are likely to desire, and the fishing is of a quality which should still earn it a place of honour in any discussion of Irish trouting.

Because Sheelin has been dragged back from disaster so successfully, costs have been high and continued vigilance is necessary. Thus the lough is not a free fishery, like the great loughs of the west, but has the special status of a developed fishery, for which a permit fee is payable, and fishers must observe a bag limit of six fish per Rod per day, with anything under 12 in (30 cm) to be returned. The dates of the trout season here are slightly different from those of the ordinary waters of the Shannon Fisheries Region, and the Sheelin season lasts from 1 March to 12 October. This starts as a fly-only water in March and April, after which spinning and trolling (from rowing boats only) is allowed.

From Lough Derravarragh to Lough Owel

Southwards from Lough Sheelin and close to the town of Castlepollard lies the third in the chain of great Midland trout lakes, Lough Derravarragh. Its 2800 acres (1100 hectares) are shallow and shaped like a hammer, with a short broad head across the north and a long handle stretching to the south. The lough is linked with Sheelin by the Inny River, which enters at the north-western corner of the lake and emerges again at the western end, from where it flows south-westwards into Lough Ree and the main Shannon system. Derravarragh is one of the trio of famous loughs – Ennell, Owel and Derravarragh – which formerly comprised the very finest of all the Midlands trout fishing. 'Hi-Regan' in 1886 called these three 'the lakes – *par excellence*', and twenty years earlier Walter Peard had visited Derravarragh and taken twenty-one trout on two May days, with fish up to 8 lb (3.5 kg) in his basket.

Sadly, Derravarragh now offers little to excite the visitor or to tempt the writer to become lyrical in its praise as a trout lake. The evils of enrichment, to which all the Midland lakes have succumbed to some degree, have hit Derravarragh very hard indeed. It was always an exceedingly rich lough, with wonderfully alkaline water and a population of trout which grew big and were

142

also numerous enough to give good fishing to the fly. The mayfly hatch on Derravarragh was the equal of any Irish lake, and the biggest trout duly came up to take them. Even so, the lake's sporting potential was not limited to the mayfly season alone, and there was good sport throughout the entire trouting season.

The naturally hard, limestone waters of Lough Derravarragh could ill afford the enriching effects of slurry, silage and nitrogenous run-off and seepage, and together with drainage, the consequence has been an unbalancing of the lake's former quality as a spawning water and as the producer of large quantities of big brown trout, nourished by the naturally abundant foods. The result has been a serious falling off in spawning and recruitment of young trout, combined with an annual tendency to a thick, dark and malodorous algal bloom in summer. This in turn suppresses fly life, makes the once-clear waters difficult to fish effectively, and seems to taint the flesh of the trout with a disagreeably muddy flavour.

There is abundant feeding for trout in the lake, especially on the generally shallow bottom, and there are undoubtedly some very large fish here. But conditions since the 1970s have steadily reduced the lake's naturally high carrying capacity for trout, which in earlier days probably rivalled that of Sheelin. The mayfly hatch still takes place, though on a much less dramatic scale than formerly, and although the waters are sometimes already becoming coloured with algae by that date in a warm spring, the big trout can still oblige. It is not uncommon for trout to 4 and 5 lb (1.8 and 2.25 kg) to be taken.

But the best of Derravarragh's fishing is probably now to be found in the early weeks of the season, up to the end of April. Water clarity should be at its best, and the lake enjoys big hatches of duckfly and buzzers. In these conditions the same tactics and fly patterns which bring such success on Sheelin should also pay off on Derravarragh. Sport can be quite lively, although the really big fish are reluctant to rise to hatching duckfly or other small insects when the lough bottom provides such rich feeding and so little competition from other fish. It is significant that the biggest trout from Derravarragh are almost always taken by trolling, although fishing a reservoir lure on a deeply sunk fly line has also been known to produce big trout from close to the bottom.

From June onwards, after the mayfly hatch has ended, the lake enjoys some steady hatches of chironomids, and sport with the fly can be good. However, the fish are likely to be the smaller individuals, and much depends upon the extent to which the water retains reasonable visibility. The severity of the algal bloom varies from year to year, and the prospects for sport with the fly fluctuate accordingly.

Sad though the recent history of Derravarragh has been, it should by no means be written off as a fishery. It still provides a good many fishers with pleasant sport. The evidence of Sheelin and other nearby Midland lakes shows what can be achieved when damaging eutrophication and pollution are checked, allowing the lakes to display their wonderful capacity for recovery. Boats can be hired locally from Castlepollard and Multyfarnham, and a

Regional Fisheries Permit is required during the season, which lasts from 1 March to 30 September.

Lough Ennell

From Lough Owel it is only a few minutes' drive by car to the last and most southerly of the five main Midland lakes. You drive back into Mullingar, turn right onto the main N52 road signposted for Tullamore, and Lough Ennell lies just west of the road after you have gone about 2 miles (3.2 km) out of the town. An alternative route is to take the quieter L14 road which leads to Dysart, and skirts Lough Ennell on the western side. From either road you can drive to one of several car parks and public jetties on the east, north and north-western shores.

Ennell has a number of interesting features to claim the trout fisher's attention. In the heyday of Midlands trouting it held pride of place, together with Owel and Derravarragh, in the triumvirate of the greatest Irish trout lakes. It had a reputation for big trout, and the biggest of them all was caught here on 15 July 1894, a trout of 26 lb 2 oz (12 kg) taken by a local angler, William Meares, trolling a traditional large Irish copper spoon off the Belvedere Castle shore. (At the time of Meares's success Ennell was generally known as Belvedere Lake.) The catching of this amazing fish must have been all the more astonishing since trout were not the quarry Meares had in mind that day, for he was actually trolling for pike. The important archive photograph of this fish and its captor is old and faded, but it shows that this was a vast, slab-sided fish, with a massive tail and relatively little overall length in proportion to the quite prodigious depth of its flanks, more like those of a bream or a carp. Small wonder that its short, thick body would not bend sufficiently to fit into Meares's pike net, and he had to play the fish until it was quite exhausted and then lift it bodily into the boat.

Another feature of Meares's specimen which can clearly be seen from the picture is the silvery, almost salmon-bright colour of the fish, totally different from the dark and heavily spotted markings we expect to find on really big lake trout of 12 lb (5.5 kg) and over, such as those which are taken almost annually from loughs like Mask and Erne. (Nor, incidentally, did it have the pike-like heaviness of head which is typical of the *ferox* type of large lake trout.) The colouring of Meares's monster highlights another point about Ennell trout, which have always had a reputation for being silvery bright. This has always been ascribed to the clear limestone water and the generally light-coloured bottom of the lake, which is sandy in many places.

Ennell therefore developed a well-deserved reputation for large, handsome trout, but the inevitable consequence of the alkaline richness of the lake made them appear dour from a fly fisher's point of view, and often difficult to tempt up to take a fly on or near the surface. The bottom feeding was simply too rich and too abundant for the fish to bother with surface feeding. The main exception to this, however, was mayfly time. Big hatches of these large ephemerids seldom fail to bring up big trout to feed on the surface, although these fish may spend the remainder of the year feeding deeper. Ennell was well known for its short but active mayfly season, which usually lasted from the third week of May until 10 June or thereabouts in normal years. Trout to 5 and 6 lb (2.25–2.7 kg) came up to the dap and the spent gnat during this brief festival, and at other times it was reckoned that a typical basket of fish taken on the wet fly would average 1–2 lb (0.7–0.9 kg).

All that came to an end in the 1950s. Ennell was always noted as being an especially shallow lake, and it could ill afford the serious drop in water levels which resulted from a drainage programme in the area. Trout numbers and the lough's ability to survive as a trout fishery were in jeopardy, and the fact that it did not die completely is largely to the credit of the local Lough Ennell Preservation Association, formed by concerned fishers and environmentalists. Their lobbying led to the intervention of the now-defunct Irish Inland Fisheries Trust, whose management worked wonders in a comparatively short time. Ennell was back to something like its old self, with lower water levels than formerly but nevertheless producing good sport and fine trout. Then a second and seemingly devastating blow fell when the lake was hit by gross pollution from nearby Mullingar. The poisonous effects of untreated sewage destroyed all that the fisheries managers had achieved, and it was scarcely surprising that the Trust abandoned Ennell in disgust and in righteous protest. The mayfly went too, further victims of the filth in the lough. By the end of the 1970s Ennell was finished as a trout fishery – or so it seemed.

But the subsequent story of Ennell has been similar to that of several other Irish Midland waters, where enrichment, pollution and radical alterations in hydrology caused by drainage schemes have been followed by some astonishing recoveries. The success of once-ruined waters like Sheelin and Owel have demonstrated what can be done if the main causes of the damage are removed or mitigated and the wonderful recuperative powers of nature are allowed to get to work – perhaps assisted by some skilful management. On Ennell the disgraceful sewage problem was first reduced and eventually eliminated by the creation of new facilities for sewage treatment, an important first step in controlling the environmental threat posed by the large and growing population of the rapidly developing town of Mullingar.

What vestiges of Ennell's wild trout population remained during the pollution period in the 1970s were remarkably quick to re-establish themselves once the lake became purer. This is due in large measure to the wonderful spawning and nursery facilities which the lake enjoys. In this respect Ennell is better endowed than any of the Midland lakes, and this is in marked contrast to the poor spawning conditions on Lough Owel, its near neighbour just a few miles away to the north. Owel, as we have seen, has superb natural conditions for growing very big trout. But its large stock of good trout is only maintained by compensating for the lack of good spawning conditions by stripping the eggs and milt from trout trying to run up its inadequate feeder streams and hatching these nearby, before returning them to the lough at a stage when they are capable of feeding and continuing their growth alongside the wild Owel trout. It has been said with some justification that if Lough Owel only had the spawning areas which exist on Ennell it would be the closest thing to a paradise fishery!

The Irish trout-fishing grapevine works with great speed and efficiency, and by 1984 there were recurrent tales of good numbers of trout being seen again in Ennell, and moreover good baskets were once again being taken on the fly. Average weights were not large at first, with trout averaging 1–1½ lb (0.5–0.7 kg) and it was also observed that there were lively rises to sizeable hatches of duckfly, from late March in mild springs through to late April, and intermittently to other chironomid hatches thereafter through the season. This follows the pattern observed on other Midland lakes, where the once-legendary mayfly hatches have virtually vanished but there have been greatly enhanced chironomid buzzer hatches.

Faith was soon restored in this lough, which many devotees of long experience on Ennell had given up for lost, and the late 1980s has been a period of steady consolidation of the wonderful regeneration of this fishery. Despite the recovery of fish numbers and quality, the essential character of the fishery has changed in some important respects. The water levels, which were lowered by the drainage activities of the 1950s, have remained much lower than they used to be, and this has brought benefits and problems for the trout and the trout fishers. Shallow water makes it easier for trout to see a team of wet flies, or a single dry fly, fished on or close to the surface, and thus it is not unknown for a fish which may be cruising and feeding on or close to the bottom to turn up and take a fly, while on other, deeper waters a bottom-feeding fish might never have noticed it. But shallow, clear water calls for a degree of precision and care in the choice of fly patterns and sizes, and in the way they are presented to the trout.

Ennell fish have more opportunity than most lough trout to give your flies a critical examination before they accept or reject them! Thus the fly fisher has a good chance of presenting his flies within sight of fish at almost every cast, but he must take additional care in doing so. It pays to use a fine, clear monofil leader in these clear waters, and experience shows that a floating line can scare fish away. The intermediate lines with their near-neutral buoyancy or the slow-sinking styles, both of which are popular with Lough Ennell regulars, leave less surface disturbance and when fished on a short line from a drifting boat do not sink far enough to cause any problems in shallow water.

Shallow waters affect the way in which a stillwater responds to natural forces like the action of wind and waves. Ennell's shallow waters mean that there is virtually no significant thermocline, and since there are more or less uniform temperatures at all levels from the surface to the bed of the lake, the trout are able to find food on or close to the surface on even the earliest and coldest days of the season, which is good news for the fly fisher who works his flies close to the surface. But although there is unusual uniformity in the water temperature throughout Ennell, the effects of the wind and the waves cause a good deal of disturbance to many parts of the bed of the lough. The churning effect can cause turbid, coloured conditions but this quickly settles again, for much of the bottom is sandy.

More lasting, however, are the effects on aquatic vegetation and the many forms of insects and other invertebrates which rely upon these host plants. Lough Owel, for example, is not a deep lough, but it is deeper than Ennell and therefore not so susceptible to the scouring and churning of wind and wave. Its coverage of aquatic vegetation is therefore fairly uniform, which in turn leads to widespread hatches of those insects which emerge from the sub-surface weed. On Ennell the water is so shallow and so constantly disturbed by wave action that many forms of weedy growth do not get a chance to become established and to nurture colonies of the many species of insects and invertebrates that trout eat.

In the absence of the stability and settled conditions that most species of lake vegetation require if they are to become successfully established, the distribution of vegetation on Ennell is patchy, and this has two effects. First it limits the total amount of good feeding areas for trout in the lough, and secondly it means that the fly fisher must take account of the character of the lake bed and fish accordingly, mindful that hatches of some types of fly will only occur over weedy areas. Many of the best such areas on Ennell are in the bays which indent the lough's western shore.

Much of the lake is fringed with reeds, which can mean two types of fishing with two very different-sized flies. Where you find reeds you invariably find hatches of what are often known as reed smuts, tiny flies belonging to the *simulium* group of insects and often referred to by the blunter name of the Black Curse. This distinguishes them from the White Curse, a sobriquet reserved for the paler-coloured *Caenis* species. Despite their tiny size, trout will feed steadily and eagerly on them, and it can be a real challenge to find and present an imitation which has the tiny, delicate appearance of the natural insect. Probably the most effective is the Goddard Smut, with a soft, sparse black hackle and an almost spherical herled body, and the smaller the hook the better! When casting such a tiny fly it is self-defeating to use the 6 or 8 lb (2.7 or 3.5 kg) leader monofil you might customarily carry for lough use. Something much finer must be used, and if you connect with a big Ennell trout you will need to remember that light leader and play him carefully, while doing your utmost to stop him from making a dash into the reeds, where a sudden parting will be almost inevitable.

Reeds are sometimes called sedges, and the hatches of big, active sedge flies on lakes like Ennell represent the other end of the spectrum from the Lilliputian smuts and midges. (Lilliput, incidentally, was not only the name of that fictional land of tiny folk created by Dublin's Jonathan Swift: it is also a placename indicating a house and a stretch of the south-western shore on Lough Ennell.) The sedge hatches begin in the late afternoons from the beginning of August onwards, and the secret is to fish along the windward shore, where the sedges are carried out onto the water by the offshore breezes. The prevailing wind here is westerly, and thus the bays from the Bog Islands northwards are all likely to be good. Ennell is not nearly such an important Green Peter lake as Owel, but that may come with time as this rejuvenated fishery continues to evolve. But other sedge imitations account for plenty of fish, and they include the Murrough, the Shredge, the G&H Sedge, the Invicta and the Red Palmer, fished dry, skimmed or twitched, as the occasion demands.

Finally, as Ennell's season draws to its end, dapping comes to the fore, as on neighbouring Lough Owel. Both loughs open on 1 March and close on 30 September, and the dapping season usually begins with the daddy-longlegs, which can be easily collected along almost every part of the lough shore, wherever there are rough grasses, field rushes, gorse or thorn bushes. Your live-bait box should contain at least eighty or a hundred insects for a full day on the lough, to allow for losses, the inevitable escapes when you open the box, drowned insects, those which the trout, big and small, will chew, and to ensure that you have no excuse for always having fresh and appetising 'daddies' on offer on your hook.

The grasshopper is the second natural dap in chronological order on Ennell, coming into its own in late August and September. Presented singly, as on Lough Owel, it can do deadly execution when conditions are right, and at the tail end of the season in September traditional wet-fly fishing is highly successful on Ennell, as the fish feed eagerly in preparation for the onset of spawning and the winter.

These five famous Midland lakes deserve serious consideration by resident and visiting angler alike. This account of some of their past glories, recent problems and more recent resurgence gives only a hint of the fascination they offer to the fisherman who does not merely wish to catch trout, but who also enjoys thinking about the waters he is fishing, and planning his tactics and his methods accordingly.

Lough Owel

An altogether brighter and happier prospect awaits the fly fisher who moves on from Derravarragh to the last two lakes of the main Midland network, the twin jewels of Lough Owel and Lough Ennell. Both have had to endure the common afflictions of slurry seepage, silage effluent and all the agriculturally produced problems which have beset the Midland loughs, and both fisheries have undergone important and fundamental changes. But they remain two of the most interesting trout fisheries in Ireland.

These two lakes lie north and south respectively of the big market town of Mullingar. (Together with Longford and Athlone, Mullingar claims to be the most central town in Ireland. Inevitably, it all depends on where you are starting from!) But from whatever point of the compass you approach, the best way to arrive at Lough Owel is along the main N4 trunk road which runs northwards from Mullingar towards Edgeworthstown and on to Longford, following the sweep of the lough's north-eastern shore. The two best public piers are at the south end of the lough, at Mullaly's Quay by the yacht club, and further along to the west, at Tullaghan, where there is a slipway and a good-sized car park. You are sure to want to fish from a boat, as is the case on

almost every Irish stillwater, and it is significant that very few local anglers fish
from the shore. For the visitor a boat not only allows effective coverage of the
water but eliminates the need to seek permission for access to parts of the lake
shore, perhaps from several different landowners.

If you look through old literature on Irish angling you will get the distinct
impression that Lough Owel was known to hold very big trout, but that they
were by no means easy to catch. That much, at least, remains just as true
today as it was a century or more ago. Lough Owel does indeed hold some very
big trout, well into double figures, although anything over 7 lb (3 kg) caught
on the fly will attract a very great deal of attention these days. And yet the local
people, and the fisheries staff, who watch the little spawning streams in late
autumn regularly see massive trout which would tip the scales at comfortably
over 10 lb (4.5 kg) and even 12 lb (5.5 kg). Perhaps it is always thus, on the
principle that the best things seem always to turn up when you cannot have
them! But there can be absolutely no doubt that the Owel wild trout run very
big indeed.

Although you may be lucky enough to see such fish at spawning time, one of
the essential features of Lough Owel is the paucity of good spawning streams.
Other Midland lakes have good, sizeable rivers flowing in and out, but Owel is
almost entirely fed by springs, its waters dimpling up, pure and with sparkling
clarity from countless natural springs percolating through the underlying
limestone. There are no worthwhile feeder streams to speak of, only five small
rivulets, two of which flow in from the northern end and the other three along
the western shore. And so we find Lough Owel to be a clear and food-rich lake,
abundantly endowed with the natural conditions which encourage trout to
grow big and heavy but sadly lacking in the fundamentally important attri-
butes of good spawning conditions. Small wonder therefore that Lough Owel
historically had a reputation for holding a small population of very big and
very elusive trout.

The natural abundance and diversity of insects and crustaceans in these
hard limestone waters are offset by poor conditions for the breeding of new
generations of trout, and the fisherman's difficulties are exacerbated by the
astonishing clarity of the spring water. This allows no margin for clumsiness or
lack of delicacy in fishing methods, and so Owel became known as a place of
massive but shy trout which had almost to be charmed out of the water, so
difficult were they to catch. In this respect, if not in the size of the lough, Owel
might be compared with the limestone lochs of Durness in Sutherland –
pellucid in their clarity, famous for big fish, and unforgiving if the presentation
of the fly is not careful and delicate.

By the 1920s Lough Owel had virtually reached the nadir of its reputation.
The official *Angler's Guide to the Free State*, published in Dublin in 1924,
described Owel as 'fallen off in recent years, and is now hardly worth
considering'. It appeared that matters had not significantly improved almost a
quarter of a century later, for *The Angler's Guide* of 1948 laconically described
Owel as holding 'some large trout' but went on to dissuade most fly fishers by
adding that 'the best baits are the loach in spring and perch fry in summer and

autumn'. Deep trolling for big trout was the order of the day, leaving little scope for the fly fisher.

Lough Owel still holds massive trout for which the best method might still be to troll a minnow in the spring or to fish deep with a perch-fry imitation at the end of the season. But it all comes back to the fundamental characteristics of this lake, with its food-filled waters and its lack of spawning facilities – a lake which is biologically unbalanced and which cannot be a self-sustaining trout fishery of the quality which the lough deserves without the help of careful management.

Like Lough Sheelin and other Midland lakes, Lough Owel has been taken under the wing of the Irish Central Fisheries Board, which has provided the scientific expertise and the practical management skills to give the wonderful natural potential of Lough Owel a helping hand. In essence the management policy has been to make an annual assessment of the lake's fish-holding capability, of the existing stocks of trout in the lough each spring, and the ways in which stocking with reared fry and more mature fish can make up the short-fall and provide a trout population which is adequate but not unnaturally abundant, and which creates the diversity of fish ages which should occur in a balanced fishery. The outcome of this is that Owel now receives annual stockings of trout fry, yearling fish and also ready-to-catch fish at or above the 12-in (30 cm) minimum for the fishery. The latter provide instant sport, while the yearling trout and the fry grow on gradually.

The stocked fish come, of course, from a fish farm, but that does not mean that they are from a different and alien genetic strain compared to Owel's wild trout. Genetic consistency is maintained by a policy of monitoring the feeders of Lough Owel, which is where the spawning runs take place, and when it is judged that there has been enough natural spawning to give an optimum level in the lough's natural breeding and nursery areas, the remaining fish are trapped and stripped of their eggs and milt. The fertilised ova are then transferred to the hatchery and fish farm nearby, for eventual release back into the lough from which they came in embryo. It is a clever and simple way of ensuring that Owel's trout population is not limited by the lough's meagre natural spawning facilities.

No stocking policy, however carefully planned or thoughtfully conceived, ever meets with unanimous acclaim, and the Owel policy has not been without its critics. Nor does any stocking operation ever produce entirely predictable results, so different are the responses of individual fishery ecosystems to the sudden arrival of large numbers of additional fish. It remains to be seen how well the fry and the yearling trout adapt to Owel, and what eventual contribution they make to the lough's 'natural' trout population after they have grown to maturity on the rich feeding there. But the larger stocked fish of takeable size are known to be free-rising and relatively easy to catch on Owel, like most stockies in the majority of waters.

Any fishery manager faced with the task of stocking a lough like Owel must decide whether it is best to put the new fish into the lake in autumn or spring. Autumn might appear to be a better time, for the angling season is almost finished and the stocked fish can apparently slip away quietly into a relatively undisturbed lough. There they can acclimatise and grow through the winter, to provide the next season's anglers with more sporting fish which have become better attuned to their new environment and acquired something of the native wariness of the wild fish. The manager is also spared the sight of his precious stockies being hauled out in large quantities by fly fishers whose flies hitting the surface trigger off the feeding responses of fish reared on scattered pelleted foods.

What is unseen, and therefore tends to be overlooked, is what goes on under the water. Although autumn stocking may seem logical and preferable to spring stocking, the reality is different. Stocked fish straight from the fish farm are accustomed to living in shoals, in confinement, and being fed with food scattered onto the surface of the water. Thus they become attuned to communal living and to looking to the area on or close under the surface as their feeding zone. But when such fish are released into a lake in autumn they are moving into an environment in which there is relatively little wild food on or near the surface. That explains why, although trout are carnivorous creatures which feed on various forms of animal life, stocked trout have been found to rise indiscriminately to unsuitable material dropping onto the water, such as seeds and berries, fragments of twigs and leaves and similar debris. That also explains why they are easy to catch with a carelessly cast fly or almost any pattern! Only experience teaches them the discriminating wariness that comes naturally to the wild fish.

On Lough Owel, and on every trout fishery, the colder weather of autumn brings an end to the insect hatches which have been going on steadily since spring, and the wild trout will be busily feeding in mid-water or along the bottom, their diet comprising more and more larvae, shrimps, snails, leeches and water lice. The wild fish have learned to change their feeding patterns with the changing seasons, but stew-bred stockies are initially ignorant of these alternative sources of food. A further disadvantage lies in the fact that the wild fish are preparing to spawn, and are feeding eagerly in preparation for the physical rigours of spawning and the long winter ahead. There can be aggressive competition for food at this time, and the wild fish can respond angrily to the appearance of shoals of stock fish in their feeding areas. The consequences can be high levels of mortality among autumn-stocked fish.

Spring stocking renders the newly released trout vulnerable to the fishermen, but their harvest can be controlled by the imposition of bag limits to curb excesses. On Lough Owel you can take up to six fish in a day, an arrangement that seems to keep everyone happy. There are excellent hatches of duckfly and other chironomids in the early weeks of the new season, and trout whose natural instinct is to feed on surface foods will find there is no shortage. Later in the season the olives, the mayfly, various buzzer species and the sedges cater for continued surface feeding, and the stocked fish develop a marked wariness before the season ends, becoming as difficult to catch as their wild cousins.

A 1987 estimate indicated that around ninety percent of the early season catch on Owel consists of stocked fish, taken chiefly during the duckfly and buzzer hatches. Few wild fish are rising readily to hatches in the early months, and even Owel's huge hatches of olives in May are largely ignored by them. There is a small but useful mayfly hatch which can always be relied upon to bring up a few of the big, wild fish which are otherwise bottom feeders, but it is not until the big sedge hatches of July and August that the wild fish really turn in earnest to surface feeding. Then you will be able to see the difference between the recently stocked fish and the wild trout, or at any rate those fish which started life as stockies and have become integrated into the population of wild, fully acclimatised trout.

The broad, powerful tails, the deep, muscular bodies and the thick, heavy shoulders tell of a free life, and there is none of the flaccid weakness or the stuntedness of fin and tail which bespeak a life in a concrete stewpond. And the proof of the pudding will be in the eating, or at any rate in the cleaning before you cook them. Wild trout from these and similar waters, or fish which have been stocked and have adapted well, will have the rich pinkness of flesh which tells they have been feeding on shrimps and other crustaceans. The recently stocked trout may have pallid flesh similar to that of a brownie from an acidic hill lough – unless the fish-farm diet has included the essential carotin colouring agent, of course!

Beginning with the duckfly, the best fly patterns to use are the various pupa imitations, the Blae and Black and the Sooty Olive, with the Fiery Brown, the ever-dependable Mallard and Claret and the Black Pennell in reserve. For each of these traditional wet-fly patterns there is an equivalent nymph or pupa version, with those hints of reddish-ginger, green or segmented greyish-white which represent the emergent stages of the various chironomids. Later in the spring, when the lake olives are hatching, the Sooty Olive moves into real prominence as a favourite, together with such obvious olive representations as the Gold-ribbed Hare's Ear and the Greenwell's Glory.

Sizes will usually be 10 or 12 when fishing in a normal Owel ripple, but in calmer conditions it pays handsomely to drop down to 14 and 16, or even smaller if you have them available, and to cast a long and gentle line with a very much longer leader than you might otherwise think of using. Twelve to 15 ft (3.5–4.5 m) is not too long when the surface of this very clear lough is really calm. Likewise you should take account of the weight of the leader monofilament used, which might be up to 8 lb (3.5 kg) or even 10 lb (4.5 kg) on a good rolling wave but which needs to be much finer in a calm. Pay attention also to the colour of the monofilament leader you use. Conventional wisdom among Owel regulars is that in those limpid waters with their remarkable clarity a clear monofil is much less likely to frighten fish than a green- or olive-coloured nylon. And beware false casting, the flash of a brightly varnished rod, or any noise or clatter in the boat, especially when the wind drops or if you are fishing a dry version of any of the Owel flies.

At mayfly time you will probably find that the main hatch of fly, and therefore the main concentration of fish and fishers, will be along the northern shore, especially from Kilpatrick's Point, just below the narrow and reedy northern bottleneck of the lake, and south-east past the shallows off Braba-

A smile of success. Judith McKelvie with a June brownie taken on fly from one of Ulster's smaller game fisheries.

zon's Point and on past the mouth of the in-flowing Portshanaghan feeder stream. All along these drifts you might productively use nymphal imitations, any of the various Gosling and Straddlebug patterns fished semi-sunk in the surface film, and a Grey Wulff tripping along buoyantly and thoroughly oiled on the tops of the ripples. The spent-gnat fishing on Lough Owel is not as productive as it used to be, but some fine fish have been taken each year, especially on a quiet evening when you may cast to individual feeding fish, using a soft-hackled pattern to simulate the spent and dying female.

Sedge hatches on Owel can be impressive, and the trout think so too. The Murrough has its following, and the Muddler Minnow takes good fish when fished quickly and with animation over a good wave. But the pre-eminent sedge pattern here is the Green Peter, and each season it accounts for more large wild Owel trout than any other pattern. The Green Peter is one of Ireland's most celebrated and successful flies, for trout, seatrout and salmon, and there are those who will rarely cast a team of flies without one somewhere on the leader. It is intended to represent one of the varieties of the Great Red Sedge, and it can be dressed small or large, wet or dry, the latter depending upon the position and angle of the hackle.

One of the commonest topics of fly fishers' conversation in Ireland concerns the dates when certain flies begin to emerge on certain lakes. This is perhaps most characteristic of mayfly chat, and some enthusiasts will go so far as to sit down with a diary and a calendar and mark up the dates on which they are certain the 'fly will be up' on this lough and that. Mother Nature seems to resist such precision in timetabling, and the weather around hatching time can make all the difference.

With the Green Peter on Lough Owel it is always rather approximate, and even the Owel regulars will hedge their dates. But it generally comes during the last fortnight of the month, tending to be earlier in warm, calm summers. The first few days of the hatch will see a progressive build-up in the numbers and size of the fish rising to take sedges. About a week after the main hatch has started is probably the peak time, with the majority of good fish showing the maximum of interest in the hatch. Provided the weather stays settled and there are no sudden snaps of cold weather or thundery spells, the sport on Owel should be at its peak of the season. The onset of twilight is the trigger for the main sedge hatch, and the best of the sport is likely to take place in almost pitch darkness. This makes certain demands on the fly fisher, not least in his accurate handling of a boat by touch and feel and sound as much as by sight, and in the fairly precise presentation of a fly and the playing of a fish (and it may be a very big one!) in the dark.

If you begin fishing from one of the southern jetties I have mentioned, as most of us do, and if there is a westerly breeze, or better still a north-easterly one, provided it is not a chill wind, the best plan will be to motor out to somewhere just below where the little Ash Ditch feeder runs in, and drift back south-eastwards past the 'eyot' or 'crannog' and along the shallows past the ruins of the old abbey church at Portloman. Here the shoreline becomes reedy and your best line may be back towards Srudora Island at the south end, not far out from Tullaghan jetty. The north-west/south-west orientation of Lough Owel also means that if there is a southerly or, less commonly, a south-easterly wind blowing, it makes it possible to take long drifts along the north-eastern shore from Church Island towards Brabazon's Point and beyond.

From late afternoon a three-fly cast fished in traditional wet-fly style is best, and when the Green Peter experts are out on Lough Owel you will usually find that they fish with a Green Peter nymph on the point, a Mallard and Claret, a Green Peter or an Invicta on the dropper, and a Green Peter or a Muddler Minnow on the bob. This brackets most likely taking situations, catering for nymphing fish, for those taking the merging sedges, and a well-worked bob fly creates the attractor disturbance on the surface which simulates the scuttling wake of a sedge and often catches the eye of a cruising trout on the feed. This cast, or some minor variation on it, may work well right into the night, but others prefer to watch for clear signs of big fish taking the fully fledged sedges off the surface with powerful, slashing rises. At this point they change to a single dry fly, bushily dressed and thoroughly oiled, fished on a fairly long line by the standards we are accustomed to using from a drifting boat, and worked in the typical sedge fashion by twitching it in a jerky movement across the water, or, if there is a good ripple, skimming it at some speed across the surface. Here the natural buoyancy and wave-creating qualities of the Muddler and other patterns incorporating deer hair can be very effective.

This after-dark fishing of a dry pattern or skimming a wake fly for fish taking big sedges is the Green Peter equivalent of spent-gnat fishing during mayfly time, and it produces the best fish of the year on Owel, especially to those who fish with the right degree of care and concentration. The gloaming and afterwards on a lough is a calm and quiet time, sounds are magnified in the stillness and across the water, and you must listen and watch for signs of individual fish feeding. When the Green Peter is hatching on Owel the lough's biggest trout come up and cruise with powerful and purposeful majesty, and the art is often to cast to a rising, cruising individual, dropping your fly ahead of him and on the correct path, and then imparting just the right amount of skittering, jerking movement to it.

The best results tend to be achieved by those who have not only the dexterity and skill to cast accurately, but who are able to manoeuvre a boat with one hand while casting with the other. A great many Irish lough fishermen spend much of the season with a rod seemingly glued to one hand and the handle of an oar firmly fixed in the other. A quick tweak here and a long, steady pull there, and they can guide a drifting boat onto the perfect course from which to intercept a feeding fish. Unless such ability to perform two skills at once comes readily to you, it is best to have a boatman, or to take turns on the oars with a fishing companion.

The take to the Green Peter, when it comes, can be savagely powerful, and it is fatally easy to respond with comparable energy and speed. This will lose you many fish, and your response must be to tighten firmly after a definite pause. This gives a large fish time to take hold of the fly and turn away and downwards with it before the backward tension of the line and leader pulls the hook firmly into position. It will come as no surprise to an Owel regular to find he is firmly connected to 3, 4, or 5 lb (1.35–2.25 kg) of splendidly powerful, wild brown trout.

As the end of the season comes on Lough Owel, a good sprinkling of big fish are always taken by dapping. The dap may of course be used much earlier in the season, although you will see little sign of it during mayfly time compared with a generation or two ago. But August and after is daddy-longlegs time on many Irish stillwaters (and some rivers too) and the dapped 'daddy', using the natural or an artificial, takes its share of good fish. So too does that unlikely cocktail of baits, the natural daddy-longlegs and the grasshopper fished together. But the small band of dedicated dappers on Lough Owel tend to favour the grasshopper on its own as the very best natural dap, and in the sunny warmth of mid-morning you may see figures carrying live-bait boxes moving among the trees and grasses along the shores, gathering grasshoppers which will lie on the traditional wisp of hay until the afternoon and evening, when the dapping rods begin to appear on the water. Some fishers still use the old live-bait hooks with their patent catches to grip the grasshopper, but the majority will mount their baits singly or in pairs on the same sort of hooks, usually size 10, on which they would tie their Green Peters and other big lake flies.

9 The Great Loughs

It is a daunting task to undertake any survey of the great game fishing loughs of Ireland. Their number, the variety of sport they can provide during each season, and the endless permutations of tackle, tactics and local hints and wrinkles which the enthusiastic angler can employ make Ireland's big lake fisheries a subject worthy of a book all to themselves. One day perhaps someone will write it. Meantime, it is important not to allow their variety, size and complexity to preclude at least some mention of these great fisheries in this general survey of Ireland and the game fishing it has to offer.

Lough Erne

On any map of Ireland you can readily locate the great natural stillwaters. Most prominent of all, of course, is Lough Neagh, which has been discussed in the section dealing with the game fisheries of Northern Ireland. Letting your eye drift southwards, the next large inland water you will notice is the big, boomerang-shaped expanse of Lower Lough Erne, tucked away in the south-western corner of Northern Ireland, and trailing off into a point at its western end. From there the whole of the vast Erne catchment, comprising some 37,800 acres (15,750 hectares) plus the many tributary rivers, large and small, drains into the waters of Donegal Bay and the Atlantic along the 7 or 8 miles (11–13 km) of the River Erne, from the outflow at Rosscor, past Belleek and into the sea at Ballyshannon.

Lower Lough Erne is under the overall management of the Department of Agriculture for Northern Ireland, and the Department's policy has been to divide the waters of the Upper and Lower Loughs into two distinct fisheries. The Upper is designated primarily as a coarse fishery, while the Lower Lough westwards from Castlehume and the mouth of the Ballinamallard River is principally a game fishery, with brown trout as the main quarry species.

It is sad almost beyond words to read the brief entry in the D.A.N.I. *Angling Guide* which tells us that this great lough holds many species of coarse fish, brown trout, 'and the occasional salmon and sea trout'. That sense of sadness stems from the catastrophic decline of migratory salmonids within the Erne system over the past hundred years.

The rot set in with a large-scale drainage and land reclaimation scheme, which was instituted in the 1890s to relieve the extensive winter flooding which annually affected the Upper Lough and a large acreage of surrounding farmland to the east of Belleek and the Lower Lough. So serious was this winter flooding that large areas of good livestock grazing were rendered useless for months on end, and there was a local saying that 'in summer Lough Erne is in Fermanagh, but in winter Fermanagh is in Lough Erne'.

A private drainage company set about improving the run-off of water from the Upper Erne catchment, and this involved the deepening and canalising of part of the River Erne between Rosscor and Belleek, which destroyed a number of famous and productive salmon pools below Eel Weir Hill on the Marquess of Ely's estate. At Belleek the falls were blasted and flood gates were installed to regulate the flow of the river. This had the effect of eradicating some of the best parts of the rod fishery, and the dedicated summer fishers who persevered on the remaining lower beats of the river were beset by serious and sometimes hazardous fluctuations in the levels of the river. Sudden opening of the Belleek gates, invariably without prior warning, allowed a flood of anything up to 10 ft (3 m) of water to surge downstream, and many a hapless angler had to scramble for the bank or risk a ducking. Matters were made worse by the nature of the pools on the river, which was wide and deep, and could only be fished to best effect by deep wading.

But despite these early drainage moves, the Erne remained a superbly productive salmon river, which came into its own from June onwards. Augustus Grimble, in his exhaustive survey of the British and Irish salmon fisheries, concluded that the Erne was perhaps the very finest summer salmon fishery anywhere in the British Isles. The numbers, and the size, of the massive, multi-sea winter salmon which were taken on the Erne, both by rod and line and in the nets, continued to be quite prodigious. Some of the best accounts of this wonderful fishery are to be found in the books of two Erne experts of the Victorian and Edwardian period, Sir Henry Seton-Kerr in *My Sporting Holidays* (1904) and (more extensively) Sidney Berdoe Wilkinson in *Reminiscences of Sport in Ireland* (1931, repr. 1987).

The real body-blow for the Erne as a major salmon and seatrout fishery, from which it has never recovered, came in the 1940s when a large-scale hydro-electric scheme was implemented. Two dams were built, at Cliff and at Kathleen's Falls, and all the finest and most celebrated Erne beats and pools vanished almost overnight under the dreary waters of the newly-created Assaroe Lough, which filled the watercourse between the barrages. There is something breathtakingly ironic in the wording of the Irish Government's official *Angling Guide* of 1948, which remarked that the aftermath of the recent damming of the Erne made it 'impossible to say what angling facilities these lakes are likely to afford'. The answer was soon painfully evident, and the hugely prolific Erne salmon run dwindled to virtual extinction.

A small number of fish annually struggle over the fish passes and into the Lower Lough, but the golden thread of annual continuity and genetic consistency upon which a salmon run depends was severed in the late 1940s and is unlikely ever to be adequately restored.

Muckross pier on Lower Lough Erne, and Ian Holman prepares to set out with a trio of Bruce & Walker lough rods.

Locally dressed flies are always best. Howard Black of Kesh dresses flies for all the finest Irish game-fishing waters from Donegal to Galway.

And yet all is not wholly lost. Each year some good fish are taken, mainly by spinning or trolling, below Rosscor and just above Belleek, and results in the late 1980s were more encouraging than for many years past. Salmon may still be the rare and delightful exception on the lower stretches of the Erne, but at least some of them are still there.

This brief digression on the sad story of the Erne salmon is in great contrast to the state of trout fishing on Lough Erne. For if we turn our attention to trout, the wild brown trout of Lough Erne, it is no exaggeration to say that Lower Lough Erne is unquestionably one of the finest and most exciting stillwater game fisheries anywhere in Europe. The lough, especially at the western end, provides consistently good sport with fine, wild fish from the very beginning of the season on 1 March, and there are excellent prospects for good baskets of trout falling to traditional lough-style wet-fly fishing right through to the season's end on 30 September. There is a catch limit of six fish per rod per day, and a minimum size of 12 in (30 cm) also applies.

The Lough Erne trouting begins, like many Irish loughs, with the duckfly fishing in March, progressing through the buzzer period of April and early May. And then comes mayfly time.

Lough Erne is one of Ireland's foremost mayfly loughs, with good hatches in evidence from about 20 May onwards in a typical season, and some superb potential for evening spent-gnat fishing on balmy evenings in early June. From Kesh westwards, especially along the northern shore of the lough, there are innumerable excellent mayfly spots; and around all the bays and islands along past Boa Island and the area known locally as 'the Gardens' and right down to Rosscor viaduct very large numbers of sizeable trout can be seen cruising and feeding with avid determination on the spent and dying female mayflies.

Lower Lough Erne offers another and equally interesting form of trout fishing – the quest for really massive specimen brown trout. Lough Erne has the space and the resources of food to allow some individual trout to grow to a great size, and each season a good number of trout weighing 12 lb (5.5 kg) and more are taken from the lough. Such fish are good for a few days' gossip among the local fishing community, but are otherwise taken somewhat for granted. But bigger individuals are also accounted for, and lough trout to 18 and 20 lb (8–9 kg) were caught with some regularity in the 1980s. Some of these fish were thoroughly documented, photographed, weighed and measured, and had all the necessary credentials to make them candidates for consideration by the official specimen fish committees. Others, alas, were not so carefully recorded, and there is absolutely no doubt that Lower Lough Erne trout of well over 20 lb (9 kg) have been caught since the 1970s. And there are other similar specimens still to be caught by those who are sufficiently dedicated and patient.

Despite the sneers of the strict fly-only trouters, specimen trout hunting is not a mindless and moronic activity, entailing little more than endless hours of trolling to and fro around the lough with deep, slow-spinning lures. Such a tedious and unimaginative procedure might be rewarded by the catching of the very occasional big trout, but modern specimen trout fishing is a serious and carefully conducted exercise, involving specialised tackle, considerable planning and much attention to detail.

American trout fishermen on the great lakes of Canada and the United States have exported much of their expertise to Ireland and the rest of Europe. Big trout are known to live and feed at depths which are closely linked to the sub-surface contours of the lakes, to the temperature gradient of the water, and to the whereabouts of the food supplies upon which they depend. For large lough trout this means other, smaller fish, and in Lough Erne this is likely to be chiefly char. The American experience has shown that careful study of the underwater geography and an awareness of the thermocline are two of the vital secrets of success in catching big brown trout.

Lower Lough Erne is a vast sheet of water, and to try to take a specimen trout simply by endless trolling is like searching for the proverbial needle in a haystack. Maps of the lough, showing the depths and shallows, are a useful starting point for research and preliminary planning, but the real advances in specimen trout hunting have come with the development of compact and accurate electronic depth recorders and fish-finders, especially when these are used in association with a monitoring of the water temperature at various depths, and the use of down-rigger systems to ensure that trolled baits and lures are fishing at the correct depths.

To apply modern technology to the catching of big fish in this way is decried by some sectors of the game fishing fraternity, who maintain it is unsporting and too much like fishmongering. This seems a little unfair. To apply an understanding of the habitat and feeding preferences of deep-living lough trout is no different in principle from the study of the insects which surface-feeding trout take. We have no scruples about changing from a floating to a sinking fly line if we feel that it is appropriate. To go further and fish your lures 30 or 40 ft deep (9–12 m) is only a matter of degree, and does not signify a difference in the ethical principles which guide our philosophy of game fishing. Such deepwater trolling may not be to every game fisher's personal taste, but that is quite different from condemning it as somehow undesirable or unsporting. And it is churlish to deny any fellow angler the reward and satisfaction of netting a specimen trout whose downfall he has achieved after a great deal of careful thought, planning and hard work.

The very large trout which are regularly taken from Lough Erne's depths each season are interesting fish in various ways, and they deserve closer study than they have received to date. They tend to be deep in the body and chunky in conformation, and are not generally similar to the lank, heavy-headed individuals which are generally referred to as *ferox* or 'cannibal' trout. These terms are too often used in a loose and unthinking way by many anglers. The *ferox* trout of, for example, Lough Melvin and certain other waters in Ireland and Britain are distinguished by a rather specific genetic make-up, and it is incorrect to assume that every very large brown trout is automatically a *ferox*. Likewise, it is simply absurd to say that one type of trout is a 'cannibal' when in fact every brown trout is avidly carnivorous by nature, and thinks nothing of devouring his smaller and weaker fellows at every stage of their development, from eggs to mature fish.

Lough Melvin

Next on our list of notable large loughs is Lough Melvin, which lies just to the south of Lower Lough Erne, and whose waters straddle the county boundaries of Fermanagh and Leitrim, and thus the border between Northern Ireland and the Irish Republic. The north-eastern corner of Lough Melvin lies within Northern Ireland, while the rest of the lough, most of its principal feeder streams, and its only outlet, the Bundrowes River, are all in the Republic.

Lough Melvin is interestingly placed in relation to two other much larger catchments, the very big Erne system to the north and the massive Shannon system, longest of all the river systems of the British Isles, which has its source in the Cuilcagh hills not far to the south-east. Melvin is a sizeable lough, almost 10 miles (16 km) long and about 2 miles (3.2 km) wide at its widest point. It is not especially noted for the great size of its fish, but Melvin is a real

Fly fishing for salmon and grilse in Rossinver Bay on Lough Melvin, where most of the Melvin–Bundrowes salmon gather from April onwards. (It is not generally advisable for either Rod to stand up in a boat when casting or playing a fish!)

paradise for any game fisher who enjoys the challenge of waters which provide plenty of lively sport with a fascinating diversity of fish types.

There are salmon, both early springers and lively summer grilse, and some of the most enjoyable lough fly fishing for salmon is to be found here. The Rossinver Fishery owns the fishing at the south-eastern end of the lough, and manages it with great skill and dedication. Much of the southern shore falls within the control of this fishery, and this stretch offers good prospects for salmon throughout the season. But the pride of the Rossinver Fishery is Rossinver Bay itself, where over ninety percent of all the salmon eventually congregate before running up the principal spawning streams. This is a carefully preserved fly-only fishery, but access can readily be arranged through the Honorary Secretary, Terence Bradley, who lives at Eden Point, Rossinver (Tel: 072-54029). Charges are moderate, and the 1989 cost of a full day's hire of a boat and an engine for two Rods was £20 sterling (IR £25).

Most Melvin salmon caught early in the season are taken by trolling, and the locally favoured lure is a green-and-yellow Devon minnow (invariably referred to as the 'yellow-belly'). Slightly lower water levels, warmer air and water temperatures and calmer weather conditions from late April and May onwards mean that fly fishing for salmon and early grilse becomes possible, and the quality of the grilse fishing in June and July is really excellent.

One of the best Melvin fly-caught salmon of the 1980s fell to the rod of Terence Bradley himself. This bright and solidly built fish of 16 lb (7 kg) was caught on a size 6 shrimp pattern in late April 1982. But fish in the range 8–10 lb (3.5–4.5 kg) represent a good average for spring salmon in Lough Melvin, with grilse in the range 4–6 lb (1.8–2.7 kg) from May onwards. Various shrimp patterns are proven killing flies on Melvin, as also are the Silver Doctor, the Jock Scott and the Thunder and Lightning. In warmer weather smaller flies, especially those with prominent yellow dressings, seem to be most successful. And many a Melvin salmon and grilse has fallen to a trout fly, especially the Green Peter and the various Gosling and Straddlebug variants.

Perhaps the greatest fascination about the fishing on Lough Melvin lies in its brown trout. Most surprisingly, this lough-and-river system does not receive any significant seatrout run. At first sight this seems surprising, for the map would seem to indicate that all the conditions are ideal – a good-sized glaciated lough set in hilly country, with direct access from the Atlantic up a few miles of river. But seatrout are virtually absent from this fishery, occurring only occasionally in the river, and then principally in the sea pool and one or two of the very lowest pools not far above the tide.

But what Melvin lacks in seatrout it makes up for in brown trout – probably four distinct species in all. For those of us who were brought up to believe that all brown trout are simply variants on the single species *Salmo trutta* this comes as a great surprise. Recent thinking about trout has tended to dismiss the Victorian anglers' and biologists' enthusiasm for identifying and naming endless different races, sub-species and species of brown trout. But the most modern research, involving close examination of the genetic make-up of different types of trout, has revealed that many waters do indeed maintain populations of brown trout which are quite distinct from one another genetically, in their distribution within the waters concerned, and in their feeding habits and other aspects of their behaviour.

Lough Melvin's brown trout have been the object of detailed study by fisheries biologists, and their clear conclusions are in general accord with what the anglers of mid-Victorian times believed. There are good brown trout of a type which conforms to the general appearance of typical lough trout in many waters in Ireland and Scotland. But there are also three more types of trout, *sonaghan, gillaroo* and *ferox*, each of these has been shown to be quite distinctive in its genetic make-up and appearance.

The *sonaghan* is a bright and lively little trout, rarely running to more than 1–1¾ lb (0.45–0.8 kg), and a good average would be just under one pound. Their basic coloration is olive shading to silver on the flanks, and the fish's body is deep in the flank and the head is small and neat. *Sonaghan* are heavily marked with large, dark spots, their tails are especially broad and square, and they have distinctively dark and rather elongated pectoral fins. This latter feature resulted in their designation by some Victorian fisheries experts as *Salmo nigrippinus*, in the days before enthusiastic attempts at rationalisation threw away all the innumerable local and variant names, deciding that every trout of every type ought simply to be known as *Salmo trutta*.

There is a good deal in the appearance and fighting abilities of these *sonaghan* to suggest some affinity with seatrout, and at one time it was suggested that these were indeed land-locked seatrout stemming from some ancient race. But since Melvin has a direct and easy link with the sea, the term 'land-locked' simply will not do, and the most recent scientific studies have concluded that *sonaghan* are actually a distinct species of brown trout, of very ancient origins, which are descended from primeval stock which colonised Lough Melvin in the immediate aftermath of the last Ice Age.

These wonderfully hard-fighting little trout are fish of the deeper water, and tend to shoal fairly close to the surface over the lough's very deepest parts. Their principal foods are plankton and insect larvae, and they can come readily to a team of flies fished in the classic lough style, with a shortish line cast from a boat drifting beam-on to the breeze. They fight with a verve and a powerful, tugging energy which is out of all proportion to their size and weight, and your first encounter with a *sonaghan* may give you a pleasant surprise by showing what a powerful fight can be put up by a smallish fish. It is perhaps natural for a fish which spends much of its time swimming and feeding over the deepest waters of Lough Melvin to react to the hook by a plunging, powerful dive into the depths. This is a characteristic of all *sonaghan*, whose first reaction on being hooked seems always to be a diving, tugging rush down deep into the water. In addition to their pleasant appearance and their sporting ways, *sonaghan* have the additional advantage of being very good indeed to eat.

The *gillaroo* is another of the lough's distinctive trout, but this is a fish of the rocky shallows and the sandy bays, and seems to have little of the *sonaghan*'s tendency to move out over the deeper water. *Gillaroo* is Irish for 'the red fellow', and the fish has a very distinctive colour, with a bright buttery-gold hue on its flanks and a liberal flecking with vivid vermilion and carmine spots, especially below the lateral line. Its flesh is a rich salmon pink, which is a reflection of its fondness for feeding among the shrimps and other crustaceans of the shallow waters around the fringes of the shore and the islands.

To digest this fare, the *gillaroo* has evolved a specially thickened and powerful stomach wall, which has often been compared to the gizzard of a fowl. Your best prospects for bringing one or two of these beautiful trout to the net is to fish close along by the shore, casting your flies right in among the very shallowest fringes. Do not be surprised if you find you are suddenly taken by something very large and powerful, for *gillaroo* run up to 4 and 5 lb (1.8–2.25 kg) and sometimes heavier still. But a more typical fish of 1–2 lb (0.7–0.9 kg) will give a very good account of itself, as handsome a brown trout as you could wish to see, and very good to eat.

Third and last of Melvin's distinctive races and species of trout is the *ferox*. Contrary to popular lore and generations of fishermen's tales, these are not always large trout, and a *ferox* does not develop with size or age from some vaguely unspecified strain of brown trout. A *ferox* is born a *ferox*, and within his genetic make-up are the basic codes and building blocks which mean he is destined to become a certain type of trout, heavy and large in the head, with few spottings or other markings on his otherwise uniformly dark greenish-olive back and flanks. He lives and feeds in the depths of the lough, and his naturally carnivorous tendencies develop early in life into a predilection for other small fish, especially small trout and char. Lough Melvin has an abundant char population, and comparisons with a number of other deep, glaciated loughs in Ireland and Scotland has shown there is a correlation between the presence of *ferox* trout and the availability of large numbers of char, often at considerable depths.

The fondness of the *ferox* for feeding deep on other smaller fish means he is seldom encountered by the fly fisher who uses traditional patterns and methods, and whose flies and tactics will readily take *gillaroo* from the rocky shallows and surface-feeding *sonaghan* over the deeper waters of the open parts of the lough. Most Melvin *ferox* have been caught by fishers trolling for salmon, and some have been very large indeed, rivalling the great brown trout from Lough Erne. Individual fish weighing up to 15 lb (7 kg) have been caught since the 1970s, and there are many earlier reports of even larger brown trout. The old term for these big Melvin *ferox* specimens was 'bracklough', apparently derived from the Irish for 'big trout', and some interesting accounts of them are to be found in two important books about Irish fishing, Sidney Berdoe Wilkinson's *Reminiscences of Sport in Ireland* (1931, repr. 1987) and Rev. Henry Newland's *The Erne; its Legends and its Fly Fishing* (1851).

The specimen trout potential of Lough Melvin has not been adequately explored or exploited, and there is undoubtedly lots of scope here for the dedicated deep-water specimen hunter who is prepared to undertake the planning and patient preparatory work, assisted by modern methods of depth and temperature monitoring, and then to go fishing at controlled speeds and depths. Some very big lough trout await such an enthusiast, and there are also char aplenty to be taken on flies and small spinner lures fished on down-rigger tackle and trolled slowly at depths of up to 60 ft (18 m) or more.

The Shannon System

Lough Allen

It is difficult to tear oneself away from Lough Melvin, with its unique trout, its excellent grilse and salmon, and its scenically delightful setting in the green hills of the Fermanagh-Leitrim countryside, with the limestone escarpments of Sligo and Ben Bulben soaring away to the south-west. This is a very special fishery, tucked away but not forgotten between those two great catchments of Erne and Shannon which flank it to north and south.

As your eye drifts southwards over a relief map of Ireland the next sizeable loughs you will probably see are those which belong to the great Shannon system itself. First and most northerly of these is Lough Allen, an elongated inverted triangle shape nestling in the Leitrim hills to the north of Carrick-on-Shannon. Not surprisingly, Lough Allen lies within the Shannon Fisheries Region, the largest Regional Fisheries Division in the Republic of Ireland, which comprises not only the whole of the Shannon catchment area, including the great 240-mile (384 km) river itself, but also important fishing areas in parts of counties Clare and Kerry. There is within this very large and varied region an enormous variety of game-fishing waters, and perhaps the most important characteristic of Lough Allen is its sheer size and the wildness of its setting, and of the weather conditions which can prevail there. Like any large lough, Allen is no place to be unless you have a good boat in sound condition, a reliable engine and someone aboard who is competent to handle a boat under difficult conditions. Everyone who knows Lough Allen is only too well aware of what a squally, windswept place it can be, so take extra care with your equipment and planning before you set out for a day's fishing.

Lough Allen can be fished from a number of centres, and the best places at which to base yourself are the villages of Drumkeeran, close to the lough's north-western corner, and Dowra, which lies a mile or two upstream on the river Shannon to the north of the lough. At the southern end of Lough Allen, and near to some of the best trout fishing areas, is the town of Drumshanbo. This is probably also the best centre in which to make arrangements to hire a boat and an outboard motor, or to arrange for the assistance of a boatman.

As a game fishery Lough Allen has been unfairly neglected for too long. This is primarily because it has a formidable reputation as a coarse fishery, producing a wide variety of species, including some excellent bream and roach, and some very large pike. The latter have a magnetic attraction for specimen pike hunters, including an increasing number of visitors from Europe, especially Germany. Pike and trout may be an uncomfortable combination on many smaller waters, but there is plenty of room for both in the wide expanses of Lough Allen, which in addition to its coarse fishing has some first-class brown trout. This lough, like so many in Ireland, follows a fairly typical and predictable pattern, with good wet-fly fishing from the start of the season on

Neat of head and deep of flank—two well conditioned brown trout taken on a Murrough pattern at sedge time in early August.

1 March, when Duckfly and other traditional dark patterns work well. The mayfly hatch on Lough Allen is not particularly spectacular, but it is certainly useful, and every year some excellent specimens are taken, including fish which would never dream of coming to feed on insects close to the surface at any other time, preferring the richer fare of small fish and various invertebrates in the depths of the lough.

By general agreement Lough Allen really comes into its own as a trout fishery towards the end of the season, especially in August and September. Sedge patterns can do deadly execution from late July onwards, and very good fish can be taken using dapping tactics, the local favourites being the natural daddy-longlegs and grasshoppers, although good results have also been achieved with suitable artificials and imitations.

The visitor to Lough Allen should be aware of the fact that this great natural stillwater is used as a public water supply, and there are pumping stations and sluice gates which regulate the flow of water from the lough. This inevitably has important implication for the movements and behaviour of the fish, and the best natural feeding areas (and therefore the largest numbers of good trout) tend to be towards the narrow southern end of the lough. Here there is a prominent landmark in the form of O'Reilly's Island, which is about just above the southern tip of the lough. There are some excellent and scenically attractive drifts to be enjoyed at this part of Lough Arrow, at which point you are invariably over fairly shallow water where trout are often free-rising, and sport can be excellent.

Lough Ree

Lough Ree is the second of the three large loughs on the Shannon system, a straggling, elongated lough which stretches for over 15 miles (24 km) as the crow flies, from the village of Lanesborough at the northern end to the town of Athlone at the far south of the lough. A glance at a detailed map will show just how convoluted and deeply indented the shore of Lough Ree is. This means there are innumerable bays, points and islands, many of which provide the kind of shallows which brown trout love, and over which productive drifts can be made.

The visiting fisher will find access to the lough is easy, with various boat slipways and piers around the shore, and the best plan is probably to make a leisurely exploration of the circumference of the lough by car, investigating the various access points, and then deciding where to set out from.

Like Lough Allen, its large neighbour to the north, Lough Ree holds a variety of fresh-water species, including a great many varieties of coarse fish, many of which are of internationally respected specimen quality. But brown trout happily co-exist with pike, bream and all the others, and the excellence of the coarse fishing still tends to mean that Lough Ree is unfairly neglected as regards its game-fishing potential. In fact, the lough holds a very large stock of excellent trout, and first-class sport can be had over almost any area of the lough where you choose to fish. However, one of the characteristics of the Lough Ree trout is their general tendency to be reluctant to feed close to the surface, something they share with the great trout of Lough Neagh in Northern Ireland. Both loughs have been known for centuries to hold very large numbers of brown trout, with some quite exceptionally large individual fish recorded. So numerous are the trout in both loughs that there used to be a great deal of commercial netting, which provided a very good living for a number of local families.

This tendency of the Lough Ree trout to feed well down below the surface can mean that a day's wet-fly fishing in traditional lough style can be rather disappointing, but that is more a reflection on those who stick doggedly to short-line, lough-style tactics, rather than modifying their methods and going deeper in search of fish. Perhaps more than any other Irish lough, Ree has great potential for those who know how to fish effectively with deep sinking lines and sunken lures. This style of fishing, so familiar to many regulars on the great reservoirs of England, is still little practised by Irish fly fishers, and Lough Ree is one very good reason for the English visitor not to leave his fast-sinking lines and deep-fishing lures behind when he comes to Ireland on a game-fishing holiday.

A notable exception to the general bottom-feeding tendencies of the Lough Ree trout occurs at mayfly time. Here, as on every Irish water which enjoys a really good hatch of mayfly, trout which otherwise rarely come to the surface cannot resist the temptation to come up and join in the brief but rich annual feast. Mayfly time on Lough Ree can begin as early as 15 or 16 May in a mild, warm season, and this makes it one of the very earliest mayfly loughs anywhere in Ireland. Mayfly time is also one of the few periods of the year when Lough Ree attracts any significant number of game fishers, local or otherwise. At other times you may almost feel you have this large and attractive fishery all to yourself.

The best hatches of mayfly and the best falls of spent gnat occur in the shallows, along the shores and around the various bays and islets. This in turn lures the trout in from the depths of the lough, to cruise and feed eagerly in relatively shallow water. To drift and fish effectively over shallow water means careful boat handling, and the visitor who is unfamiliar with the ways of the lough may find his fishing more effective, and certainly more relaxed and enjoyable, if he has the help of a good local boatman. Boats are available for hire at various points around the lough, and two of the best places to begin your enquiries are at the Anchor Hotel at Lanesborough, at the northern end of the lough, and also in the town of Athlone, which is well supplied with fishing-tackle shops and enthusiastic local fishermen. Finding a boat, and possibly securing the services of a knowledgeable local boatman, should present few problems.

Lough Ree, like so many fisheries, has its own distinctive character and its own local qualities and quirks. One of the most interesting of these is the widely held belief that Lough Ree trout at mayfly time require greater restraint in 'tightening' than on any other lough. Interminable and numerous are the theories about how you should react when a large trout comes up to take your mayfly, be it a dapped natural insect or some form of artificial. Some enthusiasts have their favourite little rhyme or incantation to recite before lifting the rod and tightening into the fish, while others try to estimate the time lag in terms of seconds – all of which is very difficult to do in a controlled and measured way when you have just had the thrill of seeing a large lough trout rise and roll over your fly! For some reason Lough Ree has acquired the reputation of having trout which require the greatest patience and self-restraint, and mayfly enthusiasts will tell you with the utmost conviction that you may tighten on a trout in Lough Erne or on Lough Derg after just two or three seconds, but a Lough Ree trout requires at least six or seven seconds. It must be an exceptionally self-possessed and cool-headed fisherman who can apply such precise calculations to his reactions where big, wild trout are concerned!

Lough Derg

The third and most southerly lough on the Shannon system is Lough Derg, a large and delightful fishery whose physical size is exceeded only by the magnitude of its worldwide reputation as a quite outstanding trout fishery, most especially at mayfly time. Like all the big loughs on the Shannon system, Lough Derg is really a generous widening out of the river's course. The profile of the lough is long and sinuous, stretching from the town of Portumna at the northern end to Killaloe at the southernmost end, with the Slieve Bernagh mountains to the west and the Arra hills to the east. Between them Lough

Derg comes to a point and assumes the character of a river once again for the remainder of its course south-westwards past Limerick and into the long and winding estuary.

Like Loughs Allen and Ree, Derg has a wonderfully rich and varied population of fish, including brown trout, numerous species of coarse fish, and a very sizeable population of pollan (which, as we have seen, are also a characteristic of Lough Neagh in central Ulster). There is also the occasional salmon, although the once-famous Shannon salmon fishery, which used to produce some of Europe's most splendid runs of really massive fish, was to all intents and purposes destroyed in the 1940s by the establishment of a hydro-electric scheme on the lower reaches of the river at Ardnacrusha. A salmon anywhere on the Shannon or in Lough Derg is indeed a bonus nowadays.

Unfortunately, the tragic deterioration of the Shannon as a salmon fishery has some parallels in the quality of its trout fishing. A century ago, or even fifty years ago, it was certainly a candidate for a place in the top ten brown trout stillwater fisheries anywhere in western Europe. Latterly, and especially since the 1970s, the quality of the lough and thus of the trout fishing has deteriorated considerably, the result of the same influences which have wrought such great changes on the famous Midland loughs like Sheelin, Owel and Ennell. Enrichment of the water by a combination of nitrogenous run-off, silage seepage, slurry escapes and the washing of fertilisers off the rich farmland which surrounds this catchment have increased the alkalinity of Lough Derg, causing its once-clear waters to become murky with algal bloom. This can be particularly acute from late spring onwards, especially if there has been a prolonged period of warm weather with light winds. The effects of this type of undesirable enrichment do not need to be repeated here, but the situation up to the late 1980s was still not hopeless by any means. The mayfly hatch, and the emergence of many other varieties of insects important to the trout and the trout fisher, especially chironomids, sedges and lake olives has dropped off somewhat, but you may find really sizeable and impressive hatches in certain places and at certain times, with superb sport to match.

Proverbially and traditionally, Lough Derg has the earliest mayfly hatch in Ireland. Foolish though it is to be too precise or dogmatic about dates, for some reason 10 May has become the magic date in the minds of those who regularly make the mayfly pilgrimage to Lough Derg. In fact, as on every mayfly water, the actual date depends from year to year on the prevailing weather conditions. A late, cold spring may delay the hatch by up to a week or more, while there have been occasions when unusually good weather in April has actually precipitated good hatches of mayfly almost a fortnight before the typical date, as early as the last day or two of April.

Lough Derg is such a large water, so sinuous and convoluted in its bays and points, with such an abundance of islands large and small, and very large areas of relatively shallow water, that the visiting fisherman may be at a total loss as to where to start. There are some useful general guidelines, however, and in very broad terms it is true to say that the northern and north-eastern parts of the lough usually provide the poorest sport for the fly fisherman, not only at

The author and friend, afloat and thoughtful on Lough Derg. Ireland's large loughs offer a wide choice of good drifts, and a rolling wave means excellent fly presentation.

mayfly time but throughout the season. To make such a statement is to invite a chorus of derision and disapproval from those who have had good sport in such places, or who have managed to locate certain spots where an excellent drift or two can usually be relied upon. But this general opinion about the north and north-east of Lough Derg is shared by a great many fly fishermen who know the lough well, and for whom the southern half, particularly the waters from Goat Island southwards, represent the best fishing on the lough.

There is excellent access to the lough, as any reasonably detailed map of the area will show. Dromineer Bay is perhaps the most obvious of these, with excellent car parking and slipway facilities close to Dromineer village. Further south there are ideal access points, piers and jetties at Garrykennedy, near Killaloe and, round on the western side of the lough, at Scarriff Bay and further along at Mount Shannon. All of these starting points enable you to set out in your boat and get onto excellent fishing water very quickly.

There is good sport to be had early in the season if you can locate one of Lough Derg's good localised hatches of buzzers and other early season insects, but it is fairly safe to assume that most visitors to Lough Derg will choose their time carefully to coincide with the annual mayfly season. Then, depending on the conditions and your personal preferences – and on what the trout appear to be preferring! – you may choose to fish with a three-fly cast comprising a Mayfly nymph pattern on the point, perhaps an Invicta or a Golden Olive on the dropper, and a Gosling or Straddlebug pattern fished as a bob fly. For this last pattern, your best bet of all may be a really bushily dressed version of the Grey Wulff. This fly pattern would have been totally unknown to earlier generations of mayfly fishermen, on Lough Derg or anywhere else. However, such has been its great success as a mayfly imitation and as a generous lough trout 'attractor pattern' that many enthusiasts place great reliance on it, both at mayfly time and throughout the season on many large loughs.

Dapping the natural insect is, not surprisingly, as effective as it is traditional, and an early morning outing along the shoreline should enable you to fill your bait box with a gross or more of good mayflies, picked up from the undersides of the leaves. Various artificial dapping patterns can also be highly successful, and at the height of the mayfly season on Lough Derg you may see a wide variety of techniques and equipment being used, ranging from wet-fly fishing with a bushy bob fly to dapping with lough rods varying in length from the typical 10–11 ft (305–335 cm) wet-fly boat-fishing rods up to the purpose-built telescopic dapping rods which can be extended to as much as 15 or 17 ft (455–520 cm).

Mayfly time on any lough is always exciting, but the cream of Lough Derg sport is probably to be had on relatively calm evenings when there has been a good fall of spent gnat. This is when you can enjoy the special excitement of taking to the water in the long gloaming of an evening in late May, watching carefully for big trout cruising and feeding among the dead and dying female mayflies on the water, and carefully casting your imitative pattern so as to land neatly ahead of one of these big specimens. This is a style of fishing which calls for careful observation, deft and accurate casting, slow and silent manoeuvring of the boat so as not to disturb feeding fish, and, if at all possible, the ability to position yourself so as to be facing into the westerly, setting sun. When conditions at dusk are calm and silent, as they should be for effective spent gnat fishing, the last thing you want is for you and your boat to be silhouetted against the setting sun, which will quickly betray your presence to these big trout, with their uncanny instincts for self-preservation. To cast up-sun is to give yourself a considerable advantage, and may make all the difference between an empty creel and a memorably heavy one.

Despite the pre-eminence of the mayfly period on Lough Derg, we must not overlook the excellent sport which this lough affords towards the end of the season, especially in September when the sedge hatches can be very productive. The really big, handsome Lough Derg trout which were tempted up to feed near the surface in May can once again be seen cruising and feeding well above their normal depth, and some really excellent baskets of big fish are taken when Lough Derg trout are 'on the sedge'. It is interesting to note that the very large sedge patterns which produce such good results elsewhere are not generally favoured by the Lough Derg experts. Instead of large Murroughs, Green Peters and various muddler-type dressings, you are much more likely to see small hackled patterns which would seem to be more at home on small rivers and chalk streams rather than on the vastness of a great Irish lough. But 'fine and small' seems to be the watchword on Lough Derg at sedge time, and some of the results achieved by local experts are abundant proof of this.

Lough Arrow

Our journey down the Shannon system, lough by lough, has taken us quite far into the south-west of Ireland, but to continue our outline survey of Ireland's largest and most important game-fishing loughs we must return to that map which has been our general guide, and double back on our tracks a little. Let's look northwards, and let's also keep our thoughts on those mayflies upon which so much of Lough Derg's reputation has been built. For among the hills of County Sligo lies another wonderful mayfly lough, Lough Arrow.

Cuckoos and blackbirds always remind me of Lough Arrow. Not that either bird is commoner there than in many other parts of Ireland. But when you are fishing from a boat on Arrow, enfolded by that gentle countryside where the green pastures and the foliage of the trees skirt the water's edge, the calls of the blackbird and the cuckoo seem to make up a more emphatic *continuo* than on any other Irish lough. Perhaps it is some trick of the local acoustics. At dawn and dusk the blackbirds are busy among the shrubby trees and along the overgrown hedgerows, their 'pink' and 'chip' piercing the half-light as you launch out from the bay or drift the shores. The dawn and dusk choruses on Lough Arrow have an enthusiastic melody and volume which gives buoyancy to your spirits at the beginning and end of every spring fishing day. It is worth remembering how many of the ancient myths and poems of Gaelic Ireland contain references to the blackbird, dapper in his livery of sable feathers and with a stream of ringing notes pouring from the startling buttery gold of his bill. On Arrow and throughout Ireland, from every hedgerow and thicket, the song of the cock blackbird comes to our ears as an expression of a living link in the continuum of the Irish countryside.

The cuckoo is at its loudest and most evident, audible if not always visible, at mayfly time on Lough Arrow. It is unthinkable that a May day's fishing on Arrow should go by without your hearing the cuckoo's repeated, sometimes maddeningly insistent disyllables, enhanced with that special quality of tonal clarity which you always seem to find when sounds carry across open water.

Lough Arrow opens for the start of the brown trout season on 1 March, and fishing continues until 30 September. In this respect, and in common with its near neighbour 8 miles (13 km) away to the north, Lough Gill, its season is slightly shorter than the statutory dates laid down for the North-Western Fisheries Region, where the trout season generally begins on 15 February. But on Arrow it is 1 March, and has been for as long as anyone can remember.

The early season on Lough Arrow can be a time of mixed fortunes and pleasures for the fly fisher. The enthusiasm of the Rod who takes to the water eager to begin a new season's fishing without delay can sometimes be matched by an equal enthusiasm on the part of the trout to take his flies. In early March they are likely to be less discriminating than at later times in the year, rising hungrily to a team of traditional and sober-hued wet flies fished 'over the front' on a short line, as you drift along the shores and through the bays. It is not unusual for wild brown trout to feed with incautious zest in the hungry weeks of early spring, eager to make up the weight and energies expended during spawning and in the cold, dark months which follow. It can flatter your fishing, this March near-madness, when the lough can seem full of trout each ready to seize your fly. It can be an ideal time to take a beginner fishing, too, for there is nothing like a day of activity with a reasonably frequent succession of rises to encourage a newcomer to fly fishing for trout.

But there are also disadvantages. Early March is seldom a time of kindly weather, the air temperature may still have a numbing wintriness, and you will do well to have even a short day's fishing without getting a blustery buffeting by the wind, or having to endure sluicings of heavy rain or even hail.

Such conditions are not conducive to the emergence of fly life, and the trout know this too. Lough Arrow is an astonishingly rich water, even by the high standards of Irish limestone loughs, and there is abundant invertebrate feeding for the trout among the nymphs and larvae along the bottom. Why should they move and try to feed near the surface, when such a feast awaits them at deeper levels? On this rich diet they recover weight and condition as rapidly as any trout after spawning, but there can still be a lacklustre lankness to a Lough Arrow trout in early March if it rises and takes your fly from below the surface film.

It is more certain and more logical to fish your flies slow and deep in the early days of the season, in the style which is familiar to the British stillwater fly fisher but which is still an unfamiliar novelty to most Irish fishers. A sinking line will take your fly or nymph down to the feeding level of the fish, and a leaded nymph on a longish leader fished on a floating line may achieve much the same effect. But your boating tactics must be modified to take account of this. There is no point in trying to fish deep and slow when your boat is drifting merrily along with a fresh March breeze propelling it. Even a drogue may not slow you up to the snail's pace at which your sunken line and nymph will work best. Against all the normal practices of boat fishing on Irish loughs, you may do best to anchor and fish from a fixed position, your boat temporarily serving as a tethered casting platform rather than as a bobbing, drifting conveyance.

It seems only sensible to be careful and selective in your taking of these early trout. They are not especially difficult to catch, especially if you fish deep, and a deeply sunk line with a suspender-type nymph working buoyantly just above the lough floor can be deadly. But a proportion of what you catch will either be undersized (there is a 12-in/30 cm minimum size limit on Arrow) or ill-conditioned, and should be returned. A pattern dressed on a barbless hook, or a standard hook with the barb flattened, makes it easy to release and return selected fish. Among the traditional fly fishing fraternity, in Ireland and everywhere else, the thought of using a fly dressed on a barbless hook seems only a degree less ridiculous than fishing with a line but no fly. Only the experience of hooking and holding fish – often big, active fish, too – on barbless hooks demonstrates how little we really depend on the holding properties of

The late Alex Perceval with a Lough Arrow trout, massive of head and splendidly marked, but lank and going back in condition.

the barb, and how much of our success is due to maintaining adequate tension and steady contact with the fish as we play it.

For easy access to Lough Arrow and its various bays, piers and boat moorings the visitor will do well to base himself in Ballinafad, which lies right at the southern end of the lough, or at nearby Boyle, Ballyfarnan or Ballymote. All are within easy driving distance, all have excellent accommodation in every degree from a comfortable bed-and-breakfast arrangement in a private house, country farmhouse guest-houses, a sprinkling of small hotels and a few larger ones. There is also the attractive option of booking your room in one of the great private houses of counties Sligo and Leitrim, handsome and sometimes massive mansions, where paying guests can enjoy the uniquely elegant and relaxed ambience of Irish country houses.

Lough Arrow is a real delight for the fly fisher who enjoys fishing from a boat. There are relatively few serious hazards compared with the rocky shallows which await the unwary or the inexperienced on many western loughs, and the long shores of Lough Arrow, with their gently sweeping bays and inlets, provide an almost inexhaustible succession of drifts for the boat fisher to try. There are a number of prominent islands, all of which help to increase Arrow's total area of trout-rich shallows, as does the long peninsula of Annaghloy Point which reaches southwards across the lough towards Drum-doe.

For much of the early part of the season Lough Arrow is quiet and almost deserted, and the start of the mayfly hatch generally signals the beginnings of real activity among local fishers and visitors from more distant parts. Arrow's mayfly hatch comes comparatively early, around 18 May in a typical year, and then you will find enthusiasts out on the lough at almost all times of the day and night. In late May there can be some superb spent gnat fishing in the long dusks, and this phase of the mayfly season also coincides with some superb (if rather localised) evening hatches of big sedges. In this western setting the dusk lingers long and it is perfectly possible to fish right through the night. As the light fails your eyes gradually become attuned to the semi-darkness, and you begin to fish as much by sound as by sight. The biggest and most challenging of Arrow's lovely trout are on the move on these velvet-soft nights as midsummer approaches, and some of the lough's most knowledgeable and successful fly fishers seem to prefer to turn night into day, concentrating on the dry-fly fishing from early evening onwards, and only setting out during the day if there is a sizeable hatch of fly in progress and a good rise of trout taking place in response to it.

But there is more to Arrow than its mayfly season, glorious though that can be, and the late season fishing can be excellent, especially towards the southern end of the lough and all across from Ballinafad Bay at the south-west corner to Andersna Bay at the south-east end. Sedge patterns and the ever-dependable Green Peter can produce fine baskets of excellent trout right up to the close of the season on 30 September.

Lough Conn

Westwards from Lough Arrow and in the centre of north Connaught lies Lough Conn. This lough and its immediately adjacent neighbour to the south, Lough Cullin, are linked to the exciting and important salmon and seatrout fishery of the river Moy, and a good proportion of the salmon which move up the Moy eventually make a westward turn and pass through the waters of Lough Cullin and thence through the connecting stream of Pontoon and into the wide and wild waters of Lough Conn.

Conn is a sizeable and very important game fishery, arguably one of the most popular and consistently productive anywhere in Ireland. (A great many of us who know and love the lough were rubbing our eyes with downright disbelief when, in early 1989, an eminent English-based sporting magazine – which ought to have known better – published an article which maintained that Conn was declining as a fishery, and becoming dour and unproductive. Tell that to the Conn regulars who annually take big baskets of fine trout, either on quiet fishing days or in the course of big national and international competitions!)

Lough Conn's orientation is approximately north-to-south, and there is some 9 miles (14.5 km) of water from its northern end to its southern extremity at Pontoon, and in width it varies from 2 to almost 4 miles (3.2–6.5 km) across. It is abundantly populated with salmonids of various species, including a very large number of char, which have been studied in a certain amount of detail by fisheries experts, but which rarely figure in the fly fisherman's basket because of the species' characteristic habit of living and feeding at depths far below those at which we normally fish. However, the char enthusiast who is prepared to use the appropriate tackle and tactics may make good baskets of char. In Lough Conn, and indeed on every Irish water where they are present in good numbers, char remain a very underrated and largely unknown game species.

However, although Lough Conn produces quite a large number of salmon and offers wonderful potential for the char enthusiast, its chief attraction has always been its brown trout. Fly fishermen, especially those who particularly favour the traditional style of lough fishing which has been such a familiar part of the angling scene in Ireland and Scotland for many generations. Few other loughs anywhere in Ireland or Britain offer such consistently reliable and exciting sport to those whose idea of a pleasant day's fly fishing is to swing their boat beam-on to the breeze and fish 'over the front' with a short line and at a cast of three wet-fly patterns.

This part of Ireland lies within the North-Western Regional Fisheries Board area of the Irish Republic, and Lough Conn comes under the Board's jurisdiction. However, there has been no need for direct intervention to regulate or augment trout numbers here, because Lough Conn has a splendidly prolific brown trout population, the equal of any Irish lough. Spawning is good, food is adequate for good growth, and these conditions, combined with the tendency of the trout to rise freely and to provide consistent and dependable sport throughout the season, means that Lough Conn has become a favourite with many individual anglers, both local and from further afield. The liveliness of its sport and the consistently good baskets of fish which it yields have also made it popular with organisers of fly-fishing competitions.

Lough Conn is readily accessible from most parts of Ireland by the much-improved road network which has been upgraded since the 1970s, and it is rare indeed to find the lough in a dour or unproductive state. The principal bases for fishing Lough Conn are the sizeable market towns of Ballina, which is a short drive away from the northern end of the lough, and Crossmolina, which is very close to the northern extremity of the lough. At this northern end there is good access at Gortnorabbey, while along the eastern shore one of the best known spots is Cloghans Bay. The main L134 trunk road passes over the bridges which separate Lough Conn and Lough Cullin at the southern end of Conn, and Pontoon is another favourite setting-out place for fisherman. The choice is simple – head north into the wide waters of Lough Conn, or south into the more intimate surroundings of Lough Cullin. Pontoon also has one of Ireland's best-known anglers' meeting places, at the Pontoon Bridge Hotel (Tel: 094-56120, which not only provides comfortable and convenient accommodation but can arrange boats, engines and local boatmen, to assist the visiting game fisher. Its situation at the mid-point between Lough Conn and Lough Cullin also makes it a natural rendezvous for anglers on both loughs, and the trunk road which passes the front door carries a constant stream of game fishers travelling to and fro to many of Ireland's finest western and north-western waters. It is probably true to say that more fishing gossip and hot news from Irish fisheries has been exchanged in the bar and the car park of the Pontoon Bridge Hotel than at any other spot in the country!

Lough Conn begins to come to life in the latter half of March when the salmon enthusiasts are out and trolling with determined dedication, often in blustery and wintry weather, for the earliest of the spring-run fish. Most salmon on Conn are caught by trolling towards the northern end of the lough, and the early part of the season is always the most productive, with salmon catches falling off noticeably from early July in most years. In the 1980s the annual salmon catch by trolling and fly fishing was estimated at around 600 fish, although the true total may have been substantially higher than this. And if we add in a goodly number as the poachers' ill-gotten portion, the final total is impressive indeed.

The wild and often blustery environment of Lough Conn is not conducive to early-season fly fishing for trout, which is permissible from March onwards but does not really get going in earnest until late April. At this stage the dependable Buzzer and Duckfly patterns account for quite a number of fish, but the activity of the trout and the trout fishers increases noticeably towards the end of May, when the first of the mayfly begin to appear. Like many exposed western loughs, the term 'mayfly' can be something of a misnomer on Lough Conn, for in a normal year the hatches of insects will not be evident until the final days of the month, and the first half of June often provides the bulk of the mayfly sport.

Lough Conn provides such consistently good brown trout fishing through-out the season that mayfly time is not an especially busy time of year on this lough, compared to the massive influxes of anglers which can take place elsewhere on other loughs. It is also interesting to note that dapping is not often practised, either with the natural insects or with artificials, and one of the most popular and effective approaches to Conn in mayfly time is to fish a three-fly cast comprising a Mayfly Nymph of some description on the point, a traditional wet-fly pattern on the dropper, and a large and buoyant pattern, perhaps with an element of deer hair in the dressing, on the bob. This formula has proved its worth over many seasons, and the large and prominent bob fly often succeeds in attracting the attention of feeding trout, which may then either slash vigorously at the top fly as it is tripped over the waves, or, perhaps more often, they may turn and take the dropper or the point flies.

All the classic wet-fly lough patterns have proved their worth on Conn, and knowledgeable local enthusiasts will rarely drop below a size 10 in fly size, or monofilament of less than 8 lb (3.5 kg) test. This may seem like large and heavy tackle on a lough where brown trout generally average around 1–1¾ lb (0.45–0.8 kg), but the vigorous, smashing take of a Conn trout can be out of all proportion to the actual weight of the fish, and there is always that pleasant but daunting prospect of encountering a salmon or a grilse, many of which are taken by trout fishermen each season.

Lough Conn falls into two natural sectors, divided by the narrowing of its waters between the eastern extremity of the Errew peninsula and the Sandy Bay and Brackwansha areas on the opposite shore, barely ½ mile (0.8 km) across the lough. The waters to the south of this have a gentle and intimate charm, although the lough is still a wide and spacious place. But the northern end of Lough Conn, from Errew Point up to Longford Bay, is especially wild and beautiful. There are excellent drifts off Enniscoe and Gortnorabbey on the western shore, and from the inflow of the Deel River down the eastern shore past Annagh Island to Cloghans. But the shoreline drifts should not be the only northern parts you try, for there is some excellent fishing over the various rocky shallows which lie in a long ridge down the middle of the lough. These can be dangerous, especially in blustery weather, and care should be taken. But most of the principal hazards – and also the best drifts – are indicated by the various iron stanchions which stick up out of the water at these shallow, rocky spots. Known locally as 'the pins', these strategically placed iron marker posts have helped many a boat to avoid disaster and, more positively, to make good baskets of fine trout.

The Corrib System

Lough Carra

There is good sport and ample scope for the visitor to spend an entire fishing holiday on Lough Conn, but let us return to our map and allow our attention to wander in the direction of some more excellent game-fishing waters which lie not far away to the south of Lough Conn. These are the trio of loughs – Lough Carra, Lough Mask and Lough Corrib – which, together with the short Galway River which forms their combined outflow into the waters of Galway Bay, comprise what is probably the largest and most varied game-fishing area anywhere in Ireland. Enthusiasts for other fisheries may question this judgement, but Corrib and its neighbours can certainly hold their own with any other truly wild game-fishing area in Europe.

Lough Carra is decidedly the baby of the trio, comprising a mere 4000 acres (1620 hectares). But that figure disguises what a good local map reveals, which is that Lough Carra is a wonderfully intricate and varied stillwater fishery which straggles in an elongated loop down from its northernmost extremity near the village of Castleburke for a distance of over 5 miles (8 km) with a prominent eastern spur which reaches almost as far north again. Carra's islands, points, bays and inlets are innumerable, and the true enthusiast for classic fly fishing for brown trout from a boat will find everything his heart could desire on this splendid lough. Historically, Carra has tended to be overshadowed by its very much larger neighbours to the south, Loughs Mask and Corrib. But more recently, however, its individualistic charms and wonderful potential as a fly-fishing water for wild brown trout have been increasingly recognised, and many more fly fishermen from Ireland and further afield now make it their regular destination throughout the season.

Mayfly time, however, is the peak period for fishing on Carra, for the hatches of these magical insects are prolific, predictable and unusually early here. Despite its western situation and its apparently exposed position, good hatches of mayfly are often apparent from the last week of April onwards, which is considerably earlier than the general tendency on Lough Derg, far to the south, which is often credited with being Ireland's very earliest mayfly lough. (In fact, and particularly in fairness to the visiting fly fisher who may have to make detailed and elaborate arrangements many months in advance, it should be said that the first emergence of mayfly hatches on all Irish waters can vary considerably, with the weather playing a critical part in the annual pattern of mayfly emergence.)

Pre-eminently among western loughs, Lough Carra is truly a lough for all seasons. This is chiefly because of its wonderfully rich insect life, the product of local rock and subsoil which is considerably more alkaline than most western areas. To a naturally high pH must be added the further advantage of great natural clarity in the water, and the fact that the lough is remarkably shallow throughout. This allows excellent light penetration, and the consequence is that Lough Carra has excellent natural feeding and therefore holds a good number of fine brown trout, with a high average weight. There is an ever-present possibility of the fly fisherman raising and hooking something really memorable, for fish of 5–6 lb (2.25–2.7 kg) are not unusual here, and exceptional specimen trout of 16–17 lb (7–7.5 kg) have been taken on the fly, which is almost unheard of on other waters, however far you may delve back into history and local lore.

The mayfly hatch is both prolific and prolonged on many Irish waters, especially where limestone is the underlying rock. Along the shore mature insects cling to the undersides of leaves for shelter.

Good fly fishing with the various Duckfly patterns is to be had on Carra from mid-March onwards, which is about a month earlier than on Lough Conn to the north, unless the weather there is unusually kindly in early spring; and there is a sizeable hatch of olives throughout April and early May. The Black Pennell and the Black & Peacock Spider both do well here early in the season, as also does the Greenwell's Glory, which is not only a celebrated wet-fly pattern on every water in every fly-fishing country in the world, but has a proven reputation here in this corner of County Mayo.

At mayfly time you may take your pick of tactics, including the use of wet-fly and emergent patterns, dapping and spent-gnat style as your choice and the conditions dictate. But there is no denying that the greatest attraction Lough Carra has to offer the true fly-fishing enthusiast is the wonderfully challenging dry-fly fishing which accompanies a good fall of spent gnat mayfly. Successful spent-gnat fishing always presupposes careful reconnaissance, some stealthy manoeuvring in the boat, and the ability to cast your fly with an accuracy and delicacy not normally essential for successful fly fishing on a large lough. But on Lough Carra you may encounter warm and calm conditions throughout the long and lingering western dusk which call for all the care, caution and stealthy subterfuge you can muster, to place a well-chosen dry fly delicately in the path of an individual cruising, feeding fish. If all goes well your reward may be a trout of a size, weight and conformation which will take your breath away.

If mayfly time gives Carra a special appeal and challenge, you must not neglect its excellent sport at other times of the year. The hatches of olives continue to give reliable sport until well into late spring, and these are followed by abundant hatches of the smaller species of sedges during summer and early autumn. Good results can always be expected from the Green Drake and the Green Peter in due season, and the Watson's Fancy and the Invicta have also proved their worth in the latter part of the season. It is worth bearing in mind that the successful flies on Carra are often rather smaller and more fully dressed than on other loughs, and where a size 10 might be wonderfully productive on Conn or Arrow, the trout of Lough Carra might have a preference for sizes 12 and even as small as size 14, and rather more fully dressed than usual for Irish lough fishing.

Late August and September is also a good period at which to expect a good response to a dapped daddy-longlegs, and there will be excellent sport right up to the end of the season, which closes here and on loughs Arrow, Corrib and Mask on 30 September.

Lough Mask

The little village of Partry lies barely a mile (1.6 km) from the waters of Lough Carra to the north and the much larger and wilder waters of Lough Mask to the south-west. Mask dwarfs its little neighbour, being approximately five times its size at around 20,000 acres (8100 hectares), an elongated, triangular

Massive brown trout are annually encountered in many Irish loughs, especially when lures are trolled deep and slow over carefully identified areas.

shaped lough some 10 miles (16 km) long and about 4 miles (6.5 km) wide at its broadest point. On Lough Mask you will find yourself faced with a vast and generous expanse of water by comparison with the intimacy of Lough Carra, and almost every inch of its shoreline affords pleasant and productive drifts on which you can fish for superb wild brown trout using traditional lough-fishing tactics.

Surveys during the 1980s showed that the average size of Lough Mask fish taken on the fly was just over 1 lb (0.45 kg), but a good representative basket of trout from Lough Mask is sure to contain one or two fish of 2 lb (0.9 kg) and over, and fish of 4–5 lb (1.8–2.25 kg) are taken on fly with some regularity. Inevitably, however, the bigger fish tend to have to live and feed at some depth to find adequate food to satisfy their much greater energy requirements, and the depths of Lough Mask, especially at its northern end, to the north of Ram's Island, are favourite fishing grounds for the specimen trout hunter. Almost every year Lough Mask produces a handful of wonderful fish weighing 12 lb (5 kg) and upwards, and fish of 17 and 18 lb (7.5–8 kg) were taken by trolling during the 1980s. Like its immediate neighbour to the south, Lough Corrib, and also Lower Lough Erne away to the north-east in County Fermanagh, Lough Mask has enormous and still largely unexploited potential for the true trout specimen hunter, especially if he can deploy the latest tactics and technology using electronic depth finders and down-rigger trolling equipment. One of these three loughs is almost sure to yield a verifiable and internationally recognised specimen of well over 20 lb (9 kg) if the necessary tactics, dedication and perseverance are applied to its pursuit.

The enthusiast for really big lough trout may find his appetite whetted by a brief glance at some of the history of Lough Mask and its very big trout. Each winter the local representatives of the Western Fisheries Board check the feeder streams and spawning grounds of Mask, to which the great trout of the lough make their way as the days become shorter and the temperatures drop as a prelude to late autumn and winter. Each year they see massive fish, brown trout of 15 lb (7 kg) and more, and individual fish reckoned at well over the 20 lb (9 kg) mark have been seen in the late 1980s. One fish of just over 13 lb (6 kg) caught in Lough Mask in the late 1950s was laconically recorded as simply 'a large lough trout', and it is worth noting the details of a letter sent in 1736 by Lady Howth to Jonathan Swift, author of *Gulliver's Travels* and Dean of St Patrick's Cathedral in Dublin. In it she referred to 'a trout . . . a yard and four inches long, twenty three inches round . . . and he weighed thirty-five pounds and a half'. Over 250 years later, massive lough trout still await the specimen trout hunter in the depths of Lough Mask.

Wet-fly fishing with the classic dark-hued western lough patterns is always reliable on Lough Mask in the early part of the season, and the lough attracts a

Lough Mask yields a typically well-muscled and leopard-spotted brown trout.

great many regular enthusiasts during mayfly time, which begins in late May and lasts until mid June in a normal year. (It is interesting to note how Lough Mask is significantly later as a mayfly fishery than its near neighbour to the north, Lough Carra.) Wet-fly fishing, dapping the natural insect and fishing a dry fly during a fall of spent gnat in the evening can all take good baskets of fish under the right conditions, and dapping tends to be a highly effective method of fishing throughout the season from May onwards, especially using natural daddy-longlegs and grasshoppers from August until the end of the season on 30 September.

When dealing with large, sprawling natural stillwaters like Lough Mask it is always rather difficult to suggest the best centre at which the visiting angler should base himself. So much depends on local conditions at the time of his visit, and also his personal preference for scenery and the conditions on various parts of the lough. The town of Ballinrobe is the largest angling centre in this area, from which all of Lough Mask (and also Lough Carra) can quickly be reached by a relatively short car drive. But the perimeter of the lough is dotted with a number of pleasant and conveniently situated villages including Partry at the extreme north, Clonbur at the southern end, and Toormakeady which is situated close to the lough's long western shore. All around the lough you will find excellent farmhouse guest-houses, bed-and-breakfast establishments and a scattering of small hotels, all of which are well equipped for the comfort and convenience of the visiting fisherman, and where your hosts will understand your requirements. As often as not you will find that you are the guest of someone who shares your passion for trout fishing, and who may be the very best of local sources of information and advice.

Lough Corrib

Wherever you go, in Ireland or elsewhere in the world of game fishing, you will find that each water tends to have its band of passionate enthusiasts. This wonderful trio of loughs comprising Carra, Mask and Corrib is no exception, and the rivalry and choice are especially acute when three such superb natural waters lie in such close proximity. Corrib is the largest and most southerly of these three loughs, and it has a worldwide reputation which few other fisheries can rival. It is a vast stretch of water, broad and spacious across its northern end and narrowing as it follows its 32-mile (51 km) south-easterly course towards Galway, the green pastures and boglands stretching away on the eastern side while purple, heather-clad hills rise to the south-west beyond that great anglers' Mecca, the little town of Oughterard.

You can start fishing for trout here from 15 February, although you will not be surprised to find that a great many trout are still rather lean, flaccid and ill-conditioned so soon after their winter spawning. Emergent fly life is also minimal at this time of year, and trolling is the norm so early in the year. In this case it is best to troll deep and slow in the hope of a really substantial specimen trout or an early spring salmon, rather than taking smaller trout which are best left to recover their energy and vigour and to provide good fly-fishing sport in the months ahead. Few wet-fly fishermen will set out on Corrib with serious intent much before St Patrick's Day (17 March), and even then a great deal will depend on the weather. Moderate or mild conditions should mean steady hatches of chiromonids from late March onwards, for which the various Duckfly patterns should be more than adequate, especially if you drift over the quieter, shallower water in Corrib's many little bays and inlets.

From April onwards almost all the lough shore gives excellent wet-fly fishing, and you will never go wrong with a box full of traditional western patterns, of which the Mallard and Claret, the Black Pennell, the Black & Peacock Spider and the Greenwell's Glory are among the most popular. Corrib shares the good spring hatches of olives which also occur on Mask and Carra to the north, but trouting here reaches its annual crescendo in the last week or 10 days of May when the annual mayfly hatch begins. Lough Mask has a magnetic attraction for many hundreds of anglers from all over Ireland, and a great many from much further afield. It is probably no exaggeration to say that it has been Ireland's single most popular mayfly resort since the late 1970s, and in this respect it has ousted Lough Derg from its proud and historic former pre-eminence, due largely to the enrichment of Lough Derg's waters and the slight falling-off in the quality of fly fishing of all kinds now to be found there.

Lough Corrib's east shore, and boats prepare to set out on a June morning. Note the long lough rods held upright in their holders.

Much of the local economy around Lough Corrib, and especially around the town of Oughterard, depends heavily on the 'mayfly industry', with a great many hotels, guest-houses and bed-and-breakfast places heavily booked from year to year; local boatmen whose services are heavily in demand so long as the mayfly hatches continue; and also the mundane but vitally important task of collecting live mayflies for the dapping fraternity. This latter task is enthusiastically carried out by successive generations of local schoolchildren, for whom the sale of early morning collections of mayflies from along the loughside bushes can represent a very welcome and substantial addition to their pocket money.

The mayfly hatch on Lough Corrib is not only sizeable but also consistent and fairly protracted, and in a normal year will last for almost a month. Food-rich though its depths may be, the large trout are never slow to realise what a wonderful feast awaits them on or near the surface, and some really magnificent fish are taken every year. A typical day's fishing on Corrib at mayfly time will produce a basket of fish averaging well over 2 lb (0.9 kg), and each season produces a good sprinkling of fish weighing two or three times as much.

By contrast with the frenzied excitement among trout and trout fishermen on Corrib during late May and June, July can often seem a rather lifeless and dour time on this great fishery. This is only an illusion, and good fish can still be taken by the enthusiast who perseveres. There is the added attraction that the lough is an altogether quieter place, and you may enjoy a long day's fishing with the sense that Corrib's wide and watery acres are almost your own private fishery. In an age of rush and bustle, peace and solitude are qualities which we increasingly value, and Corrib can offer both in abundance. In any case, it is scarcely surprising that Corrib's trout should be somewhat satiated by the feast of mayflies, but the catch rate picks up again noticeably in August and thereafter until the season's end on 30 September.

In common with all these western loughs, Corrib produces good results to the natural daddy-longlegs and grasshopper fished on the dap, and for those whose tastes are for traditional lough-style wet-fly fishing a selection of late-season sedge patterns will rarely disappoint, especially if you fish on into the dusk and concentrate on those drifts which take you close to the points at which Corrib's various inflowing streams enter the main lough. As the season advances and the trouts' instincts inevitably tend towards spawning, there is a general movement inshore to shallower water and towards the feeder streams, and some very big fish are always accounted for in the last few weeks of the season.

Elsewhere in this book we have talked at some length about the Galway Fishery, which is the general term applied to the short stretch of river through which this trio of loughs empties into Galway Bay. Corrib receives very large annual runs of early salmon and summer grilse which pass up this river, and these provide superb sport for the salmon enthusiast, especially by trolling early in the season for the bigger spring-run salmon and with plenty of grilse falling to the fly from June onwards.

Select Bibliography

Fahy, Edward, *Child of the Tides: a sea trout handbook*, Dublin, 1985
Geen, Philip, *Fishing in Ireland*, London [c. 1910]
Grimble, Augustus, *The Salmon Rivers of Ireland*, London, 1913
Gwynn, Stephen, *Fishing Holidays*, London, 1904
Gwynn, Stephen, *River to River*, London, 1937
Headlam, Maurice, *A Holiday Fisherman*, London, 1934
'Hi-Regan' (J. J. Dunne), *How & Where to Fish in Ireland*, London, 1886
Irish Free State, *The Angler's Guide to the Irish Free State*, Dublin, 1924
Kingsmill Moore, T. C., *A Man May Fish* (2nd edn.) Gerrards Cross, 1983
Luce, A. A., *Fishing and Thinking*, London, 1959
Malone, E. J., *Irish Trout and Salmon Flies*, Gerrards Cross, 1984
Maxwell, W. H., *Wild Sports of the West of Ireland*, London 1832 (repr. 1987)
McRea, Daniel F., *Fisherman's Forum*, London, 1961
Newland, Rev. Henry, *The Erne, its Legends and its Fly Fishing*, London, 1851
Northern Ireland (Dept. of Agriculture), *Angling Guide*, Belfast (annually)
O'Reilly, Peter, *The Trout and Salmon Loughs of Ireland*, London, 1987
Peard, Walter, *A Year of Liberty; or, Salmon angling in Ireland*, London, 1867
Wilkinson, S. B., *Reminiscences of Sport in Ireland*, London, 1931 (repr. 1987)

Useful Addresses

Tourist Boards

Northern Ireland Tourist Board,
River House,
48 High Street,
Belfast BT1 2DS
(Tel: 0232-231221/7)

Bord Failte Eireann (Irish Tourist Board),
150 New Bond Street,
London W1Y 0AQ
(Tel: 01-493 3201)

Bord Failte Eireann,
Baggot Street Bridge,
Dublin 2
(Tel: Dublin (01) 765871)

Irish Tourist Board Angling Representative (Paul Harris)
47 The Crescent,
Brinklow,
Nr Rugby,
Warwickshire
(Tel: 0788-833203)

Fisheries Boards

NORTHERN IRELAND

Fisheries Conservancy Board,
1 Mahon Road,
Portadown,
Craigavon
Co. Armagh BT62 3EE
(Tel: Portadown 334666)

Foyle Fisheries Commission,
8 Victoria Road,
Londonderry BT47 2AB
(Tel: Londonderry 42100)

Department of Agriculture,
Fisheries Division,
Room 19,
Hut 5,
Castle Grounds,
Stormont,
Belfast
(Tel: Belfast 63939 ext. 2283/2381)

REPUBLIC OF IRELAND

The Western Regional Fisheries Board,
The Weir Lodge,
Earls Island,
Galway
Tel: (091) 63118 (3 lines)

The Central Fisheries Board,
Balnagowan,
St Mobhi Boreen,
Glasnevin,
Dublin 9
Tel: (01) 379206

The Eastern Regional Fisheries Board,
Balnagowan,
St Mobhi Boreen,
Glasnevin,
Dublin 9
Tel: (01) 379206

The Northern Regional Fisheries Board,
Station Road,
Ballyshannon,
Co. Donegal
Tel: (072) 51435

The North Western Regional Fisheries Board,
Ardnaree House,
Abbey Street,
Ballina,
Co. Mayo
Tel: (096) 22788

The Shannon Regional Fisheries Board,
Thomond Weir,
Limerick
Tel: (061) 55171

The South Western Regional Fisheries Board,
1 Neviles Terrace,
Massey Town,
Macroom,
Co. Cork
Tel: (026) 41222

The Southern Regional Fisheries Board,
Anglesea Street,
Clonmel,
Co. Tipperary
Tel: (052) 23624

Travel

For the visiting game fisher, getting to Ireland and travelling around its innumerable fisheries is unlikely to present any problems. If you are setting out from Britain to Ireland, by far the best plan is to take your own car across on one of the various roll-on roll-off ferry-services. Fishing rods are cumbersome on aircraft; even a small selection of tackle can take up a good deal of space, and an adequate supply of clothing, boots and other comforts can amount to quite a pile of luggage. Stowed in your car at your own front door, all of this can be effortlessly transported thereafter. In any event, you will certainly require a car once you have arrived in Ireland to get you around the countryside and give you ready access to some of the most important and often remote waters.

The shortest sea crossings, taking only 2¼ hours, are from Stranraer and Cairnryan in south-west Scotland and Larne in Co. Antrim. These services are run by Sealink and P & O (British European Ferries) respectively, and there are several crossings in each direction virtually every day of the year. From Larne you have direct access to most of Northern Ireland's game fisheries within a maximum of 1¾ hours' drive, and 2 hours or so will take you right across to the west coast and the fisheries of Donegal and Sligo in the Irish Republic.

From Liverpool and Holyhead there are slightly longer crossings to Dublin and Dun Laoghaire, from both of which destinations you can quickly get onto Ireland's excellent network of trunk roads and then head north, west or south according to the fishing destination you have chosen. Allow at least 3½–4 hours to get from the outskirts of Dublin to Lough Arrow or Lough Conn, and a generous 6–7 hours to reach some of the remoter fisheries of west Connemara.

The traveller beginning his journey from southern England might find it more convenient to head directly westwards along the M4 motorway, and take the car ferry from Fishguard in south-west Wales to Rosslare in Co. Wexford, at Ireland's south-eastern corner.

The visiting motorist in Ireland will find nothing unfamiliar, except for the very much higher cost of petrol in the Irish Republic. It pays to arrive with your tank full! Otherwise motoring is as in Britain, except for the extraordinary quietness of the roads and the generally easy pace of the traffic, and of Irish life in general. Off the major trunk routes you may find yourself on some narrow and winding by-roads, and care is called for. It is all too easy to let your gaze wander to admire the view, only to find you have to brake suddenly to avoid an oncoming tractor or a herd of cows!

By air there are numerous daily flights from Heathrow, Gatwick, Birmingham, Manchester, Glasgow and Edinburgh to Belfast (International and Harbour airports), Dublin, Cork and Shannon, and the regular operators include British Airways, Aer Lingus, British Midland, Danair and Loganair. All flights can be linked to the collection of a hire car at the airport on arrival, and the two Irish tourist boards or any travel agent will be able to advise you about these increasingly popular 'fly-drive' holiday packages, which may also be linked to pre-booked accommodation.

Fishing Licences, Permits and Permission

Strictly speaking, there is no 'free fishing' in Ireland, even on those waters which are designated 'free fisheries', for in both Northern Ireland and the Irish Republic there are various legal requirements regarding licences and permits for game fishing.

The following is a summary of the regulations (as at June 1989):

Republic of Ireland

It is not permitted to fish, or attempt to fish, for salmon, trout or coarse fish without a rod and line licence. The word 'salmon' includes all fish of the salmon species – spring and summer (grilse) salmon and sea trout. 'Trout' are defined as a) all fish of the brown trout kind, b) rainbow trout and char, c) pollan or freshwater herring, and d) any spawn or fry of trout.

The schedule of licence duties payable is:

State salmon & sea trout licence (annual)	IR£25.00
State salmon & sea trout licence (21 days)	IR£10.00
Brown trout licence (annual)	IR£15.00
Brown trout licence (21 days)	IR £5.00

(The brown trout licence fee does not apply to persons aged 65 and over, or under 18 years.)

Composite freshwater licence (annual, all species)   IR£25.00

These licences may be purchased from the offices of the Central Fisheries Board and Regional Fisheries Boards, or from local tackle dealers, fisheries proprietors and managers, and some hotels.

Northern Ireland

In Northern Ireland a rod licence is required by every person over the age of 18 years intending to fish for any species with rod and line in fresh water. Furthermore, a rod licence is also required by all persons, of whatever age, if fishing for migratory fish (i.e. salmon and seatrout) anywhere in Northern

Ireland; and by all persons fishing for salmon, seatrout or brown trout in the Foyle Fisheries area.

In addition to the above general requirements for a rod licence for game fishing, a permit is usually also required. This is a document issued by a fishery owner and conferring the right to fish. Many excellent game fisheries are managed by the Department of Agriculture for Northern Ireland, which issues permits to fish individual waters or general permits for all D.A.N.I. waters, for the season, for a period of 15 days (i.e. for visitors), and for juveniles (i.e. under 18 years).

For 1989 the categories of Licences and Permits were as follows:

Northern Ireland Fisheries Conservancy Board Licences:

Season game-fishing rod licence	£13.30
15-day game-fishing rod licence	£9.20
Supplement payable by holder of a Foyle Fisheries Commission season rod licence	£10.65

Foyle Fisheries Commission Licences:

Season game-fishing licence	£12.00
14-day game-fishing licence	£7.50
Season game-fishing licence (under 18)	£6.00
Supplement payable by holder of a NIFCB season game-fishing rod licence	£8.15

N.I. licence and permit costs include vat at 15 percent.

In both Northern Ireland and the Irish Republic individual fisheries, whether state controlled or privately owned, have their own charges in addition to the statutory requirements for rod licences. Details of these are available on request either direct from the fishery concerned, or through a local tackle shop or game-angling association, or by contacting the appropriate tourist board.